HIDDEN

Secrets of the Western Esoteric Tradition

WISDOM

TIM WALLACE-MURPHY

disinformation

♉ disinformation®

Copyright © 2010 Tim Wallace-Murphy

Published by:
The Disinformation Company Ltd.
111 East 14th Street, Suite 108
New York, NY 10003
Tel.: +1.212.691.1605
Fax: +1.212.691.1606
www.disinfo.com

Library of Congress Control Number: 2010921578

ISBN: 978-1934708-48-4

Designed by Greg Stadnyk

Distributed in the U.S. and Canada by:
Consortium Book Sales and Distribution
34 Thirteenth Avenue NE, Suite 101
Minneapolis MN 55413-1007
Tel.: +1.800.283.3572
www.cbsd.com

Distributed in the United Kingdom and Eire by:
Turnaround Publisher Services Ltd.
Unit 3, Olympia Trading Estate
Coburg Road, London, N22 6TZ
Tel.: +44.(0)20.8829.3000 Fax: +44.(0)20.8881.5088
www.turnaround-uk.com

Distributed in Australia by: Tower Books
Unit 2/17 Rodborough Road
Frenchs Forest NSW 2086
Tel.: +61.2.9975.5566 Fax: +61.2.9975.5599
Email: info@towerbooks.com.au

Attention colleges and universities, corporations and other organizations: Quantity discounts are available on bulk purchases of this book for educational training purposes, fund-raising, or gift giving. Special books, booklets, or book excerpts can also be created to fit your specific needs. For information contact the Marketing Department of The Disinformation Company Ltd.

Managing Editor: Ralph Bernardo

10 9 8 7 6 5 4 3 2 1

Printed in the United States of America

Disinformation® is a registered trademark of The Disinformation Company Ltd.

HIDDEN

WISDOM

TIM WALLACE-MURPHY

This book is respectfully dedicated to my first literary collaborator, Trevor Ravenscroft. A warm, rumbustious, humanly flawed genius who knew how to turn his soul into a magic mirror to reflect his love of God on all who knew him.

ACKNOWLEDGEMENTS

No work such as this is ever produced without the help, encouragement and support of a large number of people. And while responsibility for this book rests solely with the author, I gratefully acknowledge the assistance received from: Paul Amorus of the Moulin de Soleils, Provence; Stuart Beattie of the Rosslyn Chapel Trust; Richard Beaumont of Staverton, Devon; Laurence Bloom of London; Robert Brydon of Edinburgh; Richard Buades of Marseilles; Mike Cooke of Nice; Nicole Dawe of Okehampton; Baroness Edni di Pauli of London; David Fayle of Taunton; Jean-Michel Garnier of Chartres; Thierry Garnier of Marseilles; Antonia Goodland-Clark of Cannes: Michael Halsey of Auchterarder; Marilyn Hopkins of Harberton; the late Guy Jourdan of Bargemon, Provence; Georges Keiss of the Centre d'Etudes et de Recherches Templière, Campagne-sur-Aude; the late Michael Monkton of Buckingham; James Mackay Munro of Edinburgh; the late Andrew Pattison of Edinburgh; Alan Pearson of Rennes-les-Bains; David Pykett of Burton-on-Trent; Amy Ralston of Staverton, Devon; Victor Rosati of Totnes; Pat Sibille of Aberdeen; Niven Sinclair of London; Prince Michael of Albany; that ever-patient and wise lady Dawn Bramadat of Montreal and, last but not least, Gary Baddeley and the staff at The Disinformation Company of New York.

CONTENTS

INTRODUCTION 1

CHAPTER 1
From A State Of Grace?
Prehistoric Man and the Dawn of Civilization 5

CHAPTER 2
Mute Testimony to Neolithic Spirituality 13

CHAPTER 3
Egypt – Land of Magic and Mystery 21

CHAPTER 4
The Covenant and the People of Israel 35

CHAPTER 5
The Glory Of Ancient Greece And The Power Of Rome 45

CHAPTER 6
The Initiates of Celtic Culture 57

CHAPTER 7
The Messiah And Different Accounts
Of His Teaching; The Conflict Between Fact And Faith 65

CHAPTER 8
Patrem Omnipotentem: The Rise Of A Repressive Society 83

CHAPTER 9
Buried Treasure: The Underground Streams Of Spirituality 101

CHAPTER 10
The Search For The Holy Grail 117

CHAPTER 11
The Crusade Against Fellow Christians;
And The Founding Of The Holy Inquisition 137

CHAPTER 12
Holy Mother the Church Eats Her Own Young! 155

CHAPTER 13
The Sons Of The Widow: Freemasonry And Rosicrucianism 169

CHAPTER 14
The Floodgates Open: The Rising Tide Of Ideas 187

CHAPTER 15
The Age Of Exploration:
The Destruction Of Native Cultures And Peoples 205

CHAPTER 16
Two Revolutions That Changed The World.................................... 223

CHAPTER 17
Nationalism, Imperialism And The Esoteric Revival 239

CHAPTER 18
The War To End All War;
And Some Of The Wars That Followed It.. 255

CHAPTER 19
The Modern Wellsprings Of Spirituality.. 273

CHAPTER 20
Standing At The Threshold Of The Spiritual World.......................... 285

SELECTED BIBLIOGRAPHY 307

ENDNOTES 315

INDEX 327

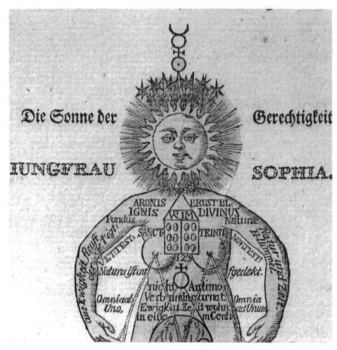

Detail from *Secret Figures of the Rosicrucians of the 16th and 17th Centuries*,
Altona, Hamburg, Germany, 1785.

INTRODUCTION

The mystery surrounding the Knights Templar and the controversies that have perpetually surrounded the Freemasons, the Rosicrucians and the other heirs to Templar traditions, have tended to disguise the fact that their common knowledge and insight predates the foundation of the Templar Order by several thousand years. This hidden stream of spirituality and that of sacred knowledge are inseparably entwined to form the single most important, continuous strand in the entire Western esoteric tradition. This tradition which, despite its hidden nature, was described by Theodore Roszak of California State University as "probably the single, most profoundly imaginative and influential spiritual tradition of European culture," exerted a seminal influence on the thinking of the builders of the great cathedrals; leading teachers in ecclesiastical schools; philosophers, playwrights and poets such as Shakespeare, Goethe, Blake and Yeats; artists and Renaissance giants such as Leonardo da Vinci and Michelangelo; and indirectly on all generations of European Christendom. It is also the root from which sprang alchemy and modern science. While there has been enough continuity to use the term "tradition" accurately, it should, nonetheless, be understood as one that is dynamic, pervasive, loose and constantly re-synthesising, disappearing from plain sight for most of the time only to be intermittently and indirectly perceived by its fruits, the achievements of its many, multi-talented and spiritually perceptive initiates and disciples.

This vibrant hidden stream of spirituality irrigated the intellectually barren wastes of medieval Europe and brought the beginnings of peace and stability to a continent riven by squabbling

feudal barons, warring kings and dominated by an oppressive clergy. The Knights Templar created the climate wherein the seeds of
capitalism could grow and flourish, and the underground streams
of hidden wisdom that were passed down by their heirs stimulated
and sustained the Renaissance. Yet despite the obvious benefits
that flowed from their insight, the Knights Templar and all who
followed in their footsteps were slandered, harried and persecuted
by Holy Mother the Church, to the point of near extinction.

It has always been a mystery how a church, supposedly founded
on the teachings of the "gentle Jesus," deliberately created a regime
of repression founded firmly on intolerance, torture and genocide.
When we examine the relationship between the Christian Church
and its supposed spiritual rivals in the light of the Dead Sea Scrolls
material, the answers emerge with startling clarity.

It is not my intent to add to controversy, to criticize or blindly praise that which I do not fully understand, but any close and
dispassionate examination of the facts soon discloses that spiritual insight is both very real and highly relevant to everyday life,
especially in the turbulent and troubled world which we now all
inhabit. Indeed, it may well prove to be the key to the very survival of mankind as a whole. Therefore this work is dedicated to
all those, throughout the ages, who kept this spiritual tradition
alive despite appalling persecution so that we in the twenty-first
century might benefit from its accumulated fruits and ennoble
our lives by emulating their example.

Cave painting at Lascaux, France.

CHAPTER 1

From A State Of Grace?
Prehistoric Man and the Dawn of Civilization

Most civilizations have evolved similarly – from the wandering band, egalitarian, co-operative, sharing resources and in awe of nature, through the tribe, to the settled agricultural community and town and so to the city, at first usually centred on religion. As numbers grow, bureaucracies evolve and, from them, secular elites. Hierarchies of rule and ownership bring the desire first to defend power and wealth, then to acquire more – by force. Each rise in numbers is led by a new order – with scope for peace and war. As we pass from the industrial into the information age, we seek a global order – but, unless we control our technology, risk global destruction.[1]   *– The Gaia Peace Atlas*

N othing arises in a vacuum. Culture, religions and civilization itself all have their roots in the past and any study that ignores this ever-present fact is valueless. Therefore in order to gain a true appreciation of the nature of esoteric knowledge and learn why it had to remain secret in the European context, as well as its long-term effects, we need to begin our research at the earliest time possible. Then, progressing forwards, step by step from that mysterious beginning we can begin to understand the nature of the massive advances and changes that have occurred in the evolution of man and of society itself and appreciate the formative role that esoteric knowledge has played in creating the culture that sustains us all.

The past is a very strange place; people behaved differently there. Even recent history is distorted in our perception by our own inability to understand the thinking patterns and basic attitudes that were the foundation of earlier cultures. It seems almost futile to try and appreciate attitudes, ideas and beliefs that have long since been consigned to intellectual oblivion on the short but misty road from those days to the present. In any attempt to resolve the problems, not merely of history, but of prehistory – the time of myth and legend – we must try to correct this distortion by whatever reasonable means that modern scientific and academic disciplines can provide.

History, as we now understand it, did not begin until the development of writing and written records. The multi-faceted and mysterious problems of the interpretation of the prehistory of our race are compounded by our own previous reluctance, or unwillingness, to concede that man himself is an integral part of the evolutionary process: a process which is not just biological in nature, but also encompasses the evolution of both intellect and consciousness. Our only guidelines in this attempt to understand our own early development as a species are the archaeological artifacts that have come to light, our present level of conscious intellectual ability and, above all, the mythology that has been handed down over the ages. Mythology used and evaluated with circumspection may yet provide some of the keys to unlock the doors that, at present at least, bar the way to a more comprehensive understanding of our cultural and religious origins.

Yet how can one speak seriously of mythology in this age of modern technology and science? Of what use can it be in our search for understanding and factual evidence? Many scientists, philosophers and historians of the present century are divided in their evaluation of the use of mythology as an historical tool. However, the value placed on myth as an indication of historical truth is undergoing a profound change. Interpreted with discretion and in conjunction with archaeological evidence or, supported by the opinions of scholars of repute, far from confusing the issue, mythology can provide insights into the developmental prehistoric era of man that stand the test of dispassionate scientific analysis. One modern scholar, Theodore Roszak, claims that: "The meaning of myths lies in the vision of life and nature they hold at their core."[2] This confirmation of the value of oft-derided myth was echoed by Joseph Campbell who claimed that: "Mythology is the penultimate truth – penultimate because the ultimate cannot be put into words."[3] This point was reinforced by Kathleen Raine, who stated that "Fact is not the truth of myth; myth is the truth of fact"[4] and by the Indian scholar, Ananda Coomaraswamy, who wrote: "Myth embodies the nearest approach to absolute truth that can be stated in words."[5] Bill Moyers remarked to Joseph Campbell, "Myths are stories of our search through the ages for truth, for meaning, for significance." Campbell replied, "Myths are clues to the spiritual potentialities of human life."[6]

The precursors of our species evolved in the heartland of Africa over two million years ago. Scientists begin to call these creatures "early man" at the stage of development they reached one million years later. It is generally believed that they lived in small family-based bands of "hunter-gatherers." These were the first demonstrable form of human organization: one within which man formed his earliest relationships with other men, with nature and with the planet that continues to sustain him. This primitive way of life persists to this day in the more remote regions of the globe, and it is doubtful if the basic manner of living of the modern hunter-gatherers differs greatly from that of mankind's distant ancestors.

Hunter-gatherers live in small mobile groups and have to adopt ecologically sustainable lifestyles. When the population outstrips the available food supply, they have no alternative but to travel on in search of new territory. Their choice is brutal – move or starve.[7] Thus we can see that early man had to devise ways to create and maintain a social organization which allowed for and encouraged a nomadic, or at best, semi-nomadic lifestyle. With continuing growth of population, these small bands had to extend their range of movement over an ever-widening area. They moved inexorably onwards and outwards until they eventually spread in ever increasing numbers, fanlike, across the face of the Earth and established themselves throughout the globe from China in the east, to Europe in the west.[8]

Archaeological evidence exists that sheds some light on the general nature of some of the belief systems that may have sustained their social organization. Burial patterns and certain other practices provide evidence that disclose the essentially "spiritual" nature of these beliefs. Cave paintings such as those at Altimera, Lascaux, Montespan and Les Trois Frères in the Ariège in France reflect the shamanistic practices of the early cave dwellers, a form of ritual magic that is still practiced today by hunter-gatherers in many parts of South America, Africa and Australia today. As man became more numerous and pressure on the available food supply became greater, it was inevitable that magic, or some form of ritual, spiritual enhancement became of greater importance. Cave paintings, burial practices and female figurines found in excavations all point to a strong and persistent belief in spiritual powers by our Stone Age ancestors.[9] In fact it is now generally agreed that primitive man lived in awe of nature, seeing some form of living spirituality in every leaf, every creature, and every aspect of their lives.

Indeed that insightful English author, Colin Wilson, suggests that primitive man had one great advantage over his modern counterpart, in that he knew that he possessed spiritual powers. Knowing this, if he wanted to develop and deepen them it was simply a question of finding the best possible method of doing so. The insight probably came first, the method followed and, as we have seen in the example of the so-called cave art, Stone Age man soon found at least one. Wilson also introduced the conception that among all peoples are natural leaders. Perhaps they are the dominant males of the animal kingdom, normally about one in twenty of any population. These he called the "Few." It is to this group that he ascribes the search to increase and pass on to succeeding generations the spiritual or magical powers designed to enhance the chance of survival of the entire band. This search for shamanistic rituals and procedures to heighten man's spiritual powers, allied to the time-consuming search for food and shelter, explains to some degree the pressures that tended to restrict prehistoric man's inventiveness and cultural progress.[10]

Until approximately ten thousand years ago our ancestors had little impact on the planet, or on the animals and plants around them. Then came a quantum leap in the development of man with profound implications for not only man himself, but for all the plants and animals and, ultimately, for the survival of the planet as a whole. In some inexplicable way our primitive ancestors found ways to domesticate animals and plants, thus entering into a new and evolutionary partnership with many of them.

No other living species has accomplished this in anything like the same manner.

Darwin's much ignored co-discoverer of the theory of "natural selection," Alfred Russel Wallace, claimed that some "metaphysical force" had directed evolution at three different and critical points: the beginning of life itself; the beginnings of consciousness; and at the start of civilization.[11] This presupposes that mankind passed through a period when man himself was not a conscious being. Julian Huxley, in his introduction to a work on the same subject by Pierre Teilhard de Chardin, states quite clearly that human intelligence and consciousness were an integral part of the evolutionary process.[12] Thus three leading scientists suggest that consciousness emerged at a critical stage of evolutionary advance as something genuinely new and startling. When it did emerge it had a dramatic effect on the course of history as the evolution of consciousness provoked significant and wide reaching behavioral changes in man, particularly the dramatic shift from the nomadic lifestyle of the early hunter-gatherers to the creation of settled communities of the earliest agriculturalists. This is the single most dramatic change in the way of life mankind has ever experienced. This massive change, which laid down the direct roots of our present civilization, did not take place instantaneously across the settled regions of the globe. It happened piecemeal and spread slowly. With this change we commenced the process that began to separate us from the spiritual heritage that was so important to our Neolithic ancestors – one that is not given substance by written records or mythology, for there are none, but by monuments that have fascinated modern man for centuries.

Throughout Western Europe, especially in Great Britain, there is a vast and imposing body of evidence testifying to the supreme value accorded spirituality by our first ancestors who began to raise crops, domesticate animals and live in settled communities. Stonehenge, Avebury, Carnac and an infinite variety of other megalithic structures stand in mute testimony to early man's spiritual beliefs.

Stakes around the Newgrange burial chamber. County Meath, Ireland.

CHAPTER 2

Mute Testimony to Neolithic Spirituality

All places that the eye of heaven visits
Are to a wise man ports and happy havens[13]

– William Shakespeare, *King Richard the Second*

S acred sites of Stone Age man are mysterious in the extreme. Irrespective of their location or size they are all imbued with a tangible mystical power that attracts awe-stricken tourists and pilgrims by the thousands. It is not simply the size of the structures erected upon them that amazes the twentieth century observer. Some innate, haunting quality seems to lie tantalizingly just beyond the understanding of modern man, puzzling him, attracting him and, apparently, satisfying some deep inner need. Is this quality something spiritual perhaps, or does it derive from the mystical power of the site itself? Even the Romans were aware of this; indeed, they used to describe it, as the "genius loci" – the spirit of the place.

The puzzle deepens if we understand that people who left no written records constructed this vast range of megalithic structures scattered right across the globe. Their compelling allure arises, in part, from the immense size of the stones used in their construction and the fact that we have no clear idea of how or why many of them were built. Some, such as the long barrows and dolmens, are quite obviously burial places but the exact function of most of the others is still beyond the understanding of modern man. The siting of these ritual monuments poses an even more intriguing problem. Their location was deliberate and calculated on sites of demonstrable telluric power. The Greek philosopher and initiate, Plato, believed that the ancients were simple people who accepted things as they were. If a particular place had a mystical appeal, a magical effect or a healing power, they used it. Did our ancestors discover the telluric energy first, or the magical sites? We will never know. What is beyond doubt is that one vitally important attribute required of a Druid was the ability to discern the Earth's sacred places.

Amateur archaeologist Alfred Watkins rediscovered strange lines of telluric energy in the early 1920s and demonstrated that man could still detect them.[14] Water divining had been known for centuries and was accepted as a "God-given" means of finding water. Now a "new" use was found for divining, or dowsing – the location of a complex network of lines of energy linking a wide variety of ancient sites. They join the sites of long barrows, dolmens, henges, healing wells, sacred grottos and many early churches – tangible and detectable lines connecting them all with amazing, yet predictable, precision. In the East, these lines of energy, or *chi*, have been known and recognized by Chinese feng shui experts for millennia, but in the Western world the ability to detect and use them had been lost for centuries.

Another enigma arises from the inexplicable, and truly amazing, precision of alignment found between so many monuments and the planetary bodies and stars. This is not an isolated phenomenon – there are many Neolithic temples that are orientated to receive light and energy from heavenly bodies. The best-known example is, perhaps, Stonehenge, but it is at Newgrange in Ireland that one of the most fascinating alignments is to be found. This Neolithic passage grave dates from 3200 BCE. It predates Stonehenge and Avebury and is several centuries older than the Pyramids of Giza. In 1963 the examination of an anomalous stone slab at the beginning of the passage led to the discovery of a "roof box" immediately over the entrance. This had been constructed in such a manner that on midwinter's day the first rays of the morning sun shine down the passageway and fall upon the burial chamber at the far end. How did Neolithic man in 3200 BCE know how to align such a vast structure in this precise manner? The precision is such that these so-called "primitive" people must have possessed an incredible degree of astronomical knowledge.[15] A study of ancient Egyptian construction proves that this knowledge persisted and developed well into the era of early civilization.[16] This precision and skill is not the only dramatic discovery we make when we study Neolithic sites and artifacts. Meticulous archaeological excavation reveals even more startling evidence of the power of spiritual insight and its effects upon human behavior, disclosing facts that flatly contradict many widely held beliefs about the essentially warlike nature of mankind.

One such settlement which had been continuously occupied from the middle of the seventh millennium to the middle of the sixth millennium BCE was discovered in 1961 at Çatalhöyük in Anatolia. Excavations brought to light evidence that amplified and transformed the whole conception of Neolithic behavior. Arts and crafts were well represented, giving a crucial insight into man's activities, appearance and dress, as well as his religious beliefs. Fragments of textiles were found that are among the earliest yet discovered. Bones discovered on the site clearly show that animals had not yet been domesticated; the inhabitants lived on the results of their agriculture, supplemented by hunting. From the evidence provided by this site much can be deduced to illuminate man's behavior at that time and even earlier.

No evolutionary development takes place in a vacuum. Each step forward is related to the habits and actions that preceded it. From detailed analysis of finds at the Çatalhöyük site we find, to our intense surprise, that war is neither a part of human nature, nor necessarily of urban life. This site has now been excavated back to the seventh millennium BCE and, surprisingly, in the eight hundred years of its occupation that have so far been studied, there is no evidence of any act of war; no sign of any sack or massacre; no single skeleton that discloses any indication that death was caused by an act of violence. This apparently startling find came as no surprise to many scholars whose opinions prior to this discovery had been devalued or overlooked. One noted writer, Charlene Spretnak, talks movingly of the culture revealed by the archaeology in such settlements in Old Europe:

> … which have revealed sophisticated art and religious symbols reflecting reverence for Mother Earth, the elements and animals; egalitarian graves; and no fortifications or evidence of warfare before the invasions of the barbarian tribes we now call the Indo European tribes from the Eurasian steppes.[17]

Jacob Bronowski gave a simple explanation as to how war came about: "But war, organized war, is not a human instinct. It is simply a highly planned and co-operative form of theft." Yet, the majority of people in the twenty-first century, working on the experience of our own time and that of history, believe implicitly that war is part of human nature. This conception is now completely untenable – for there is no firm evidence whatsoever from any source to indicate that humanity engaged in inter-group conflict or mass violence, until as late as 10,000 BCE. The first recorded war of which we have any historical certainty took place between Upper and Lower Egypt about 3200 BCE. This conflict, like so many others since, was concerned with the acquisition of land. In the hunter-gatherer societies that have survived until the twentieth century, violent and aggressive behavior is ritualized and rarely results in serious injury. It is so-called civilized man, not the primitives, who invented and engaged in war, later refining it in all its awful technological, amoral destructiveness to the point where the entire planet could be destroyed and all forms of life extinguished forever in a nuclear holocaust.

Yet is the evidence from Çatalhöyük the only basis from which we can deduce the importance of spiritual matters to our Stone Age ancestors? We have mentioned the burial practices, wall paintings and figurines that have been discovered elsewhere. There are many mythologies that tell of the "divine" origin of agriculture and handicrafts. Joseph Campbell wrote prolifically about the mythology of the North American Indians and the Polynesian peoples of the Pacific who both claimed, quite clearly, to have received agricultural knowledge as a "God-given gift."[18] Although there is no evidence whatsoever for any cultural contact between these races there is a unanimity between their myths that is truly startling. This is in harmony with the ancient traditions of all peoples who invariably speak of a "divine origin" for their practical skills. In Persia, Zoroaster learned the art of agriculture from the Sun god, Ahura Mazda; Osiris taught the Egyptians the art of growing corn; Dionysus traveled the lands to impart the knowledge of the vine; Moses received the Tablet of the Law from Jehovah on Mount Sinai; Hammurabi was personally instructed by the god Shamash; the goddess Egeria inspired Numa Pompilius to instigate the religious rituals of Rome.[19]

In each of the early civilizations an elite corps of initiates guarded and interpreted a body of sacred knowledge and magic that was then used to the benefit of the entire community, tribe or race. This elite corps of rulers, priests and kings were initiated members of the "Few" and acted as stewards of the gods. They are believed by many to be the spiritual heirs to the shamans, or medicine men, of their hunter-gatherer ancestors. The knowledge, or "gnosis," that they guarded, preserved and increased, was the very foundation of the sacred texts and rituals of the state religion and influenced the way of life of the entire people. This was as true for the civilization of ancient Egypt – which is now known to be the source of much of Western esoteric knowledge – as for that of the Chinese, Mesopotamian and Mayan peoples. In each instance this gnosis had its roots deeply embedded in the mysterious era of the prehistory of the civilization that recorded it. Its true earlier origins and evolutionary development can only be guessed at, for by the time that civilization had evolved to the point of literacy, the knowledge itself had developed a depth and complexity that is truly beyond our present understanding. Yet in our arrogance we have the temerity to describe the people who first used this knowledge as "primitive."

The Pharaoh Akhenaten depicted in painted limestone,
located at the Louvre Museum, Paris.

CHAPTER 3

Egypt – Land of Magic and Mystery

Early civilizations, all founded firmly on the new practice of agriculture, developed in five major centers around the world. The first three – Egypt, Sumer and India – developed completely independently of one another. The other two – China and Central America – came much later but apparently in the same way. Each individual center developed blindly, separately, struggling to survive, to spread and to ramify, as though each was specifically designed to transform the entire globe.[20]

Written records, so essential for an accurate understanding of the past, only came into being with the development of city building societies, with the rise of early civilization in fact. The development of writing in the first civilizations has enabled modern archaeology to expand and amplify the previously silent form of witness given by ancient structures. Interpreted with care, an archaeological site, be it the excavation of a city, royal grave or temple, when examined in the light of written records, can speak to us like the disembodied voice of truth arching over the millennia directly from the early decades of civilized man to the present. The knowledge and skill that built these memorable structures, the beliefs that underpinned both their purpose and their construction, has reached out and touched nearly every generation since that time: at first in the countries of the Middle East, then through the Roman Empire into Europe and beyond. All three of the great religions that span the globe, Judaism, Christianity and Islam, owe a great debt to their common ancestor, the initiatory religion of ancient Egypt.

Careful study now demonstrates that the reality that manifests itself within the monuments of ancient Egypt evolved inexorably from a complex basis of profound knowledge and technical skill whose precise extent and origin we still regard with astonishment. Each one of these enormous buildings not only freezes that stream of ever expanding knowledge at a precise moment in its overall development, but provides a magical "rear-view mirror" giving a snapshot of a very different culture, a distinct flavor and scent of a subtly evolving belief system founded firmly upon "sacred knowledge," at a reasonably dateable time in history; which may tend to explain why Egyptology has been such a compelling field of study for over two centuries.

The fascination of Western European academics with this ancient and mysterious world has proved both obsessive and full of controversy and dispute. Public interest has been stimulated and sustained by the splendor of the archaeological successes of the early twentieth century. The treasures of Tutankhamun and the popular mythology of the so-called "mummy's curse" which followed, brought what was then an art and is now an arcane science, to the level of "pop" culture. Is this profound and continuing interest in Egyptology so strange? Not when you consider that this ancient land, which flourished so productively along the fertile narrow valley of the Nile, has produced not only the enormous troves of treasure and intriguing monuments such as the pyramids, but also the seeds of modern science, medicine, surgery, astronomy, mathematics and civil engineering on a grand scale. It was also the land of Moses, a figure of immense importance to all three of the great worldwide religions. One way or another, modern Western civilization owes an incalculable debt to the divine gift of "gnosis," or sacred knowledge, that is the vibrant, spiritual legacy of Egyptian civilization.

One monument that reflects this sacred knowledge in its construction is believed to be the oldest masonry building in the world, King Djoser's seven-stepped pyramid at Saqqara.[21] The designer and builder of this imposing structure was a towering figure in his own right: the priest-architect and genius, Imhotep, high priest of Annu and the Egyptian astronomer general. He was granted the title "chief of the observers" and the Greeks later equated him to their god of medicine, Asclepius.[22] His wisdom, knowledge, insight and healing powers were qualities particularly prized and revered in ancient Egypt. The seven steps correspond to the seven planetary spheres that encircle the Earth. According to the ancient Egyptians the seven planets were held to represent the seven stages of ascent to the heavens through which the soul must pass after death. The comparison between this Egyptian belief in a seven stage planetary ascent after death and the Druidic belief in a seven stage purification of the soul before death is intriguing, to say the least. Some of the keys to the puzzles posed by the levels of skill and technology needed to construct the Pyramid of Djoser are to be found nearby in pyramids of a much later date. Here, texts were discovered that grant us a fascinating understanding of the depth of knowledge possessed at a very early stage of development by this complex civilization.

It is ironic that in this modern scientific age so many important discoveries come about by accident. The history of medicine, physics and the pharmaceutical industry are littered with so-called "accidental" discoveries that have changed the course of modern history. The discovery of the "Pyramid Texts" is a classic example of this. The true agent of discovery in this instance was a desert fox, an animal that has inhabited this region since time immemorial and which is, in reality, a jackal, a creature who is best remembered in Egypt for his two deified forms. One, the god Anubis, is responsible for the final judgment – a weighing of the heart – to see if the dead are worthy of admission to the court of Osiris; the other form of this jackal god is that of Wepwawet or Upuaut, the "Opener of the Ways." An uncannily prophetic title in light of what occurred in the late 1800s: an Arab head workman spotted a lone jackal outlined by the dawn's early light, sauntering towards one of the pyramids at Saqqara. Stopping intermittently, as if inviting the astonished workman to follow him, the jackal seemingly vanished. Urged on by dreams of treasure perhaps, the workman followed, finding the entrance to a small tunnel that he then entered. Eventually he reached a chamber containing not the treasure he expected, but one of far greater import to the archaeological fraternity so busy in Egypt at that time.[23]

The precise date of the discovery is not known and even which of the leading archaeologists to first see the texts is unclear. Two of the Pyramid Texts were almost certainly first examined by Auguste Mariette, the director of the Egyptian Antiquities Services.[24] Others were discovered by Gaston Masparo, who was the first European to explore the interior of the Pyramid of Unas. What is supremely obvious is that the modern four-legged incarnation of Upuaut had indeed opened the ways, both literally and figuratively. The same could be said for the Pyramid Texts themselves for they led, ultimately, to a more profound understanding not only of the priestly belief system of the time of Unas but also, more importantly, of the great depth of that knowledge that had been accrued in the era before the time the texts were actually inscribed.

The Pyramid Texts were found on the walls of several chambers within five of the smaller pyramids at Saqqara. They consist of hieroglyphic inscriptions, carved or incised in the limestone walls and decorated with exquisite gold and turquoise coloring. In all there are over four thousand lines of hymns and formulae, the greater portion of which, according to Masparo, were first formulated during the prehistoric period in Egypt. In his opinion they are, without doubt, the oldest collection of religious writings ever discovered. I. E. S. Edwards, former keeper of Egyptian Antiquities at the British Museum, wrote of them in 1947: "The Pyramid Texts were not the invention of the Fifth or Sixth Dynasties, but had originated in earlier times."[25]

There is no doubt that the texts and the astrological knowledge they embody date back to a very much earlier period. In the opinion of Masparo, they certainly predate the writing of the Old Testament by at least two millennia, and the writing of the New Testament by nearly 3,400 years. They are, in fact, the earliest known recordings of an oral tradition of secret knowledge that, in all probability, had its origins in tribal shamanism; a tradition handed down in secret by members of the "Few" from master to pupil in the process known as "initiation." The religious, ritual and esoteric content disclosed by a modern translation clearly shows that it was a highly complex and well-developed stellar cult that was being described, one in which the dead king would ascend to heaven and be ritually reunited with the stars. The definitive translation was published in 1969 by Raymond Faulkner who wrote that: "The Pyramid Texts constitute the oldest corpus of Egyptian religious and funerary literature now extant."[26]

The texts repeatedly refer to the so-called *Zep Tepi*, or "First Time," the legendary time of Osiris, the ancient era in which Egypt was ruled directly by the gods who gave the Egyptians the sacred gift of knowledge. As no archaeological or archival proof exists that gives the slightest hint as to when, or indeed what, the so-called First Time was, it is difficult to establish precisely what the texts are referring to. Many mythologists lean towards the theory that this is a reference to earlier Babylonian or Sumerian civilizations, citing the obvious parallels between the Osiris legends and the worship of the goddess Ishtar and her resurrecting consort or son, Tammuz. Perhaps more importantly, the Pyramid Texts also disclose a complex, profound and uncannily accurate knowledge of astronomy which is inseparable from the ancient esoteric concept of "as above, so below." This finds an echo in a phrase from the Lord's Prayer, "on earth as it is in heaven," in which the visible stellar reality in the heavens is matched, in this instance, by the physical and tangible geographical features of the Egyptian landscape. For example, the constellation of the Milky Way in the heavens was believed to be represented by the River Nile that brought life, sustenance and prosperity to the land known as the two kingdoms of Egypt.

According to the ancient initiates of the Egyptian priesthood, the two kingdoms of Egypt were a living temple, built by the "spirit of God," where man could play his ritual part and reunite his spirit with the divine as the result of an alchemical process. The Temple of God on Earth, Egypt itself, was patterned on an "eternal archetype" of the supreme achievement of nature – namely man.[27] This geographical representation of the human archetype had a spine, a head in the north and a body in the south. Along the serpentine spine, represented by the River Nile, lay seven great mystical centers marked by temples, which were the earthly equivalent to the seven major energy plexii or "chakras" in the human body. Each of these had specific rituals and secret teachings that directly related to their function. Those who were initiated at particular temples were expected to serve their chakral and spiritual purpose for the benefit of all who inhabited the two kingdoms of Egypt. Thus we find the fundamental concept that the fruits of initiation, sacred knowledge and wisdom were to be used for the benefit of the entire community.

The outward complexity of Egyptian religion with its multiplicity of gods masks a very different concept of ritual duty that is hard to appreciate for modern people used to the idea of public participation in religious rituals. Apart from the great festivals of each year when the public did attend, most religious duties were performed in private by an initiatory priesthood who were led by the highest initiates of them all, the pharaohs.

The growth of sacred knowledge and insight, and mathematical, scientific and astrological skill up to this point had been enormous. Secret systems of language were developed to encode mathematical symbolism, esoteric knowledge and magic. These secret languages were known as "Hieratic" for written work, and "Senzar" for the spoken form. Healing had reached a standard of subtlety and sophistication that was not equaled in Western Europe until the late twentieth century. Post-mortem examination of mummified bodies demonstrates that highly complex and effective brain surgery was common. The wealth and creative artistry of the Egyptian artisans of that time, and later, were given graphic demonstration by the discoveries in the tomb of Tutankhamun. The boy king, like all his ancestors, was not only pharaoh, but also an initiate of the Egyptian Temple Mysteries. Those who were initiated in this manner developed a solemn and resigned worldview. They had faced the goddess Isis and had partaken of her wisdom and perceived themselves as "sons of the widow" – a phrase that rings bells with the worldwide brotherhood of Freemasonry today.[28]

These royal initiates performed the duties and secret rites that ensured that divine blessings would continue to flow and nourish all the Egyptian people. The fruits of a body of sacred knowledge known only to the initiated – such as medicine, surgery, healing, astronomy, engineering and science – were then deployed to the benefit of all the inhabitants of the two kingdoms of Egypt. One man from the very heart of this tradition, who was raised as the son of a pharaoh and was an initiate of the highest degree, was to lay the foundations of a religious system that would transform the world and bring the benefits of sacred knowledge to a far wider community. The man we know as Moses.

Until relatively recently, no one had ever been able to identify Moses with any recognizable character in the Egyptian historical record, and even today there is some dispute about exactly who he was. The first breakthrough in the search for the historical Moses came in 1934 when Sigmund Freud wrote the introductory chapters to a book on Moses. They were published in the German magazine *Imago* in 1937 under the title "Moses an Egyptian?" In this article Freud not only showed that the name Moses was Egyptian but also demonstrated that the biblical mythology surrounding his birth was an inversion of the norm as described in the mythology of Sargon, where the child of rich or royal parents is brought up in humble circumstances. Freud stated that this was to hide Moses' Egyptian origins. In a later article, also published by *Imago*, the question was posed "Why did the lawgiver, if he was an Egyptian, pass on a monotheistic belief to his followers?" The father of psychoanalysis then showed the great similarities between the religion of the Pharaoh Akhenaten and that of Moses. The Jewish Credo is *Schema Yisrael Adonai Elohenu Adonai Echod* – "Hear, O Israel, the Lord thy God is One God." Freud showed that as the Hebrew letter *d* is a transliteration of the Egyptian letter *t*, and as the *e* becomes *o*, this sentence in Egyptian script becomes "Hear, O Israel, our God Aten is the only God." A prayer that can only be ascribed to the Akhenaten era.

Suffering from terminal cancer, Freud sought refuge in

London in 1938. His two published articles, plus a third, also written in Vienna, were soon published as a full book in English. He thought this would prove to be a fit and proper culmination to his life of study. *Moses and Monotheism* was published in 1939. According to Freud, Moses was, in fact, a high official in the entourage of Akhenaten called Thuthmose, who chose the Hebrew tribe living at Goshen to be his followers and then led them out of Egypt. Freud's theory was virulently refuted by many, mainly Jewish scholars, who chose as the focus of their attack not Freud, but Akhenaten and the religion he founded. They hoped that by debunking the religion of Atenism and slandering Akhenaten's reputation with the mix of abuse and invective common to all theological disputes, Freud's theories would be devalued and negated. This is truly ironic, for it has now become apparent that the most likely candidate for the role of Moses in history was not Thuthmose, but Akhenaten himself.

It was in 1991 that a meticulous scholar from the Islamic tradition, Ahmed Osman, published research proving beyond any reasonable doubt that the biblical figure of Moses was the Egyptian Pharaoh Akhenaten himself.[29] Akhenaten had tried to institute a monotheistic belief in Egypt that nearly provoked civil war; one that had within it, oddly enough, the concept of a Trinity.

> The God Aten had become a Trinity, consisting of Re, as the father, Aten as the visible form of the father, and Akhenaten – who was both the son of Re, the son of Aten and yet at the same time the father of both; and further he was both Aten and Re.[30]

After a period of considerable unrest, Akhenaten was deposed and fled into Sinai taking his serpent headed staff with him. No further mention of him is to be found in the Egyptian records. The biblical story recounts that Moses also had to flee in the same direction after supposedly killing an Egyptian.[31] Akhenaten's tomb has been discovered, but all the available evidence indicates that it was never used for a burial and no trace of his body has ever been found. With the disappearance of Akhenaten and the death of Tutankhamun, the stage was set for the rise of a new line of kings. It was the eventful years of the first two reigns of this new dynasty that became both the setting and the cause for the biblical events we know as the "Oppression" and the "Exodus." Thanks to the work of Freud and Osman, we believe that we now have a scenario that is not only in accord with the Bible, but also marries up with Egyptian history in a highly plausible manner. While there has been considerable dispute over the dating of the Exodus, a growing number of scholars have come to the conclusion that it was at, or soon after, the time of Akhenaten. They too believe that there was some direct relationship between the faith of the Israelites and the monotheistic beliefs of the "heretic king." The Name Moses itself is, undoubtedly, Egyptian. This is not so surprising; even if we take the biblical account of his birth and upbringing as absolute truth, the name could have come from his royal, adoptive mother. To refute the claim that Akhenaten was not the rightful heir to the twin thrones of Egypt, his followers called him the "Son," that is the rightful heir to Amenhotep III. The Egyptian word for son is *Mos*.[32]

Osman's identification of Akhenaten as Moses is still debated. For instance, Egyptologist David Rohl suggests that the Exodus took place during the reign of the Pharaoh Dudimose, the 36th ruler of the Thirteenth Dynasty. Despite this, two early twentieth century Jewish scholars, Karl Abraham and Sigmund Freud, as well as the more recent Muslim researcher Ahmed Osman and the

Christian academic Robert Feather, are all in agreement that those who led and took part in the Exodus originated among Akhenaten's entourage and believed in his distinct form of monotheism.

> The strange desertion of Amarna and the sudden disappearance of all who lived in it imparts a high degree of plausibility to this new vision of the Exodus. Not only did the nobility and priesthood vanish but also so did all the artisans, craftsmen, workers and servants. Akhenaten's Egyptian priests, scribes and notables – the national elite – were the first true monotheists in humanity and believed in one god, Aten.[33]

Other dissatisfied Egyptians as well as various foreign residents, which the Bible describes as a "mixed multitude," joined Akhenaten's religious and political entourage. This view of the so-called early "people of Israel" is not new. That renowned medieval Jewish scholar Rashi wrote that they were a mixture of nations newly converted to monotheism and described them as a "mixed multitude."

One other important matter has puzzled all scholars who have vainly tried to correlate the Egyptian records with the biblical account of the Exodus. How could such a vast migration of people take place under such bizarre circumstances without any mention of it being recorded in Egyptian history? Many Egyptologists and biblical scholars, including modern Israelis, have voiced the unpopular belief that there are such grave doubts about the historicity of the Exodus that the entire account may simply be a matter of myth and legend.

Indeed Sigmund Freud declared that he could find no trace whatsoever of the term Hebrew prior to the Babylonian Exile when the scriptures were first transcribed from oral legend into written form. This was over seven centuries after the events described in Exodus and Kings, and the modern Israeli scholars Messod and Roger Sabbah claim that there is no proof of the Hebrews' existence as a nation or tribe at the time of Moses as described in the scriptures. The voluminous and extensive Egyptian official archives record the power achievements and knowledge of the pharaohs and priests; defeats, however, are largely ignored. Any pharaoh's actions that brought the state into disrepute were never mentioned. In the matter of Akhenaten's heresy, this idea was taken even further; the name of the heretical pharaoh was deleted from statues and temple walls in an attempt to remove all trace of him from the records. Akhenaten had become a nonperson. Thus his emigration would pass unrecorded and would be quietly expedited with all speed.

The treasure carried by the "people of Israel" as they left, the "jewels of silver, and jewels of gold" recorded in the Bible, were a strange and inexplicable burden for supposedly newly emancipated slaves to carry. Robert Feather claims that this treasure was composed of Moses' personal wealth and the treasure of Amarna and compensation for Akhenaten's claim to the throne. The Sabbahs believe that the right to settle in Canaan went along with the right to export the Atenist treasures of Amarna, and as Canaan was an Egyptian province, this too was part of the compensation package.

The fact that early post-Exodus Judaism was, ethnically and spiritually, clearly Egyptian in origin has been known by scholars for years, but this has not impinged upon the public consciousness because of the theological blinkers that limit the perceptions of fundamentalists of Judaism, Christianity and Islam. The devout in all three great faiths need to recognise the essentially Egyptian nature of their religious beliefs. Judaism, from the time of Moses until the time of Jesus, was constantly evolving and owes much of its development to the influence of polytheism and paganism and the ancient system of the transmission of sacred wisdom than most modern theologians would care to admit.

Moses led his new people, a strange mixture of the descendants of his grandfather, the patriarch Joseph, and his loyal Egyptian followers, from Succoth to their first camp at Etham and then through the wilderness towards the Reed Sea. Because in the Egyptian and Hebrew scripts there are no written vowels, this was later mistranslated as the "Red Sea." For much of the year, the Reed Sea is passable on foot, but it is subject to sudden inundations by tidal waves of enormous proportions. It was one of these that swamped the pharaoh and his army, who by this time were in full pursuit of Moses and his followers.[34] The Israelites, under the leadership of Moses, then left the shores of the Reed Sea and, according to the Bible, spent forty years in the wilderness before their eventual entry into the "Promised Land."

The Visionary Ezekiel Temple plan,
drawn by the 19th century French architect and Bible scholar Charles Chipiez.

CHAPTER 4

The Covenant and the People of Israel

The only evidence we have for the Israelites forty years wandering in the wilderness, their invasion of the Promised Land and their history up to the time of the invasion by the Assyrians in 722 BCE is to be found in the Bible. Despite the fundamentalist belief that the entire work is "the inspired word of God" it is, nonetheless, a highly unreliable historical source. The vivid and detailed descriptions of these events were not written in anything like their present form until many centuries later, during the Babylonian Exile that lasted from 586 until 538 BCE. Indeed, the Exodus itself along with the sojourn in Egypt, has been described by one serious historian of the Jewish people, Norman Cantor, as having been "… fabricated in later centuries for some ideologically conditioned or socially advantageous purpose."[35]

The alleged conquest of Jericho and the rest of Canaan by the people of Israel has long been viewed with outright scepticism by scholars. Indeed Sigmund Freud described this particular period as one that "is particularly impenetrable to investigation."[36] The rest of the so-called historical content of the Bible covering the period up to and immediately prior to the Exile is equally dubious in its accuracy. Only two sources of independent verification for any part of it exist in the archaeological or archival records of neighboring states. The first is a stele erected by the Egyptian Pharaoh Merneptah in 1207 BCE that records his victory against the people of Israel and which reads "Israel is laid waste." The second can be found in the annals of Sargon II, king of Assyria who wrote in 722 BCE, "In the beginning of my royal rule, I have besieged and conquered the city of the Samarians [the capital of the northern kingdom of Israel] ... I have led away 27,290 of its inhabitants as captives."[37] Apart from those corroborations, we must read the historical events described in the Bible with a large grain of salt. David and Solomon, despite their alleged wealth and power, passed signally unrecorded by any other states. The Dead Sea Scrolls scholar, John Allegro, described this entire period as one in which "We are in a shadowy world, where the hard facts of history fade off into Mythology."[38] The American historian, Norman Cantor, was even more direct: "... such is the Biblical story whose verification defies the course of historical and archaeological science. It is a romantic fantasy."[39] This leaves any serious student of the Bible, or of history, with one very pertinent question: what can we believe from our scriptural analysis? To even begin to answer that we have investigate the manner in which the scriptures were composed; who wrote them and what were they trying to achieve.

The Old Testament that we know and revere only began to take shape during the Babylonian Exile as a devout compilation of earlier material both oral and written. It included one book of the Law, most probably Deuteronomy, which had been discovered in rather suspect circumstances immediately prior to the fall of Jerusalem and the Exile that followed.[40] It is apparent from the account in Chronicles that this detailed exposition of the Law of Moses was an entirely novel idea to the king, the priests and the people of Israel at that time. Most scholars then deduce that, apart from the Ten Commandments and the Gnostic traditions they had brought with them from Egypt, all pre-Exilic Jews, including David and Solomon, had lived and died without the benefit of this Law (which, according to Deuteronomy, had been binding on all of them as an essential part of the Covenant with God, the *Berit*).

During the Exile, combining this new source along with oral tradition and other unidentified documents, the scribes began to create the basis of the scriptures we know today. According to the modern "Documentary hypothesis" at least four major sources can be discerned in its composition. Two, the J and the E, are each so described, according to whether they refer to God as Jahweh or the Elohim. These are believed to originate from oral traditions or documents dating from about the eighth century BCE. The most predominant sources are called the Deuteronomist and the P, or Priestly school, and are both believed to have been written during and immediately after the Exile.[41] Furthermore, the traditions being transcribed disclose the intertwining of two different and distinct sources of spiritual inspiration. In common with all early nomadic tribesmen, the Jews had their own "shamans," or prophets, whose mystical insight was one of the most revered sources of revelation; the second and equally important source of revelation was a direct inheritance from their Egyptian ancestors, the sacred Gnostic tradition that inspired Abraham, Melchizedek and Moses, all initiates of the Temple Mysteries. Subtle Babylonian influences can also be detected which may have developed during the Exile itself.

The scribes and priests who took on this mammoth task were undoubtedly spiritually inspired, but they also had their own personal and professional agendas to protect. It is apparent that the scriptures developed during and after the Exile, enhanced and stressed the role of the priesthood, especially the twenty-four *ma'madot* or priestly families who took turns to discharge the high-priestly function at the temple. Eligibility for membership of these privileged groups was seemingly dependant upon provable descent from Zadok, the Jebusite priest appointed to serve at the Temple by King David. In writing the "history" of their people, the priestly scholars had projected their own, newfound importance backwards across the centuries so that the scriptures read as if they had maintained their role from the time of King David at least. Furthermore, their insistence on the validity of the newly written Law of Moses gave them an ingenious explanation for the trauma of the Exile. Namely that Israel was suffering because the entire nation, individually and collectively, had ignored the Law that lay at the heart of its sacred covenant with God. Therefore, if individual behavior came into conformity with the new 613 strictures of the Law, God would smile upon them once more and restore the nation to its former glory.[42]

As the Temple in Jerusalem had been destroyed and the leading people of the Jewish nation were now exiled in Babylon, a new form of worship had to be developed. Thus the synagogue was born as a meeting place for the exiles, one where the new scriptures could be read, God could be praised and where prayers replaced the rituals and sacrifice that had been the central function at the temple. The exiles learned and used Aramaic as their spoken language and Hebrew was reserved for the scriptures. Indeed, according to Freud at least, the term Hebrew as an indication of race now came into use for the first time.[43] The overall effect of these new habits of worship, the insistence on the primacy of the Law and the reverence for the scriptures changed Judaism completely, from a nature loving, rather tolerant, loosely monotheistic religion into a strictly conformist, legalistic and tightly structured and exclusively Jahwist cult that continued unabated until the destruction of Jerusalem by the Romans some six hundred years later. The historian Karen Armstrong summed this up when she wrote: "Yahweh had finally absorbed his rivals in the religious imagination of Israel; in exile the lure of paganism lost its attraction and Judaism had been born."[44]

Understanding the circumstances that shaped the writing of the scriptures gives us a particular insight into what the priestly scribes really held to be of prime importance. The mystical tradition that sustained the prophets was given considerable prominence and while they certainly distorted and exaggerated their own historical importance as a race, they were brutally honest about the religious back-sliding of the past, those lapses into paganism that seem to have been endemic from the time of the Exodus to the beginning of the Exile. Above all, the overriding importance of wisdom was repeatedly stressed. The Hebrews obviously held their Gnostic heritage in reverence. From the miracle of the parting of the Red Sea to the end of the reign of King Solomon, wisdom is referred to again and again. The Pillar of Cloud that led them during their forty years in the wilderness was now interpreted as the very seat of Wisdom herself.[45] Wisdom was also described as becoming unto them a covering in the daytime and a flame of stars throughout the night.[46] In Proverbs we read that, "She built her house, she has set up her Seven Pillars of Wisdom."[47] Wisdom was also described as a consort of God, a somewhat bizarre idea for any true monotheists to consider. Later this eternal principle of divine wisdom was understood to be an attribute of God himself, similar to the "Glory of God."[48] Ask any Bible reader for the most distinguishing attributes of King Solomon, surely the most mythologized character in the Old Testament, and they will invariably reply, "his wisdom." It is as though wisdom above all was the sole route to righteousness, to the revelation of God's will for his people and the major source of national and spiritual unity.

The new insistence on the supreme authority of the scriptures as the record of God's plan for his Chosen People, changed the nature of Judaism in another, far more lasting way. The Jews, who had always had a high literacy rate, became completely focussed on their sacred books, which, because they were formed by the amalgamation of differing strands of tradition, were, as often as not, vague, contradictory and difficult to understand. Not to worry, the priests were always on hand to guide, interpret and explain. The English historian Paul Johnson described this situation in the following terms:

> The Jewish scriptures, formidable in bulk and often of impenetrable obscurity gave employment ... to a vast cottage industry of scribes and lawyers, both amateur and professional, filling whole libraries with their commentaries, enmeshing the Jewish world in a web of canon law, luxuriant with its internal conflicts and its mutual exclusions, too complex for any one mind to comprehend, bread and butter for a proliferating clergy and an infinite series of traps for the righteous.[49]

This complex and ever proliferating process of scriptural exegesis and interpretation started during the Exile in Babylon and continues to this day. Each individual Jew was expected to be able to read the holy books and started at an early age to learn Talmudic disputation, an adversarial form of debate, disputation and analysis. Thus Judaism began to take on even more contradictory aspects. On the one hand it became completely dismissive of other religions, while on the other, because of the multiple, and often contradictory interpretations that could be discerned not only in its scriptures but also in its law, it became increasingly tolerant of differences of opinion on religious matters among its own people. This gave rise to the old Jewish aphorism, "Where you have two Jews, you will have three arguments."

The Exile was merely one issue among others in the catalogue of disasters that befell the people of Israel between 734 and 581 BCE. Between those years there were six different and distinct enforced deportations of the Israelites and many other Jews fled voluntarily to Egypt and elsewhere for safety. Thus these events marked another major and transformative turning point in Jewish history for, from that time onwards, the majority of Jewish people would live outside the Holy Land. The Diaspora had begun in earnest, which gave further impetus to synagogue worship, for who could reach the Temple in Jerusalem from distant lands?

The Babylonian Exile therefore was a mixed blessing, for this major dislocation in Jewish life stimulated the writing of the scriptures, the foundation of synagogue worship and the transformation of Judaism into the highly legalistic, formalized cult that we recognize from the accounts in the Bible. These lasting effects tend to mask the fact that the Exile was remarkably short, lasting about seventy years. It ended in 536 BCE. The Babylonian Empire was conquered in its turn by the Persians, a race who took an even more tolerant and pragmatic view of the Jewish people and their homeland than the Babylonians. The return and the rebuilding of the temple in Jerusalem was led by Sheshbazzar,[50] the son of King Jehoiachin of Judea, and Zerubbabel, the king's grandson.[51] The apocryphal scriptures record that the return came about as a result of Zerubbabel's ability to answer a riddle that was posed in a dream experienced by the Persian King Cyrus, an almost identical replication of the mechanism allegedly used by Joseph to attain rank and power in Egypt centuries earlier. The answer to the riddle set in the dream was "Wine is strong, Women are stronger, Kings are stronger still, but Truth conquers all."[52] The Persian king soon made the following proclamation:

> Thus saith Cyrus King of Persia, the Lord God of heaven has
> given me all the kingdoms of the earth; and he has charged
> me to build him a house in Jerusalem which is in Judah. Who
> is there among you of all his people? His God be with him
> and let him go up to Jerusalem, which is in Judah, and build
> the house of the Lord God of Israel (he is the God) which is
> in Jerusalem.[53]

As a result, the return to Jerusalem began along with the slow, intermittent and tedious rebuilding of the Temple, the city walls and with them, the identity of the Hebrew people.

After many trials and tribulations, the Temple was rebuilt and the religious and commercial life of the people of Israel started to attain some semblance of normality based firmly on the 613 strictures of the Law of Moses. The Jews learned to accommodate their lives to their new masters and, after them, to the Greeks against whom they eventually rebelled. Throughout this period of several centuries, worship in the Second Temple continued to play its central role in Jewish life. Despite the strictures in the Law against building other temples to rival the one in Jerusalem, others certainly existed. One was sited at Yeb, or Elephantine, on the River Nile and the form of worship there pre-dated the Exodus;[54] another was founded in Leontopolis, again in Egypt, in 174 BCE, by the deposed high-priest Onias[55] and a third was constructed by the Samaritans at Gezarim in about 200 BCE.[56] Meanwhile in the ever-growing Diaspora spread around the coast of the Mediterranean, sizable Jewish communities flourished and multiplied under the protection of the Roman Empire.

The Olympian gods; work by Monsiau (1754–1837).

CHAPTER 5

The Glory Of Ancient Greece And The Power Of Rome

Abstraction, logic, reasoned choice and inventions, mathematics, art, calculation of space and time, anxieties and dreams of love – all these activities of inner life are nothing else than the effervescence of the newly formed centre (of consciousness), as it explodes onto itself.[57]

—Pierre Teilhard de Chardin, *The Phenomenon of Man*

The ancient world did not make one sudden, inexplicable leap from primitive hunter-gatherer societies to the breathtaking architectural glories and intellectual pinnacles of Athens. The speed of development of differing cultures varied from community to community, depending primarily on the quality of the spiritual insights that fueled their drive towards civilization. Archaeological evidence indicates that while powerful kings and emperors ruled the East, settlements developed in Europe which had their own sophisticated art forms, crafts, weaving skills and religious symbols displaying somewhat different concepts of gods and their relationship to man. Evidence, though scanty, is beginning to accumulate that clearly demonstrates that our Neolithic ancestors in Europe had a profound reverence for "Mother Earth," for plants and animals, for the very elements themselves. Little is known as yet about the various forms this worship may have taken, but sufficient evidence exists for scholars to delineate some of the myths associated with Gaia, or Mother Earth.

With the passage of time, Mother Earth took on new names and was married in mythology with the stars or the sky. New lesser gods emerged, replacing the spirits who had previously been believed to inhabit different plants and animals, until by the early years of classical Greece a complex pantheon of gods were believed to exist in the heavenly abode of Mount Olympus, with Zeus, the god of thunder, rising above them all. These gods were held to be capricious, mischievous and in conflict with each other, treating men as mere pawns as if in some complex, irrational, heavenly chess game.[58]

With increasing influence from the empires of the East, another trend, which was to be uniquely Greek, began to develop in a new and significantly different way. Its effects were to indirectly, but completely, change the world. The importation of initiation cults and their development into the "hidden" Mysteries, or "hermetic" cults, created a fertile seedbed for the flowering of philosophy, science, art and architecture.

The hidden Mysteries all have a common origin. We have spoken of Colin Wilson's conception of the "Few" – the natural leaders who knew of their innate spiritual powers and deliberately sought means of extending and strengthening them. The Mystery cults of early man arose when the "Few" tried to gain knowledge of the three apparently inescapable facts of life that confront all mankind: pain, toil and death. Pain that occurs in every birth; the necessary toil to survive in the face of hostile nature and, finally, the death that ensues in all created beings. This conception is the foundation of many, far older religious systems, in which it was called "primal karma." Only two basic attitudes are possible towards this fate of mankind: it can be regarded as a curse that has arisen from a blind evolution; or it can be regarded as a purposeful blessing at the hand of God.[59] The original path of initiation arose from the latter view in which pain, toil and death were regarded as the means through which humanity was protected from evil. As I have written elsewhere: "The first known system of initiation appeared in ancient Persia around 7000 BC when Zarathushtra divined the conversion of these three primal necessities."[60]

Initiation was restricted to a privileged few and the novice was introduced and taught by a "hierophant," or revealer of holy things. Initiation rites and the ceremonies of the Mystery cults were secret. The participants were granted knowledge of the spiritual world during the ecstatic periods of these rituals, which were held to be so sacred that they could not be revealed to outsiders except on pain of death. Some of the Greek cults, just like the Essenes of Israel, developed a deeper cosmology and, oddly enough, characteristics which were replicated in the early years of Christian belief and practice. Baptism by fire or water, the confession of sins, a period of purification and fasting, and a ritual meal of bread and water or wine. All of which were, in one form or another, part of initiation rites.

Two of the earliest, and perhaps the purest, of such Mystery cults were the Magi of Persia and the Orphic cults in Greece. The Orphic Mystery religion was supposedly founded by the legendary singer Orpheus, an approximate contemporary of Zarathushtra, known also as Zoroaster. It provided a vital, reforming and moderating influence on the savagery of the later city-states of the first waves of civilization. Its doctrine tends towards asceticism and emphasizes mental ecstasy. By this it was hoped to achieve "enthusiasm" (*entheosism*) and as a result gain mystical knowledge.[61] Little is known for certain of the Orphic Mysteries of initiation, but perhaps something can be inferred from what we do know of the rites of Eleusis. These began with a cleansing in the sea followed by the imparting of occult knowledge. In common with all initiation rites it certainly involved tests or trials – probably wandering through underground passageways with carefully prepared surprises designed to try and test the fortitude, faith and courage of the novice. Scholars suggest that the ceremonies ended with the ritual garlanding of the new initiate. The cult had a body of sacred texts and held its followers together by bonds of shared belief. It produced a philosophy which directly related to real life and the temporal world, and which provided just the vibrant conception that was needed for a passionate search for truth and beauty.[62]

Many of these early Mystery cults, such as those pertaining to Dionysus and Demeter, had a well-established "ecclesiastical year." Seasonal festivals were inherited from earlier religions – and were usually closely associated with the sowing and reaping of corn or the production of wine. Each cult or Mystery school, despite their stress on the values and reality of the spiritual world and its distinct superiority in importance to the temporal world, clung closely to the well-established links between the divine and the earthly. A close study of the Egyptian Isis cult reinforces these close links between the teaching of the Mystery schools and the cycles of growth and regeneration of the Earth in all its fruitfulness.

The supposed author of the earliest Mystery texts still extant is Hermes Trismegistos, usually identified with the divine Hermes – the messenger of the gods – or with the Egyptian god Thoth, who was also the scribe of the gods. This may be why Hermes Trismegistos is reputed to be the author of the hermetic texts, which only came to light in the third century of the Christian era. The similarity of some of their contents with Christian ideas at first led to accusations of forgery, neo-Platonists usually being held to be responsible. However it is now generally accepted that

HIDDEN WISDOM

the contents of the texts themselves, or at least of such fragments as have survived, are authentic and confirm the linkage between Greek hermetic schools and the Mystery cults of ancient Egypt.[63] This is reinforced when we study the first Greek initiate who can clearly be identified as an historical figure. This supreme individual, a mathematician, the founder of a school, a religious mystic who was interested in everything and who had a truly formative influence on Greek thought, science and philosophy – was the legendary Pythagoras.[64]

Pythagoras was born on the island of Samos about 570 BCE. His family sent him to Egypt to be initiated into the Egyptian Temple Mysteries. Diogenes Laertes wrote that Pythagoras was initiated at Thebes, where excavations in 1888 revealed a statue of the god Kabeiros with a hammer in his hand.[65] Some scholars believe that Kabeiros was worshipped by the Egyptian-Hebraic sect of the Kabeiri, early precursors of the Therapeutae and the Essenes.[66] Pythagoras was later associated with the Persian Magi and the Chaldeans. He is also reported to have spent ten years in Babylon studying the Mesopotamian Mysteries. According to Posidonius, one of Pythagoras' principle teachers was Abaris the Druid, who came from Scotland.[67] After more than thirty-four years away from home, mostly spent in the East, Pythagoras developed an oriental form of mysticism that shows through clearly in his later philosophical works.[68] He founded a school in Crotona in Southern Italy, shortly after his return to Greece. This was a school for mystics whose initiation rites were both lengthy and rigorous, and it was here that he developed his own brand of philosophy[69] that became, over the centuries, one of the most profound and lasting influences over the entire field of mysticism and the occult. Colin Wilson claims that:

> Instinctively Pythagoras … never lost his secure grasp on the mystical, "The One" – what Hindus would call Brahman – but he tried to understand the "one" by the use of his intellect.[70]

Under the influence of the Pythagoreans the verifiable rise of the Mystery cults began. With them came the close identification of the gods with nature and all its bounty, and an all-consuming curiosity about life before and after death. This led to the further development of philosophy, mathematics and science. Under the influence of the Pythagoreans, the old Olympian religion began to be displaced and a new distinctly spiritual outlook took its place. The newly emerging beliefs had something in common with those of most early cultures. The power and spirit of nature lay at their very heart and the Earth itself was described as a goddess under various guises: the great goddess of harvest and vegetation was worshipped as Ishtar, Isis, Demeter, Cybele or her pre-Hellenic name, Gaia.

The outpouring of art, philosophy and literature that accompanied and sustained the emergence of Greek civilization has been passed down to us virtually intact. Greek culture quickly developed all of the literary forms that we now regard as classic. Experience, knowledge, inquiry and expectations, were all recorded and passed on. This irreversible accumulation, the very art of storage and transmission of ideas and experience, constantly both augmented consciousness and acted as a catalyst for further evolution. An evolution which, in its turn, transformed human life itself.

The power and cumulative influence of the Gnostic initiatory culture that developed in ancient Greece, pervaded, sustained and influenced all the cultures that followed for over two millennia, including the so-called modern advances of the twentieth century. Never is this more clearly demonstrated than when we move on from the works of Pythagoras to the time of Socrates and his pupil Plato. At this time in the Greek city-states, citizens recognized that laws were made by men alone solely for the benefit and governance of men.[71] The new philosophy held that thought, philosophy and politics would inevitably lead to the knowledge of the "Good, the Beautiful and the True," and the law – man-made terrestrial law – was the ultimate expression of this. Law was thus given the twin accords of respect and a capacity for ultimate perfection as the expression of the state and therefore of man himself. The humility of Socrates was such that he held that he himself knew nothing, yet he believed that knowledge lay within the reach of all who earnestly sought it. He believed that sin derived from man's lack of knowledge and if only man had sufficient knowledge he would not sin. As the overriding cause of sin was ignorance, to reach the "Good" we must attain knowledge.

The sacred and indissoluble link between the "Good" and knowledge became one of the hallmarks of Greek thought and philosophy for many centuries. The contrast between this philosophical concept and the dogmas of early Christianity could not be more stark, for the medieval Christian ethic is quite opposed to the ideas of Socrates. The early popes, and all those who inherited their mantle for many centuries to come, held that the most important quality was a pure heart and a capacity for implicit belief, and that therefore these qualities were more likely to be found among the ignorant.[72]

After the death of Socrates, Plato took refuge with many of Socrates' followers in Megara. Then began a period of exile and travel that lasted until 387 BCE when he finally returned to Athens. There, in a grove to the north of the city, on land dedicated to the memory of the legendary hero Academus, he founded a school which from this time forth, like many centers of learning that succeeded it, became known as the "Academy." Its organization was modeled on the Pythagorean school in Southern Italy which was still flourishing, and which Plato himself had visited during the course of his travels. These two schools became the direct ancestors of all our universities, serving as role models for them from the Middle Ages to the present day.[73] The curriculum of the Academy was a direct product of the central teaching of the hermetic initiates who had exerted such a formative influence on Pythagoras many years before. The aim of the course of instruction was to turn the thoughts of men from the constantly changing world of experience, the temporal, phenomenal world, to the framework that lay behind it, the spiritual world: from becoming to being!

The Academy gained such importance, power and influence over the minds of thinking men that it lasted for far longer than any other center of learning established before or since, surviving for over nine hundred years, until it was forcibly closed by the Christian Emperor Justinian in 529 CE.[74] Justinian, like many blind, intolerant and bigoted men before and since, had failed to learn that closing or burning schools, or men for that matter, has proved singularly ineffective in stamping out ideas regarded as unorthodox or heretical. The influence of the Platonic Academy is still felt today.

No brief discourse such as this can possibly begin to trace in detail the full flowering of art, literature, philosophy and the new sciences that took place during this truly seminal era. All I can do is to give some flavour of the complex and vital development of the many intertwining strands of thought that still influence us to this day. The Greek city-states were fragmented, each proudly autonomous, each at war from time to time with its own immediate neighbors, yet also sometimes in alliance with them against the hostile empires of Persia, and later Rome. How was the concept of the "Good, the Beautiful and the True" able to spread and ramify its undoubted influence throughout the known world, not only at that time but even down to the modern era? To answer this question we must turn our attention to a newly emergent empire, one established by military force and alliances which created a stability, power and influence that the Greeks themselves, for all their achievements, never attained. This was an empire based on military might, the rule of man-made law, and concepts of order and stability that had never before been sustained for so long or over such a wide area, providing the perfect vehicle for the transmission of ideas – the Empire of Rome.

Rome took to its very heart the full flowering of the first fruits of consciousness and spread them throughout the world, not only then, but through its profound influence on Christianity, throughout all time. Thus, two distinct and separate national characteristics, firstly that of the sublimely gifted, inspired creators and innovators, the Greeks, became allied to the second, that of the sharp-eyed, innovative, pragmatic and powerful Romans, combined to develop and sustain a political and intellectual climate within which were refined the ideas that became the very foundation for Western culture in the two millennia that followed.

By the time of the birth of Jesus, the Roman Empire, which had doubled in size every generation since its foundation, encompassed nearly all the then-known world. It comprised the entire Mediterranean Littoral and had pushed its borders well beyond: westwards into Spain, France and Britain; and northwards into Germany. Although imposed by force, it was in many ways a liberal empire, for having gained territory by force, it maintained its rule by military might twinned with tolerant acceptance of local customs and religions – as long as the Roman law was upheld and lip service given to the state religion.[75] For the first time there arose an imperial establishment which brought not only stability but also widespread peace, freedom of movement and trade, tolerance to old religious forms, local customs and new philosophical ideas. Ideas were far from regimented and stultified; indeed their propagation and exchange were actively encouraged. Thus Rome absorbed the art, philosophy and religious culture that was the glory of Greece, raised it to a pinnacle of respect, and became the means whereby Greek culture, religion and ideas were transmitted throughout the world.[76]

Mystery cults began to infiltrate Roman life during the Republic. Some cults took root in their original form, others became modified with the latinization of the original Greek names, or the identification of Greek gods with specifically Roman deities. Certain cults eventually degenerated into social clubs for men only, and few of the truly great initiation cults lasted for long, with the notable exceptions of the Persian cult of Mithras and the Egyptian cult of Isis. In the two centuries following the birth of Christ, Mithraic solar worship under the protection of the god Sol Invictus grew in popularity.[77] Knowledge of these various gods and their cults spread widely, providing a confusing multiplicity of religious ideas that, as often as not, intermingled, spawning new ones all the time.

Transcending all religions and ideas of tribe or nationality, and rising above them all in the Roman Empire, was the respect accorded to education – the perfect vehicle for the new philosophical and spiritual ideas from Greece. Theology was inseparable from philosophy. Had not the first philosophers of note been initiates into the spiritual worlds? Rhetoric became the handmaiden of both; Greek the common language of the educated empire. Thus religion became, through its main derivative philosophy, the guide to intimate personal conduct, responsibility and moral virtue and, as a consequence of the Greek hermetic and philosophical influence, an age of personal religion dawned, in sharp contrast to the collective state or tribal religions of the recent past.

Greek culture provided an ambience, within which the intellect was used to transform religious ideas, but they were all ideas that came from other cultures and other times, such as Babylon, Persia and Egypt, that were now re-synthesized in Greek forms. The Greek cosmology, such as it was, derived directly from these ancient sources, as we have seen in the case of Pythagoras and those who followed him. Thus, the Roman Empire permeated by Greek culture, created and sustained a world of religious tolerance, high levels of culture and art and a deep respect for the values of education. Only once was Rome known to persecute the religion of one of its subject states, and that was in the far west of the empire, in the land of the Celts.

Two Druids. Bas-relief found at Autun, in Burgundy, France.
From *Old England: A Pictorial Museum* by Charles Knight (1845).

CHAPTER 6

The Initiates of Celtic Culture

Thus philosophy, a science of the highest utility, flourished in antiquity among the barbarians, shedding its light over nations. And afterwards it came to Greece. First in its ranks were the prophets of the Egyptians; and the Chaldeans among the Assyrians; and the Druids among the Gauls; and the Samanaeans among the Bactrians; and the philosophers of the Kelts; and the Magi of the Persians.[78]

– Clement of Alexandria, *Stromata*

There is considerable debate as to whether the Celtic people had their origins in the northern part of India or in the Middle East, but it is known that they migrated slowly westward, spending much time in Galatia, close to biblical Israel, the Lake Balaton region of Hungary and later, Northern Italy, before settling on the western fringes of mainland Europe and the British Isles. Their beliefs, rituals and practices have much in common with the recorded practices of the prophets and certain esoteric groups in biblical Israel. Some authorities claim not merely common practices, but common racial and esoteric roots, a theory which links the early Druids with the Hebrew esoteric group known as the Kabeiri.[79] The Celtic culture and social structure is well known to us for they left us a vast store of mythology, legend and literature that has served modern archaeologists and historians as a vital tool in gaining an understanding of this fascinating people. Like many peoples of their era their chiefs were guided and advised by an initiatory elite, one whose fame has spanned more than two millennia.

The initiates of the Celtic peoples of Western Europe were the Druids. To twenty-first century man, the mere mention of the Druids gives rise to images of solemn processions of long-robed figures practicing dramatic Bardic ceremonies amidst ancient megalithic monuments. Images that, in truth, owe far more to modern imagination than to any demonstrable historical fact or record. In the Celtic lands of Western Europe, Druidic teachings were handed down secretly from initiate to novice during a twenty year apprenticeship. Some of the spiritual perceptions that arose from this teaching gave rise to the energy inspiring whorls and circles of Celtic design and dance that are familiar to us today. The Celts had an alphabet, Ogham script, yet despite this, their lore was not the only knowledge transmitted orally. All Celtic mythology was handed down in the same manner and was not given written form until after the Christian conversion – the earliest manuscript copies date from the seventh century CE.

Like the ancient Egyptian initiates before them, the Druids showed surprising skills in healing and surgery. Archaeological evidence for this is to be found in the Brighton Museum, in an exhibit known as the "Ovingdon trephined skull." It was discovered by accident in January 1935 off England's south coast, by a fisherman who trawled it up in his nets. This skull has two holes cut into it over the brain and has been dated to the pre-Christian Celtic period. What is remarkable is that the ancient surgeons had cut into this person's skull on two separate occasions. The healing of the bones around both holes indicated that the patient survived the first operation, but died of sepsis some weeks after the second one.[80] Similar finds have been made in France and Ireland. To perform such operations with the patients surviving, indicates an advanced degree of medical knowledge. Most views on Druidic practice and magic are founded on folklore and myth, the traditional methods of preservation of the essential truths of primitive peoples. In a somewhat more suspect source, the records of the Romans who conquered and then colonized the Celtic lands of Western Europe, Julius Caesar recounts that the Druids:

> ... worship the God Mercury; of him thy have many images, him they consider the inventor of all arts, as the guide of ways and journeys ... After him they worship Apollo, Mars, Jupiter and Minerva.[81]

Ammianus Marcellinus described the Druids as men of great talent and members of the Pythagorean faith characterized by searching into secret and sublime things and who also believed in the immortality of the soul.[82]

This well respected Druidic culture and tradition was oral in nature. The sublime secrets of initiation, Druidic lore, magical practices and ritual were handed down among their priestly ranks as gnosis enshrined in poetic form. A similar culture pervaded the people they served. Celtic myth, which contained the folk history of the tribes, their gods and heroes, was sung, or possibly chanted to the accompaniment of a harp. It is, in fact, a form of epic poetry. This mystical and musical storehouse of magic, myth and legend provides us with a mine of information about Celtic society, describing in vivid terms the Celts' love of spectacle, food, wine and battle. This oral tradition proved to be very powerful and pervasive in its long-term effect and it helped to shape many later cultural forms and ideas. The rules of conduct of its martial heroes contributed to later medieval codes of chivalry. The constant and repeated references to the many gods attest to the sacred nature of all Celtic mythology. Both the mythology and the later Roman invaders refer to sacred sites dedicated to the planetary oracles of Mars, Venus, Mercury, Saturn, the Sun and the Moon. The Celts believed that the temporal world they inhabited was permeated and controlled by the spiritual world of the gods and it was as mediators between these two different spheres that we find mention of the Druids.

Druidism, shamanism and the Brahmanism of the Hindus have all been described as close variants on an identical theme. Diogenes Laertes equates the Druids with the Persian Magi.[83] We have mentioned how Posidonius reported that Abaris the Druid was one of the principal teachers of Pythagoras. Robert Graves, the poet and internationally renowned expert on Greek mythology, discerned that Pythagoras influenced the Essenes. Thus Druidic knowledge may well have originated in biblical Israel, flowed through the teaching of Abaris to Pythagoras and through him back to the Hebrew esoteric sect on the shores of the Dead Sea.

Like the initiates of earlier Neolithic cultures, the Druids were highly skilled astronomers. Cicero,[84] Caesar, Diodorus Siculus,[85] Pliny[86] and Tacitus[87] have all paid tribute to Druidic knowledge, especially in the field of astronomy. Pomponius Mela[88] spoke of the high regard in which the Druids were held due to their ability to "speculate by the stars." According to Cassiodorus the Druids knew the course of the twelve signs of the zodiac and traced the planets as they passed through them. Their priestly role among the Celtic tribes was also highly dependent upon their gifts of prophecy. Druids were more than mere priests however; they were also the sacred custodians of their culture, teachers, lawgivers, judges, bards and interpreters of the divine. They believed in cosmic balance. Both Julius Caesar and the Roman poet Lucan[89] were intrigued by the Druidic belief in reincarnation. Lucan suggests that this may well explain the Celts' bravery in war, as death appeared to hold no fear for them.

Druidic use of pre-existing megalithic sites was widespread and commonly reported in folklore. Like initiates of all valid spiritual pathways the Druids recognized, used and revered the sacred sites of antiquity. They knew that these centers of telluric energy were made more potent by the structures sited upon them. The megaliths themselves acted as a form of "Earth acupuncture," accentuating and concentrating the natural energies detected there. These telluric forces were known to the Druids as the "Wouivre." The Sarsens, or standing stones, at Avebury, for example, have been described as acting like a series of giant resonators, amplifying the telluric forces and vibrating them heavenwards in order to fructify the surrounding terrain.

Another strange and mysterious monument, whose purpose still baffles archaeologists and mystics alike, is to be found near Avebury. Known as Silbury Hill, its internal structure has been excavated and examined in detail. The central core is a man-made, seven-stepped structure in limestone replicating the form of Djoser's pyramid, which it predates by several centuries. This spiritual symbolism, like the spiritual realities it represents, is remarkably similar despite the different cultures from which it arose.

Seven is a magical number in all known spiritual paths. Ancient initiates knew of the vital importance of the seven chakras, or energy centers, in the human body and knowledge and insight into their working was an essential part of the Mystery wisdom of the Druids. In their mystical insight the Druids knew that similar chakras existed in the body of the Earth itself. It was on these powerful and mystical points that they founded the seven oracles representing the chakras of the Earth. These were often in grottoes found amongst the sacred groves of oak. It was here that they initiated their novices into the hidden secrets of the planetary Mysteries. They were also used for rituals of fertility, with sacrifice offered as part of those rites, or to propitiate the gods.

The magic of seven is not the sole link between spiritual paths from different cultures. Fertility – and the rites and symbolism associated with it – is one that is far more common and basic to all. One of the first independent written references to Druidic practice is about precisely this aspect of their beliefs. Julius Caesar describes, in *Commentarii de Bello Gallico*, the veneration accorded to a fire-blackened, female figurine which was worshipped at a sacred grotto at Carnuntum between the rivers Loire and Eure – a fertility symbol, supposedly of a virgin about to give birth, which he called *Virginii Pariturae*.[90] Thus confirming that the Druids also worshipped the "Eternal Feminine" as the source of all fertility.

Archaeology has now clearly demonstrated the surprisingly adventurous nature of the Celtic peoples. Evidence has been discovered which proves beyond all reasonable doubt that Celtic, Phoenician and Egyptian expeditions made prolonged contact with the American continents and created settlements there.[91] The Phoenicians traded between the Near East and Celtic Cornwall for tin. How much cultural influence flowed in either direction however, remains a mystery. In the late nineteenth century one scholar, M. Pictet, suggested that the Phoenicians introduced the religion of the Kabeiri into Ireland. Certain Welsh writers also claimed a Kabeiric association for their Druids, for they practised the same religion. The trade between the Phoenicians and the Celts gives a degree of plausibility to the legend that tells of the visit of Joseph of Arimathea and the infant Jesus to Britain not long after Julius Caesar crossed the English Channel.

When Caesar conquered Gaul he brought with him all the benefits of the *Pax Romana*, a peace founded firmly on law, military might and a surprising degree of tolerance for traditional forms of religion, local tribal customs and beliefs. Under the rule of Rome any man, however bizarre his beliefs, could live, worship and prosper – unless his behavior threatened the peace and stability of the state, when retribution would be swift and terrible. Rome's own religion was simply a matter of strict, outward observance of simple ritual duties for the benefit of the state. This posed no great burden of belief upon its adherents, who then had the freedom of choice to follow a second or third religion.

Religious toleration allowed a wide freedom of choice for all who enjoyed the benefits of Roman rule. Apart from religions of Roman origin, each subject tribe or people had their own gods. The only real interference with tribal religious practice was the hijacking of certain sacred sites. In this the Romans were simply following in the footsteps of the Druids themselves. Sadly this era of toleration and respect for the tribal gods was, in this instance at least, to be short lived. The Romans vigorously persecuted the Druids, as they feared their potential as a unifying force among the warlike Celtic tribes. Soon, however, another vicious invader was to arrive, traveling on the coat tails of a declining empire. One which was neither tolerant of the religious beliefs nor of the traditions and mythologies of the tribal peoples. This intolerant and subversive invader was a religion that was to transform emergent Europe into a seemingly unified, narrow and repressive society. The new religion of Christianity was, in the name of love, peace and redemption, to persecute and burn all those who followed more tolerant paths of revelation. Sadly the centuries that followed would be remembered for all time as the "Dark Ages."

Saint James the Just.

CHAPTER 7

The Messiah And Different Accounts Of His Teaching; The Conflict Between Fact And Faith

The Task of giving an authentic interpretation of the Word
of God ... has been entrusted to the living teaching office
of the Church alone.[92]   – The New Catholic Catechism, 1990

Heresy inevitably arises from the exercise of God's gift of
free will and the use of discernment in matters of Christian
history, faith and morals.[93]   – Tim Wallace-Murphy, *Custodians of Truth*

S
tudents of Christian religious history often have great difficulty in understanding the real causes of the bitter conflict
that has its roots in the two distinctly different versions of
the life, teaching and death of Jesus of Nazareth. This dispute
commenced in an era of vitriolic and abusive intolerance and
later culminated in the Roman Church's persecution and suppression of all its rivals. The bitterness and persecution that the
early Church employed sits ill on the shoulders of an organization
that claimed to follow the teachings of the man they called the
"Prince of Peace," an allegedly "Divine Redeemer" whose sacrifice, according to Church doctrine at least, was for the forgiveness
of all the sins of mankind. Yet the sins of the Gnostics were, for
some peculiar reason, deemed unforgivable. What was so appalling about the Gnostics? What sin was inherent in this way of fol-

lowing Jesus that could possibly justify centuries of repression, torture, burning and outright genocide?

In trying to understand the Church's attitude, one vital issue needs to be grasped; the Church knew that the Gnostics had direct knowledge that absolutely refuted the somewhat fanciful stories on which the Church had based its system of dogma and control. They knew the truth that could rock the Christian Church to its foundations and destroy its hold over its congregation forever. It may seem bizarre to state that the self-proclaimed "Guardians of Divinely Revealed Truth," the Church hierarchy, had based their entire theology, dogma and power over people, on a version of events preached by one who had never met Jesus, a man known to the original disciples as the "Spouter of Lies." This dubious foundation was then forcibly imposed upon the populace at large and supported by a repressive regime whose standard weapons were fear, torture and ritual killing.

The idea that the teachings of Jesus the Nazarene could ever be regarded as the foundation for a new and distinctly different religion, was one which never occurred to his family or his followers, much less to the apostles who walked and talked with him throughout his ministry. Without exception they were, and always remained, strict, devout, fundamentalist and nationalistic Jews who, after the execution of their leader "continued daily with one accord in the Temple"[94] – strange behavior indeed for those supposedly starting a new religion. The only distinction between them and their neighbors was their fanatical adherence to Jesus' interpretation of the Law, underpinned by their faith in the Messianic nature of his role. There was absolutely nothing in his teachings, as understood by them, to cause any breach with traditional Judaism. On the contrary, as the Kingly Messiah, Jesus the Nazarene was the fulfillment of Jewish religious thought and belief.[95] The Christian

Church has tried to camouflage this fact by describing this great prophet as Jesus of Nazareth, conveniently ignoring the fact that Nazareth did not exist at that time. Jesus was in fact the leader of the Nazorean or Nazarene sect of the Essenes. Considerable conflict arose between many of the priestly and Sadducee factions and the followers of Jesus, because those in a position of power felt that his teachings undermined their priestly authority and threatened to bring about the revolutionary overthrow of the hated Roman occupiers to whom both the Pharisees and the Sadducees owed so much of their privilege, position and power.

The so-called divine origin and nature of Jesus that later became such a divisive and controversial issue, was not a problem among those who knew him. Nowhere is it written, either in the Gospels or elsewhere, that Jesus claimed to be divine. His family and the disciples knew from their own first-hand experience that he was a simply a man who was spiritually inspired by God. No one among them took the teachings of Jesus as an indictment of Judaism, nor was the crucifixion regarded as a means of salvation.

Let us first examine the Gospel account of the birth of Jesus. Few of the millions of children who have thrilled to the Christmas story, fewer still of the priests, pastors and preachers who tell it with such love and reverence, realize that within it lies another that flatly contradicts firmly held present-day beliefs. Mainstream churches now, as in the past, find the concept of spiritual initiation, astrology or the practice of magic to be abominations, yet, there for all to see at the very beginning of the Christian experience, this so-called abomination is recorded for all time; initiates being praised and used to reinforce the cosmic nature of the birth of the infant in the Bethlehem manger. "Now when Jesus was born in Bethlehem ... behold there came wise men from the east."[96]

According to esoteric tradition these wise men from the East were initiates of one of the oldest orders in the world, an order of profound humility and purity and perhaps the last surviving Eastern esoteric order of any real validity still functioning outside of Judea, the Magi of Persia.[97] The Gospel recounts how, having received foreknowledge of this momentous birth by virtue of their spiritual insight, these men traveled an immense distance for that time, simply following a star that moved steadily until it came to rest over a stable in a small Judean town: how they made a dangerous and prolonged journey over difficult terrain, carrying gifts of great value through country infested with robbers, and laid them at the feet of the newborn son of the young wife of a simple carpenter, Joseph, of the House of David.

If few who marveled at the story of the Magi have bothered to make the connection with the later Christian condemnation of spiritual insight, clairvoyance or fortune telling, how many realize that the story itself has been stolen from the legends attending the birth of one of Jesus' contemporaries, namely John the Baptist, and not to the birth of Jesus at all? Like so much more in the Gospel accounts it was adopted, doubtless, for very pious and sincere reasons, to add color and a sense of the miraculous to the mythology of Jesus.

Trapped by its own strange beliefs over the nature of Jesus' "miraculous birth" and the alleged "perpetual virginity" of his mother Mary, the Church had painted itself into a corner from which there was no escape. How could one who was dogmatically declared to be "ever virgin" be described as having a large family? Outright denial was not the tactic employed by the Church hierarchy, and in the light of the Gospels, how could it be: "Is not this the carpenter, the son of Mary, the brother of James, of Joses (or Joseph), and of Juda (or Judas) and Simon? And are not his sisters here with us?"[98] In another Gospel account we read: "Is not this the carpenter's son? Is not his mother's name Mary and his brethren, James, and Joses, and Simon and Judas?"[99] Marginalization, omission and evasion were the tactics used by the Church in response to their self-imposed conundrum of "How could a virgin have such a large family?"

There are repeated statements both in the Gospels and in the various lives of the saints that James and John were the sons of Zebedee. But two further questions then arise concerning these important characters. Firstly who was their mother? Secondly what was their relationship to Jesus? Were they simply pupils following the divinely inspired prophet? Or could the relationship have been one of consanguinity? Did they, in fact, exist at all? For answers to these vexatious issues let us first of all turn to the one source even the Church itself dare not question, the Holy Gospels themselves.

One possible key to this puzzle is contained in a seemingly innocuous sentence: "Among which was Mary Magdalene, Mary the mother of James, and Joses, and the mother of Zebedee's children."[100] It seems probable from this statement that Mary may have married Zebedee after the death of Joseph and therefore the sons of Zebedee were also the sons of Mary the supposedly "ever virgin" mother of Jesus. Remarriage after the death of a spouse was common; how else was Mary to support her family? If this is so then James the Great and John, the sons of Zebedee, were half-brothers of Jesus, while James the Just, Simon and Joseph junior were his full brothers and sons of Joseph.

Confirmation of this theory came from an unlikely source: the "guidebook" to Santiago de Compostela. In the Church's somewhat jaundiced eye, someone has blundered, for the book describes the reliquary of St. James the Less in the following terms: "The most important silver bust is that of St. James the Lesser.

The cranium of the saint, the brother of St. James the Greater, was brought from Jerusalem to Braga in the 12th century." Thus in an official Catholic publication the two Jameses are described as brothers. James the Less, known also as James the Just, is described in the Gospels as the Lord's brother. It now looks certain that Mary was the mother of the sons of Zebedee.

One modern and insightful scholar who has worked extensively on the "Dead Sea Scrolls" has also come to a conclusion that again shows up Pauline theology in a very poor light. Robert Eisenman claims that the so-called "sons of Zebedee" are creatures of pure invention. Working from New Testament sources Eisenman claims that the stories about the sons of Zebedee are "Patent dissimulation, but dissimulation towards a very clear goal, to downplay the role of and finally eliminate the other James – not James the Less but James the Just – from Scripture."[101] He goes on to say that "… traces of the originals of many of these reworkings are still there, lying just beneath the surface, and with a little enhancement they are restored with some ease."

There was also another brother, whose true relationship to Jesus the Church has suppressed: Didymus Judas Thomas. He is the Judas referred to in the passages quoted above. He is also the undoubted author of "The Gospel of Thomas," one of the so-called Gnostic Gospels. Thomas' role has been cleverly devalued in teachings deriving from a passage in the canonical Gospels that has resulted in him being known for two thousand years as "Doubting Thomas."[102] This simple phrase casts doubt not only upon his commitment and spiritual insight, but also upon his personal knowledge of Jesus himself. Why should this slander be cast upon one of the apostles? The translation of the word Didymus gives us a vital clue to Thomas' real importance – in Greek, *didyme* means TWIN!!

The Gospel of Thomas was an important document that circulated widely for the first three centuries of Christian history. It was a serious rival to the canonical Gospels as a source of authority and gives us further proof as to why the Church was running scared about the importance of Thomas. It was eventually suppressed by the Church and disappeared from sight for nearly fifteen hundred years until it was rediscovered at Nag Hammadi. In one translation of it we find the following:

> The disciples said to Jesus:
> "We know that you will depart from us,
> Who is to be our leader?"
>
> Jesus said to them:
> "Wherever you are,
> You will go to James the Righteous,
> for whose sake the heaven and the earth,
> came into being."[103]

Reflect deeply on these words of Jesus. Do they not indicate, as many esoteric scholars and initiates have known for centuries, that James' role as the Priestly Messiah was at least as important, or perhaps even superior in some way to that of Jesus as the Kingly Messiah? It certainly indicates that James the Just was of far greater importance than either of the men we know as St. Peter and St. Paul.

After the crucifixion, James, assisted by the Apostles Peter and John, was indisputably the leader of the new Jesus sect in Jerusalem. This triumvirate of religious leaders, almost certainly all brothers of Jesus, corresponded exactly to the ruling trio of the Essene community from which they and Jesus sprang. They were even called the "pillars" by Paul: "And when James, Cephas and John who seemed to be pillars, perceived that grace was given me, they gave to me and Barnabas the right hands of fellowship."[104] One vitally important aspect of all of this seems to have escaped the notice of the early Church theologians. According to the Gospel of Thomas, Jesus appointed James as his heir to the leadership; the New Testament itself confirms that he was the first "bishop" of Jerusalem, so where does that leave the Church and their doctrine about Peter as being the foundation upon which Jesus built his Church? Thus the whole question of "Apostolic succession" for the so-called heirs to St. Peter is now in serious dispute. Indeed the papacy's claim to authentic scriptural authority can now clearly be seen to rest on extremely shaky foundations.

No explanation is offered as to why the new "Christian" community formed in Jerusalem at that precise time, much less how a handful of Galilean peasants and fishermen could create such an elaborate form of communal government with such speed. The proof of its effectiveness is apparent from the "Acts of the Apostles," which describe how this seemingly ad hoc structure sustained a rapid influx of thousands of Jewish adherents from throughout the Diaspora. From where did these simple people develop the practice of communal meetings on the first day of the week? Whose idea was it to create such a complex and efficient system of governance? One headed by a triumvirate assisted by area supervisors, or bishops, and administrators, or deacons.

All organizations, however novel, owe a debt to their predecessors. In this instance a well-tried and tested model was available in existing Essene organization and practices. Jesus and his close followers were, of course, Essenes. Even Pentecost was not a new event: it had long been celebrated as the Jewish festival of *Shavu'ot*, which the Essenes celebrated as the "Convention of the

Community."[105] Yet Christian theologians claim that Christianity, its beliefs, rituals and feasts, including Pentecost, are unique and different from previous religions!

Jesus was the Kingly Messiah in the tradition of David and his followers were Jews, Jesus people, not Christians as we now understand the term. Nothing in the words or actions of their master, in his teachings or in the scriptures – which they, as all devout Jews of the time, especially the Essenes, knew intimately – gave them any cause to think otherwise. According to Aristides, one of the early apologists for the Christian faith, the worship of the first Jerusalem "Christians" was fundamentally more monotheistic than even that of the Jews. After all, Jesus' brother, James the Just, was a high priest who was still granted entrance to the "Holy of Holies" in the Temple. Like their alleged cousin John the Baptist, both Jesus and James were Levites through their mother's family line.

The mysterious figure of James had taken on the role of the Priestly Messiah, a role previously held by John the Baptist until his execution by Herod. James exerted great power and authority for many years after the crucifixion of Jesus and was clearly acknowledged by all the apostles, including Paul, as a far more significant figure than the later Christian Churches have ever dared to admit.

He was of the lineage of David ... and moreover we have found that he officiated after the manner of the ancient priesthood. Whereof also he was permitted once a year to enter the Holy of Holies (i.e. on the Day of Atonement), as the Law commanded the high priests, according to that which is written; for so many before us have told of him, both Eusebius and Clement and others. Furthermore he was empowered to wear on his head the high priestly diadem as the aforementioned trustworthy men have attested in their memoirs.[106]

The pre-eminence and importance of James is referred to many times in a variety of ancient documents, many of which are to be found in the writings of the early fathers of the Church. Why then has his role been distorted and minimized by the Church to such an extent that the laity and most of the clergy know little about it? Church teaching about him, scanty though it is, has been deliberately left vague and inconclusive. Two characters called James are described – James the Great and James the Less. Why have the actions and importance of James the Just at that time been either suppressed or glossed over? Why was his importance diminished by being called James the Less? Why does the truth about Jesus and his family conflict so dramatically with the doctrine of the Church that was supposedly founded to promote his teaching?

To a world completely immersed for centuries in the teaching that Jesus is God, it is perhaps difficult at first to accept that Jesus himself never claimed divine status. He and all his disciples were ultra-orthodox and devout Jews who were well steeped in esoteric, Hebraic Gnosticism that could trace its roots back to the Egyptian Temple Mysteries. The origin of the name Essene is held by many to mean "Those with the Light Within," and Jesus was an Essene initiate. In the Koran, our Muslim brethren call the man we know as Jesus by the name of "Issa." The derivation of this name is also of interest, not only to students of mainstream Christianity, but also to scholars studying the beliefs of the Knights Templar. One translation of the name is "an initiate of Isis." It is known that Jesus did spend time in Egypt as a very young child but he most probably would have been initiated in Israel. The Egyptian Mysteries pervaded the entire esoteric belief system of biblical Israel from the time of the Egyptian initiate Moses onwards. Isis was undoubtedly an object of adoration by the later Knights Templar, who venerated her in the guise of the Black Madonna. Another translation of the name Issa that is often put forward is "an initiate of Light." Was Jesus not called the "Light of the World?" Furthermore the Knights Templar, along with other Gnostic initiates, claimed to follow the "True Teachings of Jesus" in complete contrast to the Pauline doctrine of Holy Mother the Church.

The Messiah may indeed have been referred to as a "Son of God," a phrase which, to the Jews of biblical times, meant something very different indeed from that understood by Christians today. To the Jews this title ranked Jesus with the many other "Sons of God" mentioned in the Old Testament, such as Adam, Abraham, Moses and David.[107] The status of "Son of God" was held to be attainable to all of those who followed Jesus' teaching and who gained initiation.

There is no doubt whatsoever that it was St. Paul, who never met the living Jesus, who was the first to preach the doctrine that Jesus was divine – a doctrine that would be considered as blasphemy by Jesus and his disciples! He is also the probable author of an extremely dubious doctrine that would have made the true followers of Jesus turn in their graves: the idea of communion wine representing the "blood of Jesus." Jesus and all his immediate followers, the apostles and all who listened to his teaching, were strict, fundamentalist Jews with a great veneration for the Law of Moses. According to the Law there was an absolute prohibition against the ingestion of blood in any form. All meat had to be killed in a ritual manner that drained it of all blood. No Jew could drink blood, even in allegorical form, without being in breach of the covenant with Almighty God.[108]

Paul's other major, fundamental, and theologically important, divergence from the beliefs of James and the apostles is demonstrated by the phrase "Christ died for us." Since the staying of Abraham's hand on Mount Moriah, the notion of a vicarious human sacrifice of this nature would be viewed as outright blasphemy by devout Jews, but such an idea was totally in keeping with the traditions of the Greeks and Romans to whom Paul was preaching. To them a noble, sacrificial death would be extolled and the concept of deification of an extraordinary human being would have been accepted without question. It is for these reasons, among others, that many modern scholars hold the view that Paul may well have been the "Wicked Priest" referred to in the Dead Sea Scrolls, a character also described as the "Liar," the "Scoffer," and the "Spouter of Lies." Many of those who knew Jesus personally would have agreed with that, for Paul was despised and disliked by James and most of the other disciples. As this view will appear extreme to many sincere Christians, let us see if there is any supporting evidence to back it up.

There is at least one other document of similar age to the synoptic Gospels that repays careful scrutiny. It was written in the early years of the Church when the effects of Paul's teaching had already become all too evident. It originated among the Ebionites, or Nazoreans, the very sect from which Jesus came and whose teachings he elaborated as a basis for his own. They were the people who were closest to him throughout his ministry and were certainly the sect with the deepest understanding of his teaching. This vitally important document is known as the "Kerygmata Petrou." In this, the followers of the true teachings of Jesus describe the "Apostle" Paul, venerated by the Church as the "Father of Christianity," in very different terms that one would hardly expect to hear from his spiritual brothers. Paul is called, unequivocally the "Liar" and, more strongly, the "hostile man who falsified the true ideas of Jesus."

Paul was obviously only too well aware of these critical views, and his angry refutation of them in the Epistles effectively and accurately dates the accusations themselves:

Am I not free? Am I not an apostle? Have I not seen Jesus our Lord? Are you not the result of my work in the Lord?

Even though I may not be an apostle to others, surely I am one to you! For you are the seal of my apostleship in the Lord.

This is my defence to those who sit in judgement on me.

Don't we have the right to food and drink? Don't we have the right to take a believing wife along with us, as do the other apostles and the Lord's brothers and Cephas?

Or is it only Barnabas and I who must work for a living?[109]

It would seem from this quotation, and from other comments that he makes later in the same letter, that Paul is concerned not only that his apostleship is being called into question, but that he is also being accused of taking some sort of financial advantage from it. In another letter he once more brings in the blasphemous concept of human propitiatory sacrifice and stresses the "legitimacy" of his apostleship yet again:

... For there is one God and one mediator between God and men, the man Christ Jesus, who gave himself as a ransom for all men ...

And for this purpose I was appointed a herald and an apostle – I am telling the truth, I am not lying ... [110]

When one reads all the Epistles of St. Paul at one sitting, this whinging, self-pitying, defensive tone and the constant need to rebut criticism originating among the elders of the Church in Jerusalem becomes ever more apparent. Read them one immediately after the other and see for yourself. But that is not all; the events on the road to Damascus and Paul's claim to have received spiritual teaching by Christ were also scornfully condemned by the Ebionite document as "visions and illusions inspired by devils."

Furthermore, it is also now becoming apparent that Paul's arrest was for very different reasons than those given in the Acts of the Apostles. One scholar with an international reputation for Dead Sea Scrolls translation, Robert Eisenman, as a result of his meticulous study of the New Testament and other contemporaneous documents has arrived at a startlingly different conclusion. Paul, who was a member of the Herodian family, was taken into custody by the Romans to protect him from the angry mob in Jerusalem after Paul had attacked and severely injured James the Just, the first bishop of Jerusalem and the heir to the mantle of Jesus.[111] Further evidence of this attack is to be found in the Pseudo-Clementine Recognitions.

In view of Paul's relationship to the Herodian royal family, his Roman citizenship, the protective custody and the way he completely inverted the teachings of Jesus, there are strong grounds for suspecting that he was acting as an *agent provocateur* who had deliberately infiltrated the fundamentalist and nationalistic group led by James that was firmly founded on the true teachings of Jesus.

After the many disputes with James and the elders of the Jerusalem community, Paul found himself involved in conflict with evangelists accredited by James. Due to this competition Paul began to lose ground steadily throughout the missionary field.[112] James had issued letters of accreditation to all who preached the true teachings of Jesus to the Jewish community in the Diaspora. Paul never had such official recognition; in fact the Ebionites and all in the Jerusalem "Church" were brutally dismissive about Paul's claim to the rank of apostle. According to them this title was reserved solely for those who accompanied Jesus during his ministry. In one early document we find confirmation of the principle of letters of accreditation and the supreme position of James. The words are reportedly those of Peter:

> Our Lord and Prophet, who has sent us, declared to us that the evil One, having disputed with him forty days, but failing to prevail against him, promised He would send Apostles from among his subjects to deceive them. Therefore, above all, remember to shun any Apostles, teacher, or prophet who does not accurately compare his teaching with (that of) James ... the brother of my Lord ... and this even if he comes to you with recommendations.[113]

Bitter disputes originating from the differences between the true teaching of Jesus and the version preached by Paul continued well into the second century. The Ebionites knew that Jesus as a man had come to reveal the true path to initiation in the age-old Hebraic/Egyptian tradition, a pathway to enlightenment. Paul, on the other hand, claimed that Jesus was divine and had come to redeem the world through his supreme sacrifice at Golgotha. There was no middle ground that could bridge this yawning spiritual divide. It led to some crazy theological convolutions later, which would be amusing if the circumstances of Church debate had not spawned such tragic results.

For example, Irenaeus, the bishop of Lyon, condemned the Ebionites, the earthly followers of Jesus, as heretics for claiming that

Jesus was a man and not God, as defined by the new Pauline form of Christianity. He admitted that the Ebionites rejected the Pauline epistles, and even rejected Paul himself as "an apostate of the Law." Irenaeus showed the mental convolutions that only a Pauline theologian was capable of, in that he claimed that Jesus – whom he believed was divine – had been in error, practising the "wrong religion" while on Earth.[114] Reflect on this. Jesus is defined as being divine and therefore incapable of error, yet, according to this Pauline theologian, God himself had erred and followed the wrong flock!

However fate took a hand and this picture was to change dramatically. The influence of James and the Jerusalem community was to be negated in a dramatic way. The traumatic hand of history was soon to virtually erase their very presence from Church records.

With the murder of James the Just in Jerusalem, the stage was set for disaster. The killing of the Priestly Messiah who had inherited the mantle of John the Baptist lit the fuse that eventually led to the explosive revolt of the Israelites against the hated Roman oppressors. Reflect carefully: if Jesus was of supreme importance among his people, why was it that his murder passed without comment or civil commotion and yet the murder of his brother initiated the complex chain of apocalyptic events that resulted in the destruction of the Temple and the dispersion of the Jews? The traumatic fall of Jerusalem and the enforced dispersion of the Jewish people removed from the Roman Empire the one group which had any real chance of preaching the true teachings of Jesus – the Essenes: initiatory, nationalistic, fundamentalist and fervent Jews.

With the death of James and the dispersion of his followers, the stage was left almost entirely at the mercy of the man we know as St. Paul. He embedded his distorted vision of the divine redemptive sacrifice of Christ within a form of Zoroastrian cosmic theology that Judaism had inherited while under Persian rule.

In bringing his new "gospel" to the Gentiles, Paul used all the skills with which he was undoubtedly blessed and his teaching rapidly became the foundation for all Christian theology. When the Church grew and became "established" by the Edict of Milan, its flawed Pauline theological base became the foundation for a sustained campaign of repression directed against all of its rivals – pagan temples, local deities and the wide range of Mystery cults and Gnostic groups, Christian or otherwise.

A gold multiple of Constantine with Sol Invictus, minted in Ticinum, 313 CE.

CHAPTER 8

Patrem Omnipotentem: The Rise Of A Repressive Society

The idea of a sky god, of a distant father in heaven, is gradually emerging as one of the most widespread conceptions in early religion. The Australian Aborigines and many African tribesmen have such a sky god, while the Chinese had an ancient sky god, of whom the emperor was the representative on earth, and the Greek Zeus and the Roman Jupiter appear to have developed out of such a conception. In general however the sky god remained distant and remote from men's lives.[115]

– H. R. Ellis Davidson, *Gods and Myths of Northern Europe*

The emerging Christian Church, based almost completely on the teaching and theology of St. Paul, spread widely and rapidly throughout the major centers of the Mediterranean world. Yet Paul himself left no organizational structure or fixed dogma behind him. How could he? He claimed repeatedly that the "Holy Spirit" was working through him and others; man therefore could not be expected to regulate what the Spirit would accomplish. The Pauline Church thus became an inversion of normal organizational practice, no laws or regulations were required because the Church and its individual members were led by the Spirit. Leaders exercised their authority through the gifts of the Spirit and both Church members and leaders alike were all equally open to its sublime gifts of prophecy and teaching.

Worship was not formalized or under any set ritual or control, its only regular elements being the Essene practice of a communal supper of bread and wine with the new addition of the preaching of his own, very personal gospel of the "Risen Lord."

The new Church was susceptible to infiltration by earlier hermetic and Gnostic groups who possessed their own valid spiritual insights. This situation was compounded even further because the Church itself sprang from a variety of evangelical roots. Congregations developed in widely scattered cities as the result of missionary efforts by a disparate mix of disciples, each preaching his own oral tradition based loosely on the teachings of Jesus. Thus the Church was, in truth, a collection of heterodoxies rather than a unified and cohesive body. The greatest perceived form of danger came from the various Ebionite groups who followed the original "Way" originating from the practice of James and the early church in Jerusalem. The Temple had been destroyed and the followers of James had fled; some had sought refuge among the Jewish and Christian settlements in the Diaspora. From these various sources a multiplicity of Christian texts appeared, each embodying the oral tradition of one group or another. Many were contradictory, the whole body confused by a documentary profusion that only began to be resolved as a result of the actions of one theologically eccentric man, Marcion of Pontus.[116]

Marcion brought to the complexity of these early written documents the principles of comparative scholarship and, thereby, became a forerunner of Renaissance scholars of over a thousand years later. Using rationalism combined with historical and critical analysis, he ruthlessly pruned this massive body of contradictory texts of all that he considered false. Essentially he stripped the New Testament down to its Pauline bones and rejected all the books of the Old Testament on the grounds that they were speaking of a rival God; a vengeful, bloodthirsty, judgmental God, one substantially different to the loving *Abba* or "Father," of whom Jesus had spoken so movingly. He fervently believed a loving God would not rely on fear and terror to compel obedience, but that divine love could provide both the motivation, and the means, whereby a true Christian life could be lived by any individual. This caring message was soon to be denounced and buried by the massive repression of the Church. This devout scholar was denounced as a heretic by Tertullian, who felt that without fear and punishment man would rapidly degenerate into sin and orgiastic practices. Thus Tertullian was among the first, but by no means the last, of the Christian witch-hunters.[117] Yet, Tertullian in his turn was denounced as a heretic.

It is bizarre that this vituperative past-master of *Odium theologicum* – the ritual heaping of abuse, calumny and falsehood on one's theological opponents – the veritable scourge of heretics in his day, would become a heretic himself. However this is no more strange than that the idea of a canon of approved literature, or holy books, proposed by Marcion, another heretic, should eventually become the yardstick adopted by the Western Church itself in judging heresy. Crazy contradictions such as this abound in the early history of the Church. There was an almost perpetual atmosphere of confusion, underscored by the unremitting conflict and slander of those first theological disputes.[118] Personal abuse, insult and invective became the accepted substitutes for intellect, spiritual guidance and the precepts of Christian love and charity, thereby setting a pattern of violent intolerance that, sadly, has strident echoes in many sectors of the Christian community today. The Church's very need to survive caused it to refute anything it viewed as heretical with increasing venom. It also led to the rise of dogmatic, supposedly agreed, statements of belief which papered over areas of dispute and disbelief with a dictatorial rigidity, one that sprang not from God to whom it was ascribed, but from power-hungry, manipulative men.

Although the priesthood referred to him as "Our Father," Almighty God was redefined as a distant, strict and vengeful figure who ruled by dint of the terror of eternal punishment. Now it is a simple fact that religious systems based on fear and a punitive God inevitably give rise to religions with a strong sense of social order which do not generally encourage contemplation, debate or speculation. This was certainly the case with the emergent Christian Church. The Roman Church could brook no rivals. When it gained real power and control it was to sweep away all knowledge of the spiritual world and campaign vigorously for the destruction or closure of all the temples and centers of worship of rival faiths, hijacking these sacred sites wherever possible for its own use. The great Greek Mystery Temples were soon to be ruthlessly closed and the oracles silenced for all time, with the adherents of the ancient initiatory Mystery cults being forced to go underground in order to ensure their own survival.

However it would also be grossly misleading to imply that there was any real degree of uniformity in the Christian Church much before the union with the Roman Empire had been well established. An accepted canon of New Testament writings only began to emerge during the course of the second century, to confirm and validate the large body of oral tradition that existed alongside it.[119] In reaction to the doctrines of Marcion there was a distinct widening of the canon, thereby strengthening the hand of the ecclesiastical leaders in their battle against heresy. A more inclusive canon allowed the church to appeal to a wider congregation – including potential heretics – and to include within its all-embracing arms the followers of many divergent traditions.

Once these people had been absorbed and strengthened in faith and humble obedience to approved doctrine, documents of controversial origin that the various groups had previously revered were simply declared "non-canonical" and excluded. The majority of Essene, initiatory and Gnostic documents were presumably suppressed and disappeared in this manner.

The man primarily responsible for the movement towards the gradual evolution and eventual tightening of the canon was Eusebius[120] He wished to demonstrate beyond all doubt that the written documents of the Church were the true credentials for its teaching. This hastened and reinforced the move to an institutionalized Church with enforceable authority. Obedience to the Church became both an implicit and explicit part of belief. The creation of a universalist, international church of absolute authority was supported and reinforced by the institution of bishops. Origen aided this authoritarian development by creating an entirely new synthesis from both profane and sacred knowledge that completely ignored the pagan ideas of ancient Greece.[121] He gave to the world, for the first time, a theory of knowledge that arose solely from completely Christian origins, thus reinforcing and strengthening the Church's claim to be the fount and guardian of *all* knowledge.

With the establishment of a definitive body of doctrine and the creation of a strong hierarchy, the Church began to grow, consolidate and prosper. Within a very short time it acquired considerable property and wealth, giving it good cause to ensure that its members were regarded as good citizens of the state, as good behavior tended to ensure security of tenure over the Church's new-found temporal possessions and, as a result, despite a series of minor persecutions under Caligula, Nero and Domitian, Christians were not subjected to serious and systematic oppression until late in the second century. At that time the growing power of the

Church was perceived as a threat to the authority of Rome itself. This wave of persecution was, like all exercises of Roman law, brutal, swift and effective. Many Christians compromised, tempted by their newfound prosperity. The martyrdom, torture and persecution of the truly faithful had unforeseen consequences however. Public sympathy was aroused by their courage and fortitude and the wave of resentment that arose against the state even extended into the ranks of the army.

When Constantine triumphed in the civil war and passed the Edict of Milan,[122] granting tolerance and freedom to the Christian Church, he restored to it the property confiscated during the persecutions and granted exemption from taxes to its clergy. One inevitable result of the Edict was to increase the existing tendency of the Church to accumulate wealth, which led in turn, to corruption. New bishops were soon being appointed for their high birth, personal wealth or administrative skills rather than for their piety or righteousness. This new edict changed the face of history. From that day forward, Christianity in all its forms would exert a varying, but always predominant, influence – sometimes, outright control – over the governments of Europe for nearly seventeen hundred years. The immediate value of Christianity to Constantine, however, was threatened by the bitter theological disputes current at that time. The Church was of little use to the emperor as a unifying factor if its internal divisions prejudiced the social unity and good order of his realm.

A political solution to these spiritual problems was forcibly imposed upon the squabbling bishops and theologians by Constantine himself. This supreme politician, general and follower of the pagan cult of Sol Invictus, convened an ecumenical Council of Nicaea. To put matters simply, the emperor banged a few ecclesiastical heads together and imposed his political will upon the quarreling clerics. He was also not above outright bribery and corruption, each participant received a present appropriate to his rank from the emperor. Some claim that it was Constantine who first mastered the art of holding and corrupting an ecclesiastical conference.[123] One theological result of this political interference was the Creed. This, for a time, solved the intense theological disputes resulting from the clergy's confused and contradictory attempts to define the nature of Jesus and his relationship to the Father by introducing the concept of the "Holy Trinity."[124]

This apparently new idea of a doctrinal definition of a Trinity within monotheism was in fact of considerable antiquity for it arose from the ideas of Akhenaten.[125] The "heretical" pharaoh was in some ways the first true monotheist, yet he had described the Aten in one of his hymns, as a Trinity. Thus another Sun worshipper, the Emperor Constantine, had both a model and a royal precedent for his Trinitarian ideas. The Creed was not the only distortion to creep into Church doctrine and activity as a result of the actions of Constantine the Great. As a direct consequence of this unholy alliance between the pagan emperor and the Christian Church, the so-called men of God were called upon to validate and sanctify an activity that sat ill upon the conscience of many Christians, one that was in complete contradiction to their own accounts of the teachings of Jesus. That activity was war.

This sad reversal was first demonstrated by Emperor Constantine himself who, in reality, became the first "Holy Roman Emperor." His motives were to use Christianity to unify the Roman state and perpetuate its martial aims. He facilitated the transformation of a religion of love and passive resistance into a form of militant imperialism in which nation would confront nation, culture would conflict with culture, religion persecute religion throughout the coming centuries in bitter wars, each convinced that "God was with them"[126] – all in the name of Jesus who, in the Gospel accounts, told us to "Love thy neighbour as thyself" and "Love thine enemies."

The theological justification for this perverse inversion of Christ's loving doctrine arose from the fertile mind of a bitter, yet devout, father of the Church who brought with it another doctrine that was to have a devastating affect on Christians of all denominations – the doctrine of "original sin." This dogmatic institutionalization of guilt made entire populations the pliable, fear-ridden puppets of their priestly, spiritual masters. Both the justification of the "Just War" and the guilt-inducing distortions of the concept of original sin sprang from the mind of a man who was so in touch with God made manifest in nature that he ascribed the main cause of sin to nature and man's appetites, thus negating the Judaic idea that God was to be experienced in nature and in the history of man. This man, St. Augustine of Hippo, so loved all of God's creation, that he described women as "vessels of excrement." However, it is far from clear, whether this devout theologian included Mary, the mother of Christ, in that category.

> The mother church of Western Christianity inherited the Roman Empire with the Edict of Milan in 312. In that century the patriarchal and dualistic theologian Augustine of Hippo put forward a theology that legitimized the ... conscription of Christians into the military, "just wars" in the name of Christ, coercion of minority groups such as Donatists, and rendering women into shadows and scape-goats. ("Man but not woman is made in the image and like-ness of God") ... Only today are we beginning to free our-selves from this abortion of the maternal in the womb of the church begun sixteen centuries ago.[127]

Augustine was the first theologian to claim that membership of the Church was an absolute and inescapable pre-condition for the salvation of any soul, however holy. He used all his many gifts to defend the Church against heresy and to make what is, perhaps, the most significant and influential individual contribution to Christian doctrine of all time.[128] This bitter and twisted, yet devout, theologian also used a somewhat dubious scriptural basis to justify his theological position on coercion. By taking one phrase from the Gospel of Luke – "Compel them to come in" – this "saint" justified physical coercion of non-believers on a massive scale[129] thereby establishing the theological foundations for centuries of repression, religious war and the unspeakable iniquities of the Inquisition. This man of meticulous and all-embracing intellect did not fail the proponents of secular war. He was nothing if not all-inclusive. His doctrine of the Just War was to be used by nearly every belligerent from that time up to the present century.

Heresy and the justification for war were not his sole preoccupation either; sex was another concept that haunted his fevered and formidable intellect. Original sin was, according to St. Augustine, passed on from one generation to another by the sexual act. Sex was not a God-given gift to mankind but a lustful and sin-ridden means of procreation that transmitted sin throughout humanity for all time. With the sole exception of Jesus himself, every man was now known to be sinful from birth – by virtue of that very birth – and from this perilous state of potential damnation the Church, and the Church alone, could save him.[130]

What drove Augustine to develop the idea of original sin? Where did it come from? In the opinion of many scholars, ancient and modern, there is no biblical justification for it at all.[131] It is not mentioned anywhere in Judaism, either in the scriptures, commentaries or in the enormous store of rabbinical works. It does not hold

sway in any of the Eastern churches. Augustine made no claim that
any form of spiritual revelation had been its inspiration. The modern Jewish prophet and theologian Elie Wiesel states unequivocally
that, "The concept of Original Sin is alien to Jewish tradition."[132]
Many Catholic theologians are just as vehement in their denial that
there is any scriptural justification for this doctrine.

> The doctrine of Original Sin is not found in any of the writ-
> ings of the Old Testament. It is certainly not in chapters one to
> three of Genesis. This ought to be recognized today, not only
> by Old Testament scholars, but also by dogmatic theologians
> ... The idea that Adam's descendants are automatically sinners
> because of the sin of their ancestors and are already sinners
> when they enter the world, is foreign to holy scripture.[133]

> Traditional ideas concerning human nature, especially the doc-
> trine of Original Sin, have led us into all sorts of disastrous ac-
> tivities. This is the price we have paid in the West for beginning
> our cultural activities with the doctrine of original sin.[134]

The Eastern Church has always regarded the Roman Church's
slide into the doctrine of Original Sin with regret and profound
suspicion,[135] a particularly well-founded suspicion, for this guilt-
inducing and truly distorted view of God's love became the starting point of man's complete alienation from the supreme gift of
God: nature itself. Sadly that was not the only devastating consequence of this marvel of saintly theology. Herbert J. Muller's
analysis led him to the belief that:

> Throughout Christian history the conviction that man's
> birthright is sin has encouraged an unrealistic acceptance of

remediable social evils, or even a callousness about human suffering. It helps explain the easy acceptance of slavery and serfdom, and a record of religious atrocity unmatched by any other religion.[136]

Armed with the guilt-inducing doctrine of original sin, the Church was able to exert a highly efficient form of spiritual blackmail over all its flock. The hierarchy claimed that all truly divine revelation was by now firmly enshrined in Church doctrine and, above all, that the Church, and the Church alone, was the sole guardian of the only means of personal salvation.

Heresy was defined more restrictively by Augustine as "the distortion of a revealed truth by a baptized Christian or unbeliever." This was embedded in a form of circular argument that gave the Church total power over its people. As we have already mentioned, "revealed truth" was itself redefined by the Church's own theologians, as "What the church itself had declared to be revealed truth." In the ensuing battle against heresy, St. Augustine became the main theorist of persecution. The doctrines inspired by this brilliant, but aberrant, intellectual bigot created the theological foundation for the brutal persecution of heretics and the subsequent obscenity of the Inquisition. Augustine also proclaimed that: "The necessity for harshness is greater in the investigation of heresy than in the infliction of punishment."[137]

One of his doctrines was to become the foundation for the abuse of civil rights that characterized all totalitarian states in the centuries to come. He proposed that it was not merely necessary to search out actual heresy, but also incipient heresy.[138] From then on, both state and church became inseparable allies in the ruthless suppression of all forms of dissent, and it was according to this "divinely blessed" set of rules that the Christian states of Europe were developed.[139]

The Church was now the self-appointed guardian of all knowledge. The clergy were literate; the laity, kings and commoners alike were the spiritual and illiterate serfs of the all-powerful hierarchy. The Church became the major lawmaker in the declining Empire. Much of the customary law of the people of Europe was absorbed and codified into civil law by the clergy. Being the sole literate guardians of history, the priests wrote down the oral legends, myths and stories of the various peoples, adding their own gloss, omitting all that was offensive to accepted doctrine, retaining this, adding that, subtly changing the histories and forming the mold for a new, essentially Christian, culture. In this pervasive way the Church was able to modify and distort the histories of entire cultures, devaluing for all time any potential rivals in the field of religious beliefs – all in the name of accurate history!

Christianity had inherited a passionate concern for the historicity of belief from its Judaic roots. In a way that contrasts sharply with other religions and spiritual traditions, written or oral, Judaism had placed its prophets, kings and mythical heroes in a written history, which gave scriptural events a distinct sense of real time and place. This is a completely different approach to that of the ancient myths of the tribal peoples, where events and heroes are spoken of as if in a "dream time, long ago." What happens in historical times, so the Christian clergy asserted, really happened. Ancient and treasured tribal myths and legends were reduced to stories; mere fiction completely stripped of all power and validity. Thus the Church increased its grip not only on the current reality of the tribes, but also on their past and on their ancient cultural heritage. This escalating process was continued by the wholesale incorporation and perversion of pagan festivals into the new Christian calendar. Thus the festival of Astarte became the Christian feast of Easter; the winter equinox the important Christian celebration of Christmas; and the summer equinox the feast day of St. John the Baptist.

It was not only the doors that gave access to the spiritual and cultural heritage of the people that were slammed firmly shut by the hierarchy. In its deliberate march towards absolute power and authority, the Church feared any access to the realms of either sacred, or secular knowledge that they did not themselves monopolize and control. Who knows what might happen if people were encouraged into education, intellectual adventure and inquiry? Education was thus restricted to the clergy. Holy orders became the essential prerequisite for basic literacy. By restricting access to books, education, understanding and the world of the spirit, the Church revealed its real aims and objectives – total power and control over kings, emperors and princes; over territories, peoples and individuals; over this life and entrance to the next. All because the Church, and the Church alone, assumed unto itself, the sole right to decide who would be saved and who would be eternally damned. These barriers that were erected against education and investigation were in complete contrast to the respect for learning that had existed in pagan Rome, yet imperial Rome had also been an authoritarian state. The philosopher, Bertrand Russell, comments: "What is significant is that the function of [the Christian] religion was not conducive to the exercise of intellectual adventure."[140]

The fathers of the expanding Christian Church believed that they could legislate away all knowledge of the spiritual world, that they could persecute and terrorize all those who had knowledge of it and that they and they alone could control and monopolize all access to spiritual powers. This delusion continued to influence the thinking of Church leaders and popes for many centuries. The only tangible results that have come down to us in the record of history are the truly horrendous stories of the persistent and vicious persecutions that were the inevitable result of such an illusion.

Legislation, dogmatism and keeping the laity in a state of perpetual ignorance undoubtedly bred a silent and fearful obedience to the diktat of "Holy Mother the Church," but it did not remove spirit from the world or knowledge of the spirit from the folk memory of mankind as a whole.[141] Control over the minds and beliefs of man does not bring in its train control over super-sensible reality. The Spirit of God continued to inform, pervade and sustain the temporal world. Whilst the Church tried to modify the outward attitude of the majority of men, there was no way that the dogmatic denial of spiritual reality could ever be one hundred percent effective. Papal decrees and Church council decisions could neither change the reality of the human spirit nor abolish it. Knowledge and beliefs that gave access to Spirit continually invaded the sacrosanct domains of the growing and ever-more powerful Church. The atavistic insights of the newly Christianized Germanic tribes of the North sustained this tendency: the natural spirituality of the Celtic nations of the West strengthened it, and despite vigorous, sustained and hideous persecution, the old gnosis of the Greeks and Egyptians continued to make inroads into the Christian world. In the East, the entire Greek Orthodox Church was a vibrant and perpetual reminder of the eternal truth of man's ability to access and use the gifts of the spirit; while in the West, the hidden streams of spirituality that preserved the true teachings of Jesus used the ancient and revered rites of initiation under a veil of secrecy, to irrigate the barren intellectual and spiritual desert that was Christian Europe. The followers of the new Christianity of the Holy Grail also strove steadfastly to explore the realities of the spirit. Their secret search, camouflaged and hidden, lay behind the seemingly blind obedience that was the public face of clerical scholarship.

In seeking to monopolize all access to the sacred and claiming sole rights over all spiritual gifts, knowledge and insight, Holy Mother the Church had backed a loser, the terrible cost of which was the bloody butcher's bill of centuries of persecution and the endless litany of names that list the innocent victims of the dreaded Inquisition. Heretics, actual and potential, were sought, tortured, tried and burnt. Whole populations were put to the sword for heresy, the Cathars being the most notable. The Church was mainly corrupt, and its influence on intellectual and spiritual life, stultifying.

After the death of Charlemagne, political problems multiplied apace. Feudal barons quarreled with their kings; kings fought with one another or squabbled with popes. Actual, imagined or potential heretics were sought vigorously. The Church itself was totally corrupt, amassing wealth that was blatantly flaunted in the face of its poverty-stricken congregations. Until the twelfth century, its influence on intellectual life was completely stultifying. The clergy were literate, wealthy and powerful; the laity were kept illiterate, ignorant, and with the exception of the nobility, impoverished. Holy Mother the Church deliberately kept it that way. One modern philosopher compared the respect for knowledge common in the classical world of Socrates to the attitude that prevailed in the Christian sphere of influence.

(of Socrates) ... Though he always says he knows nothing, he does not think that knowledge lies beyond our reach. ... He holds that what makes man sin is lack of knowledge. If only he knew, he would not sin. The one overriding cause of evil is therefore ignorance. Hence to reach the Good, we must have knowledge, and so the Good is knowledge. The link between

Good and knowledge is a mark of Greek thought throughout. Christian ethics is quite opposed to this. There, the important thing is a pure heart, and that is likely to be found more readily among the ignorant.[142]

The absolute power and control exercised by the Church over education, culture, and access to the world of the spirit had far reaching consequences. Absolute power meant power and control over kings, emperors, princes and populations. All deriving from the simple fact that man was born in a state of sin, and the Church alone had the sole right of decision as to who would be saved and who would be sentenced to eternal hellfire and damnation. As kings ruled by divine right, the Church, as God's representatives on Earth, possessed higher authority than kings, emperors or princes. This attitude of Christian humility, buttressed by the doctrines of the Just War and "Compel them to come in" became the rock solid foundations for a vigorously repressive and persecuting society that grew steadily until it produced the dubious benefits of the *Index Librorum Prohibitorum* ("List of Prohibited Books"), the Holy Office of the Inquisition and that awe-inspiring manifestation of "divine love" – burning at the stake. Yet, within this period, were born some of the most deeply spiritual men and women yet seen on Earth. Followers of the hidden streams of spirituality, the true spiritual heirs of Jesus, the mystics and initiates who simply, humbly and wholeheartedly dedicated themselves to God and who sought the Holy Spirit wherever they could.

Chartres Cathedral, detail of south elevation,
from G. Dehio (died 1932) and G. von Bezold (died 1934), *Die Kirchliche Baukunst des abendlandes*, Stuttgart, Germany, 1887–1902.

CHAPTER 9

Buried Treasure:
The Underground Streams Of Spirituality

When a person has true mystical experience, he may boldly drop external disciplines, even those to which he is bound by vows.[143]

– Meister Eckhart

The leaders of the Western Church believed that they could, by blind, bigoted, dictatorial dogmatism, legislate away all knowledge of the spirit, persecute and terrorize all those who had knowledge of it, and that they and they alone could control and monopolize all access to spiritual powers. This delusion continued to exert a dominant influence on the thinking of Church leaders and popes for centuries to come. The only tangible results were the persistent and vicious persecutions that were the inevitable result of such an illusion. The ultimate and eventual culmination of this policy of arrogance was the later doctrine of "papal infallibility."[144] Thus the society that developed as a result of the merging of the Church and the Empire of Rome was one in which the Church itself became the sole arbiter of religious belief. It had become, by its very nature, a compulsory and persecuting society and all within its boundaries had to adhere to the same centrally established system of belief.

Dogmatism, persecution and keeping the laity in a state of perpetual ignorance bred a silent and fearful obedience to Holy

Mother the Church, but it did not remove the spirit from the world, or knowledge of the spirit from the folk memory of mankind as a whole, for spirituality continued to inform, pervade and sustain the temporal world. Whilst the Church tried to modify the outward attitude of the majority of men, it could neither change the reality of the human spirit, nor abolish it, for there was no way that the dogmatic denial of spiritual reality could ever be one hundred percent effective. Knowledge and beliefs that gave access to the world of the spirit continually invaded the sacrosanct domains of the Church, and the Gnostic spiritual teachings of Jesus that were continued by James and the original disciples in Jerusalem, continued in secret despite vigorous and hideous persecution.

In the fluctuating chaos of Europe after the fall of the Roman Empire, the Church was the only institution with any clear and determined idea of where it was going. The wealthy land-owning classes of the old empire had completely taken over the episcopate, so that the hierarchy alone possessed all the skills needed to bring order out of chaos. As the Gothic tribes settled in Italy and beyond, the Church made its first successful forays into the tribal hinterlands and began to convert the Franks and the Burgundians. Bishops became not only spiritual leaders, but also the military commanders of many districts, thus reinforcing the Church's reputation for establishing stability and order. An extensive bureaucracy sprang up in Rome, founded around the need for documentation of saints, doctrine, dogma and decrees. This body of clerical scribes soon acquired considerable, valuable expertise in matters of civil administration and as a result, the answers to all problems, civil or religious, seemed to lie in Rome.[145]

With the election of Gregory the Great as pope in 589 CE, the Church gained a leader who did much to bring about the expansion of the Christian Church in lands previously regarded as barbaric, including Britain.[146] With the missionaries went the administrators bringing the benefits of civilization along with the somewhat dubious blessings of Christianity. The abbots of the various Christian monasteries kept meticulous accounts and as a result were able to discover the most cost-effective manner of operation, not only for themselves, but also for other landowners. It was for reasons of economic efficiency that slavery began to vanish, not out of Christian love. It was found to be more productive and economical to colonize land with peasant tenant farmers than to employ slaves, so slavery disappeared. The basic physical landscape and society of Europe was molded and created by the cumulative actions of early monasticism, moderated of course by its reaction to outside, barbaric forces beyond its control, such as the Vikings.

By the end of the twelfth century the medieval Christian Church had proved that it was, without doubt, the most intolerant, dogmatic and repressive authority that Europe had ever experienced in its already long and bloody history. Due to the ever present suspicion of the hierarchy, all who openly ventured opinions or beliefs which contradicted it, or even differed in the slightest from its teachings, were harried, persecuted, excommunicated, tortured or burnt. Skills of dissembling and disguise became the vital prerequisites of survival for those of independent spirit who wished to avoid the unwelcome attentions of the Inquisition and the warm embrace of the stake.[147]

The power of church and state spread its ever-more penetrating tentacles downwards from pope, emperor and king to feudal lords and barons.[148] Few people in Europe escaped its all-pervading grasp. Under the rule of the Church in the early Middle Ages, feudalism developed a stability that enabled it to last, in some parts of Europe at least, until well into the twentieth century. The safety and security of the towns and villages under their feudal rulers provided a firm foundation for a second wave of monastic agricultural expansion in the tenth to twelfth centuries. On this occasion it was the new Order of the Cistercians who took the lead. They refused to accept grants and bequests of towns, villages, churches and rents, insisting instead on receiving grants of agricultural land only. They deliberately took on the role of frontiersmen, extending the areas of cultivation and pasturage beyond the limits of known civilization. They became the "agricultural apostles" in the Christianization of an ever-expanding Europe. On their estates they abolished the peasant tenant farmers, replacing them with the *conversi*, lay brothers to whom salvation was the guaranteed reward for earthly obedience. Men who could be moved at will from estate to estate according to need; men who expected no wages – highly motivated and disciplined slaves in the silent service of God.

Monks founded estates, towns, abbeys, churches and cathedrals, and were important cultural carriers, but not innovators or creators. With one or two notable exceptions they simply transcribed and codified existing, approved knowledge. The Church continued to reserve for itself absolute power and control over knowledge and education. Most of the culture and philosophy of pagan Greece was excluded from the hierarchically approved list of available learning. Scriptures, neo-Platonism, dogma, revelation and doctrine were all that interested the Church. A carefully edited history of contemporary events was also recorded by the monastic scribes, but in the main they were scriptural copyists, not original thinkers. One exception to this is the single known instance of a realistic attempt to publish the philosophical works of the ancient Greeks. *The Consolations of Philosophy* was actually written by Boethius while he was awaiting trial on charges of heresy for which he was eventually executed.[149]

Greek philosophical influence came back to European scholarship much later and, curiously, by a circuitous route. When it did arrive it had to be translated not from Greek, but from Arabic. Knowledge of ancient Greek culture and thinking had been preserved in the Arab lands of the Middle East whence many classical scholars had fled after their expulsion by Church authorities. The Arab respect for education and philosophy and their intellectual and religious tolerance, was a startling contrast to the bigoted views of the European hierarchy. Even after the rise of Islam, the heirs to the philosophical traditions of Greece survived and prospered. Knowledge of Greek philosophy and science and the more recent advances in mathematics and medicine slowly crept back into Europe via the Moorish conquests in Spain and contributed to the scholastic revival in Europe that arose in the eleventh and twelfth centuries. It was at this point that education slowly started to spread from its narrow clerical base into the European aristocracy. Within this oppressive period were born mystics and initiates who humbly dedicated themselves to God, and who sought the Holy Spirit wherever they could.

The Church's innate distrust of the mystical experience that occurred within the framework of medieval Christianity and their confused yet dogmatic refusal to acknowledge the validity of this essentially spiritual phenomenon was extraordinary to say the least. While the Church was only too ready to accept the validity of the spiritual insight of the biblical mystics and prophets, in stark contrast it was only too eager to condemn similar experience among the devout in its own ranks. Mystical experience imbues one with a sense of justice; consequently in any rigid, dogmatic and unjust system, the mystic is viewed as dangerous and is usually in trouble. This certainly proved to be the case in the Middle Ages.

Hildegard of Bingen, the medieval mystic so revered today, was, at the age of eighty-one, held in such regard by the Church that she was excommunicated along with her entire convent of nuns. St. Francis of Assisi had his order forcibly removed from his control while he was still alive, provoking in him what we would now describe as a nervous breakdown and the manifestation of the stigmata. This physical identification with the wounds Jesus suffered on the Cross was later used, paradoxically, as a sign of his true sanctity. The premature death of St. Thomas Aquinas was certainly hastened by his constant battles with the Church hierarchy. Things got so bad for this renowned theologian that in the last year of his life he had a nervous breakdown of such severity that he could neither write nor speak. Few people today are aware that he was condemned for heresy, not once, but three times before his eventual canonization. Mechthild of Magdeburg was driven from town to town without pause because she criticized the clergy for their greed and their indifference to the plight of the poor, the young and the sick. Meister Eckhart was condemned for heresy after he died. This man, probably the greatest mystic in Christian history, is still on the condemned list today. The English mystic, Julian of Norwich, was simply ignored, not only during her lifetime but for more than for two centuries after her death.[150]

True mystical experience engenders the capacity to transcend the accretions of dogma and return to the same spiritual realities experienced by the shamans of the hunter-gatherers and the revered initiates of Egypt and biblical Israel. The writings of the medieval mystics disclose the same joy in God's gift of nature that runs through the Judaism of ancient Israel like a river. Let them speak for themselves. First let us read the words of Meister Eckhart, one of the many formative influences on Martin Luther.

What is the test that you have indeed undergone
this spiritual birth?
Listen carefully. If this birth has truly taken place within you,
then every single creature will point you toward God.[151]

You can never trust God too much.
Why is it that some people do not bear fruit?
It is because they have no trust,
Either in God or in themselves.[152]

And compare his spiritual insights with those of another
great soul, Hildegard of Bingen.

The word is a living being, spirit, all verdant
greening, all creativity.
This word manifests itself in every creature.[153]

Holy persons draw to themselves all that is earthly.
The earth is at the same time mother,
She is mother of all that is natural,
mother of all that is human.
She is the mother of all,
for contained in her
are the seeds of all[154]

Hildegard of Bingen and Meister Eckhart were not alone; other
Christian mystics of the Middle Ages have also left us messages of
justice and love.

I know well that heaven and earth and all creation are great,
generous and beautiful and good ... God's goodness fills all

his creatures and all his blessed works full, and endlessly over-
flows in them ... God is everything which is good, as I see it,
and the goodness which everything has, is God.[155]

All praise be yours, my Lord, through sister Earth, our mother,
who feeds us in her sovereignty and produces various fruits and
coloured flowers and herbs.[156]

The day of my spiritual awakening
was the day I saw
– and knew I saw –
All things in God
and God in all things.[157]

Despite the persecution and condemnation of the medieval mystics, their teaching had a profound and wide reaching effect among
the admittedly small number of literate scholars of their time.
One such was Jacob Boehme, the cobbler of Gorlitz, whose work
Signatura Rerum – the "Signature Of All Things" – follows directly in the mystical tradition of his medieval forbearers. His works
gained wide circulation and were translated into many languages.
His vision can be interpreted in a number of ways, but all seem to
come back to the same central conception shared by Hildegard of
Bingen, Mechthild of Magdeburg, Julian of Norwich and all the
others. He writes movingly of the overpowering vibrant, "spiritual meaning" that is to be found existing in nature. Colin Wilson
described this in the following terms:

Boehme spoke of the "signature" of things, meaning their inner symbolic essence, which makes it sound as if he caught an
intuitive glimpse of Dr. David Foster's notion of a universe of

coded information in which all living things are the expression of a vital intelligence.[158]

Boehme's own words reveal his intent:

This book is a true mystical mirror of the highest wisdom. The best treasure that a man can attain unto in this world is true knowledge; even the knowledge of himself: For man is the great mystery of God, the microcosm, or the complete abridgement of the universe: He is the *mirandum Dei opus*, God's masterpiece, a living emblem and hieroglyphic of eternity and time; and therefore to know whence he is, and what his temporal and eternal being and well-being are, must needs be that ONE necessary thing, to which our chief study should aim and in comparison of which all the wealth of this world is but dross, and a loss to us.[159]

It is in the *Signatura* that he expounds his cosmological theories, and it provides the best start with which to gain an idea of his central teaching. It is almost axiomatic that Boehme's spiritual insights did little to endear him to the hierarchy of his time, or later, but despite all attempts to suppress his work, it was widely read. He influenced Emanuel Swedenborg and, in the English-speaking world, his thinking had a profound influence on George Fox, the Father of Quakerism and on the Cambridge Platonists who were to gain their most coherent disciple in William Law. His profound and spiritual insight also influenced two later mystics, the poets, William Blake and Johann Wolfgang von Goethe. It was by sharing the strength and the experience of the reality of the spirit with their fellow man, despite all the persecution, repression and condemnation that was their earthly reward, that the mystics of the Middle Ages carried the torch of spirituality to later generations, and through them, to us.

Thus the medieval mystics, like the prophets of biblical Israel before them, were by the very nature of their spiritual experience the divinely inspired messengers of peace, justice and the knowledge of God's presence in every part of creation. And just like the biblical prophets of old, they were far from popular with those who reserved to themselves all power and authority over the sacred. Mysticism is one of the great cornerstones of religious experience, yet the Church was terrified of the medieval mystics and their message. The hierarchy knew that all of humanity have an intrinsic capacity for mysticism as part of their spiritual heritage, which is precisely why the Church leaders tried to eliminate the concept of the human spirit from the consciousness and memory of mankind.[160]

The medieval mystics were not alone among the Christians of Western Europe in their search for spiritual truth. One well-hidden spiritual academy flourished at a site revered for its spiritual power from the days of the Druids. The medieval Mystery school of Chartres was founded soon after Bishop Fulbertus rebuilt the cathedral after the fire that destroyed the original building. His pupil Bernardus founded the esoteric and initiatory academy at Chartres, which centered around the new cathedral.[161] Under the guise of studying the seven liberal arts, the pupils of Bernardus developed the seven senses of the spirit. Outwardly they were learning about *Gramatica, Dialectica, Logica, Musica, Mathematica, Geometrica* and *Astronomia*, but these medieval students of the Mysteries were also inwardly developing and bringing to fruition the clairvoyant senses which open to a direct vision of the spiritual world. After a long period of probation the students underwent a time of purification in order to overcome the lower and instinctive nature in the soul that blinded them to the existence of the divine within themselves and within nature. Each soul was known to be capable of developing a greater degree of "spiritual perception," and discipline and meditation were the means by which they could be developed: this was the central issue of Jesus' original initiatory teaching that was outwardly taught under the guise of the liberal arts. After probation and enlightenment, the seven ascending degrees of initiation were attained, leading to a conscious involvement in the spiritual reality that underpins the world of the senses.[162]

The spiritual senses not only unveil to clairvoyant perception the thoughts and mentality, the sentiments and disposition of other souls as well as their talents and capacities, but also give a deeper insight into the laws of all natural phenomena and reveal the very unity in nature that is the mainspring of all creation. It was from this deep understanding of the spiritual realities that underpin the tangible world of nature that the initiates of Chartres divined the importance of the goddess *natura* in the divine plan for man's enlightenment. This was their reason for carving a replica of the pagan statue, *Virginii Pariturae*, which had been the center of worship at Chartres in pre-Christian times.[163] A modern replica of this statue in the guise of Mary, the Mother of God, now rests in the crypt. Another is carved in the place of honor above the main portal of the cathedral, from whence it was soon copied on most of the leading cathedrals and churches throughout Western Christendom. It is perhaps ironic, to the uninitiated at least, that one of the major dogmas of present day Roman Catholicism should have been reinforced and strengthened from the spiritual understanding and perception of the hidden initiates of the Middle Ages, who would themselves have been liable to persecution by the same Roman

Church for the heretical nature of their beliefs had they been known at that time.

Hidden among the other secret orders of initiates who retained the knowledge and capacity for spiritual vision was one anonymous group of orders that carried the traditions of initiation to the very verge of modern times, the *Compagnonnage*, known in England as the Craftmasons. Not, as so many historians suggest, just craft guilds who regulated the terms of employment of its members, but orders of initiation and humility which claimed to trace their origins right back to the building of the Temple in Jerusalem by King Solomon. Robert Graves, in his introduction to Idries Shah's work *The Sufis*, claims that the architects and builders of Solomon's Temple were neither Phoenician nor Israelite, as is commonly believed, but Sufis. This would tend to suggest a much earlier attribution for both the Sufis and the Craftmasons than is popularly believed. Many other devout followers of Jesus, including those who sought the Holy Grail, found spiritual truth and inspiration in a book of the New Testament, which has both fascinated, puzzled and sometimes appalled its readers for the last two thousand years. This much misunderstood work of immense power is known as the Revelation of St. John.

The mystery of the Revelation starts with its reputed author, St. John the Divine. It is commonly believed that St. John was the supreme pupil of Jesus who played a leading role in the Jerusalem church, and is recorded as having traveled with Peter to Samaria to lay hands on new converts there. Two independent sources place him as having lived for a long time at Ephesus. One of the early fathers of the Church, Irenaeus, tells us that John was exiled by the Emperor Domitian, during a period of persecution of the early Church in the late 80s CE. It was in a small cave on a mountainside on the penal island of Patmos that John is reputed to have written the Revelation. This cave, or rather the one legend relates is the cave of St. John, exudes a strange mystical, yet almost oppressive, peace to this day. This mystic, known in the Eastern Church as John the Theologian, wrote prolifically. The Gospel of John, three letters and the Revelation have all survived virtually intact but no one knows how much more has vanished or been suppressed – such as the "Acts of John," which was condemned by the Council of Nicaea. The Gospel according to St. John is regarded by many Christian scholars as an initiation document. It was particularly sacred to the Cathars who knew it as the "Gospel of Love." It was called the "Spiritual Gospel" by one of the early fathers of the Church, Clement of Alexandria. This is a conception that is in total keeping with the visionary origin of the disciple's other work that we now call the "Revelation."

The Revelation is a strange, compelling, yet puzzling apocalyptic book written with a truly fantastic imagery; a fascinating blend of Essene apocalyptic tradition, Babylonian mythology – including a duality of evil – and astrological fantasy derived from the Persians and the Egyptians. The whole work is made more puzzling by its obviously prophetic nature – but the prophesy seems as if it were written in a complex code, deliberately designed to obscure rather than reveal. For what sense can the rational mind of today make of this mysterious work which clothes the destiny of mankind in a framework of seals, trumpet blasts and vials of wrath? The strange symbolism and mythological imagery of the Revelation of St. John became for many devout mystics a kind of magic mirror in which they could discern reflections of both the past and the future. It was as though the divinely inspired author of this mysterious and puzzling work had seen the advent of the Christian era of repression, censorship and dogmatism and had encoded the steps of initiation to divine truth and revelation as a spiritual antidote to the coming distortions of the true teachings of Jesus.

Sevenfoldedness is one of the keys to unraveling the complex coding inherent in the Revelation. The whole mysterious work seems to advance in rhythms of seven. There are the seven stars; the seven golden candlesticks; the seven messages; the seven angels of the seven churches; the seven seals; the seven trumpet blasts and the seven vials of wrath. Seven seems to be the magical, key number of time that pervaded all the ancient schools of magic and each and every one of the respected systems of initiation. It was a number of supreme significance for the religions and initiatory systems of all the civilizations that preceded the time of Jesus, whether their origins had been Mesopotamian, Egyptian, Greek, Celtic, Roman or Christian. In the Eastern world, the Buddhists speak of Nirvana – the seventh heaven. Whatever our culture, irrespective of our era, seven appears to be the magical number we absorb with our mother's milk. As children we learn of the seven wonders of the ancient world; the seven hills of Rome; the seven colors of the rainbow; lucky seven and the superstitions surrounding the seventh son of a seventh son.

Approaching the end of the first millennium of the Christian era devout scholars and mystics found in the Revelation of St. John, the seven-fold key to a new system of Christian initiation known to history as the "Search for the Holy Grail." It is the number that recurs time and time again, repeating itself mystically in the seven spirit senses, the seven chakras, the seven planetary oracles and the seven great European cathedrals that stand on the seven planetary sites revered by the Druids.[164] Its magical influence can also be detected in the conditions to be fulfilled by an initiatory novice, and in the number of degrees of initiation sought by the noble Knights of the Templar Order – the true initiates of the Holy Grail.

Emblem of the military Order of Templars.

CHAPTER 10

The Search For The Holy Grail

Lucid discernment reveals the essential and can encourage us
to discard everything hampering its development, so that we
can advance on the path of initiation, the noble path of
human accomplishment.[165]   – Frederic Lionel, *Mirrors of Truth*

The perceptive and controversial nineteenth century scholar,
Karl Marx, clearly demonstrated that the infrastructure of
any state is always designed primarily to buttress and support the aims and policies of the ruling class. History, the written
record that has come down to us from the past, is always part of
just such an infrastructure. History is almost inevitably written
by the victors in any conflict or dispute, be that dispute physical, intellectual or spiritual. Therefore, the religious history of
the Middle Ages, as it was originally written, is the reflection of
the aims and values of the theologians, popes and bishops. Their
voluminous written record should not disguise the fact that in religious matters there are two separate streams of history running
parallel to one another. One, the outwardly visible or exoteric, is
commonly known as "history"; the other, hidden to all eyes but
those of the initiated, is the esoteric spiritual stream which continually influences it, reacts against it and thus shapes it further.
This is as true today as it was in the Middle Ages.[166]

From the thirteenth century onwards Christian Hermeticists

began to synthesize a Christianized version of the Jewish Kabbala, which originated from the Hebraic/Egyptian Gnosticism that inspired Jesus, although in the Middle Ages it was thought to be part of the Law as given to Moses. For this reason it was called tradition or "Kabbala." The *Sefer ha-Zohar* or "Book of Splendor" expressed its principal aspects, which were mainly Jewish Gnosticism, Sufi initiatory mysticism, recently synthesized neo-Platonism and magic. It was written about 1280 and spread slowly into the hidden esoteric streams of Christian Europe from the Rabbinical schools in Moorish Spain, but it did not gain wider circulation until the invention of printing. Among the esoteric streams in the early centuries of Christianity were Gnostic cults, mainly of Greek, Egyptian or Essene origin, who were persecuted mercilessly. One in particular, the Manichees, originated in Persia and yet was Christian; Augustine of Hippo was at one time a member of this sect.[167] It spread into Eastern Europe and flourished from time to time, despite being subject to continual and vigorous repression. So-called Manichean derivatives, such as the Bogomils and later the Cathar communities, were repressed with savage brutality.

In the latter part of the "Dark Ages," another new and completely Christian initiation order arose in great secrecy. We first find written indications of this new cult in the ninth century when the legend of the search for the Holy Grail became a vehicle for coded references to a scripturally based, pure, Christian path of initiation. The Grail sagas first became widely known in Europe in 1190 when they took the form of an unfinished epic, *Perceval* or *Le Conte del Graal* written by Chrétien de Troyes,[168] a subject of Count Hugh I of Champagne. He originally dedicated this work to the count's wife Marie, who was the daughter of King Louis VII of France and Eleanor of Aquitaine.[169] Both King Louis and Count Hugh were members of a mysterious and secretive group of families known as *Rex Deus*. They claim to be the direct lineal descendants of the twenty-four *ma'madot*, the high-priestly families of biblical Israel, direct descendants of Zadok the Priest, the true heirs to the Hebraic/Egyptian Gnostic and initiatory tradition.[170] Following the death of Hugh of Champagne, Chrétien re-dedicated the work to another member of the same group of families, Philippe d'Alsace, the Count of Flanders who was the cousin of Payen de Montdidier, one of the co-founders of the Knights Templar. *Le Conte del Graal* was followed some time later by the epic of *Parzival*, an allegory written by the wandering Minnesinger Wolfram von Eschenbach, which recounts the story of the characters who sought the Grail.[171]

These stories tell, in an allegorical way, of the search for enlightenment. Under the guise of describing a search for a holy relic, supposedly the cup or chalice used by Joseph of Arimathea to collect Jesus' blood after the crucifixion, the stories reveal, in coded form, the pathway of initiation taught by Jesus.[172] In stressing the concept of a search for the holy relic that was used to catch the blood of Jesus at the crucifixion, the Church, as biblical authorities, erred badly in contradicting long established Jewish traditions about men not handling corpses in this manner. Bear in mind also that the crucifixion took place on the eve of Passover and if Joseph, or any other man, had handled the body of Jesus they would have had to undergo a prolonged period of ritual purification that would have debarred them from playing any active part at the feast. Furthermore the orthodox custom of that time demanded that the body be buried as whole as possible and this would have made it a matter of blasphemy to keep the blood and bury the body.[173]

Far from being a search for a relic, the Grail quest is, as Trevor Ravenscroft so brilliantly describes in *The Cup of Destiny*, a coded guide to the seven steps of initiation. Even if one accepts the Church's explanation of a search for a relic, one important question remains to be answered. Why should any Christian knight set out in search of the "Holy Grail," when in every chapel he had, through the act of communion and transubstantiation, direct access to the body and blood of his beloved Savior, the Lord Jesus Christ?

The Grail quest was not a search for a holy relic at all; it was an allegorical description of an individual, inner adventure in spiritual experience in the true initiatory tradition.[174] According to the internationally renowned mythologist Joseph Campbell, "The Grail represents the fulfillment of the highest spiritual potentialities of human consciousness." The validity of the Grail quest was confirmed by the contents of the Nag Hammadi scrolls that include many early Christian initiatory documents long thought lost or suppressed. In the "Gospel According to Thomas," Jesus is reported as saying, "He who drinks from my mouth will become as I am, and I shall be he."[175] This, in the view of Campbell, is the whole point of the Grail.[176]

Links have been established between the troubadours singing the Grail sagas and certain of the Sufi poets of Islam who were on the same quest. Indeed, it is within the history of Sufism that we can find the earliest and most complete record of the transmission of spiritual knowledge from master to initiate. Their legendary patron "El Khidir," who is a composite and mythical figure based upon both the prophet Elijah and John the Baptist[177] – the teacher of Jesus, was known as the "verdant one," green represents the color of initiation. The English poet Robert Graves described the Sufis as: "An ancient spiritual Freemasonry whose origins have never been traced or dated although the characteristic Sufic signature is found in widely dispersed literature from at least the second millennium BC."[178]

Sufi teaching in Europe reached its zenith with the Sufi Mystery schools of Spain in the ninth century, from where their teaching slowly began to permeate into Christian Europe – a process that gathered great momentum with the formation of the Order of the Knights Templar, who were initiates of the Holy Grail. Like the Sufis before them, the Templars sought spiritual enlightenment using their insights for the benefit of the society in which they moved. Furthermore both Islamic and Christian initiatory paths sprang from the same common, Hebraic/Egyptian parent.[179] The grandson of Judaism's greatest thinker, Moses Maimonides (1135–1204), also states that the Sufi tradition is Hebraic in origin when he wrote that Sufism is "the pride of Israel bestowed upon the nations."[180]

When we turn to the two main Grail sagas themselves, we find within them the symbolism of the seven degrees of initiation. The Raven was the sign of the first degree, symbolizing the messenger of the gods. The Peacock signified the second degree, its many splendored plumage demonstrating the capacity for powers of moral imagination. The Knight became the symbol of the third and warrior degree and knighthood was bestowed for the attainment of it. The Swan was the sign of the fourth degree, not only because of its purity but also because the swan song represented the death of self and the inner realization of the divine within the human breast. The fifth degree was depicted by the Pelican, the bird that wounds its own breast to feed its young. Such an initiate lived for the perpetuation of his own people and dedicated his life to their service. The Eagle denoted the sixth degree in which an initiate gained the capacity to move and communicate in the spiritual world. The Crown was the symbol of the "King of the Grail" who had achieved the very highest degree. To him was revealed the secrets of time and an understanding of the laws at work within human destiny.[181]

It is this "direct inner knowing of God's will" transformed into physical action in the temporal world which highlights the main difference between the conformist Christian behavior and the actions of the true initiate of the spiritual world. One definition of the word Grail is that it is a corruption of "gradual" – a religious term for a step-by-step, formal process of learning. In this case a gradual preparation for the process of ever-more profound, spiritual enlightenment.[182] All known initiation cults have been recognized for their ability to sustain long-term, collective, spiritually based action dedicated, through service to others and society as a whole, and thus to God.

The Grail initiation continued in secret and exerted a direct influence on the formation of the Knights Templar in Jerusalem. It is claimed that the Templars were founded in 1119, after the success of the First Crusade. The modern consensus among historians with respect to this date is almost entirely based on the work of Archbishop William of Tyre, who wrote a history of the crusader states between 1165 and 1184, some seventy years after the Order's alleged foundation. Frequently displaying a distinct anti-Templar bias in his work, he nonetheless, wrote that the first Templars were a group of noble knights, "devoted to God, religious and God-fearing," who entrusted themselves into the hands of the patriarch (Warmund of Picquigny) to serve Christ. However another religious scribe, the monk Simon of the monastery of St. Bertin near St. Omer, wrote in around 1135–1137 that the first Templars were simply crusaders who stayed in the Holy Land after the First Crusade instead of returning home. Allegedly on the advice of the princes of God's army, they dedicated themselves to God's Temple under this rule:

... they would renounce the world, give up personal goods, free themselves to pursue chastity, and lead a communal life wearing a poor habit, only using weapons to defend the land against the attacks of the insurgent pagans when the necessity demanded.[183]

The English historian Helen Nicholson admits that this account was written within a generation of the founding of the Templars and thus must be given some credence.[184] Another near contemporary, Anselm Bishop of Havelburg, writing in 1145, dates the foundation of the Order to the time of the First Crusade. In 1153, yet another monk, Richard of Poitou from Cluny, dated the foundation of the Templars to 1109.[185] Thus, none of the contemporaries or near-contemporaries of the Order's foundation were sure precisely when the Order of the Temple was really founded. In the opinion of Nicholson, they also did not know why it began or who was truly responsible for its foundation.[186]

Among modern commentators, while many accept the work of William of Tyre, there are also those who tend to disagree. Baigent, Leigh and Lincoln claim an earlier date for its foundation, citing a letter from a leading Catholic Church dignitary in support of their claim. Indeed, in 1114, Ivo, bishop of Chartres, wrote to Count Hugh of Champagne, rebuking the count for abandoning his wife and vowing himself to the "Knighthood of Christ," *militiae Christi*, a name later used to describe the Templars (and it must be remembered that the Templars were the first military order in Christendom, so who else is the bishop referring to?) The bishop continued his tirade against Count Hugh by accusing him of taking up "that Gospel Knighthood," *evangelicum militiam*, by which two thousand may fight securely against him who rushes to attack us with two hundred thousand,[187] a distinctive phrase later used by Bernard of Clairvaux in describing the Templar Order. Prince Michael of Albany dates the foundation of the Order to circa 1094, but sadly does not cite any verifiable data to support this theory.[188]

Ostensibly the Templars were founded with papal blessing to protect pilgrims to the Holy Land but the real reason remained hidden, concealed behind a deliberate web of obfuscation and misinformation. One of the earliest recorded references to the Order is a tract written by St. Bernard of Clairvaux in 1128, entitled *In Praise of the New Knighthood.* It was to St. Bernard, the most powerful man in Europe in the early twelfth century, that the Order accredits the formulation of its rule. A protégé of his, Pope Innocent II, issued a papal bull in 1139 that placed the Templars under no earthly authority but his own, making them independent of kings, princes and the Church hierarchy. They were thus accorded a freedom of action that literally made them a law unto themselves.[189] The first Knights Templar were quartered in the former stables of King Solomon beside the site of the ruined Temple. Graham Hancock states in *The Sign and the Seal* that the Templars made prolonged and deep excavations under the Temple Mount in Jerusalem, after its capture by the Christians. We now have reason to believe that these excavations resulted in the re-discovery of the ancient knowledge of sacred geometry and building skills that spawned the sudden outburst of cathedral building in the twelfth and thirteenth centuries.[190]

To the uninitiated there is indeed a puzzle that lies behind the mysterious and sudden outburst of cathedral building that gave us those majestic and powerful "prayers in stone" that still adorn the European landscape. To answer the baffling questions as to what provoked this enormous expenditure of resources or from where the new technology, engineering and architectural skills that spawned the "rise of the Gothic" came, we have to turn to one of the Churches traditional enemies, Gnosticism, and examine the actions of some of the medieval European initiatory orders who had been influenced by this pervasive form of dualistic thinking.

St. Bernard of Clairvaux, who played a major, if somewhat mysterious, role in the foundation of the Knights Templar, was the originator of much of the Cistercian worldview. His profound interest in the initiatory teaching of sacred knowledge led him to preach over one hundred and twenty sermons on the biblical adept Solomon's "Song of Songs." He also played a formative role in the development of the initiatory tradition of the branch of the *Compagnonnage* known as the "Children of Solomon." Bernard personally attended the Council of Troyes, which gave both the rule and an increased legitimacy to the new Knightly Order of the Templars. The Templars are now widely recognized to have been an initiatory order and in the mystery surrounding their foundation it is possible to discern strong and distinct Gnostic influences operating right from the start. The other initiatory orders were the men known in England as the Craftmasons who built the great cathedrals. In France this was far from an homogenous group as there were at least three such fraternities – the "Children of Father Soubise," the "Children of Master Jacques" and the "Children of Solomon." Their spiritual heirs are now known as *Les Compagnons du Devoir du Tour de France*.[191] Some followed a path of initiation, some did not; but all observed a moral tradition of chivalry within their craft and a submission to work that must be done. By one definition companions are men who share the same bread but, according to Raoul Verges, they are men who know how to use a pair of compasses. Men who share the same bread form a community or fraternity; by contrast, those who know how to use a pair of compasses are initiates granted insight into the laws, knowledge and harmony of sacred geometry that admits them to the status of "Mason."

Their Masonic traditions were deep-rooted and expressed at the craft level in a hierarchy of three degrees; apprentice, companion and attained-companion or master. As those who have vital, God-given work to do, they refused to bear arms and, in the manner of "Grail Knights," have always refused to build fortresses or prisons. Apprentices learnt their trade under the direction of companions, while moving from yard to yard in the course of a *Tour de France*; they underwent initiation by their hierophants, or masters, privately, in "cayennes." The three fraternities, which are now amalgamated into one single association, had different duties and techniques in their early days. The Children of Father Soubise were founded in the very heart of the Benedictine monastic system, where those engaged in the Craft were taught and initiated. They mostly worked in the Romanesque style and their "signatures" differ widely from those who built in the Gothic style, even when their work is contemporary.

The Children of Master Jacques became the *Compagnons Passants du Devoir*. They were founded by Master Jacques, the son of Jacquin, a master-Craftmason who attained this status after his journeys in Greece, Egypt and Jerusalem where, it is alleged, he made the two pillars of the Temple of Solomon, of which one is actually called Jacquin. The term *passants* designates men who "gave passage" – according to some authorities this implied a role as bridge builders; however we may have cause to review this definition later. It is possible that the Children of Master Jacques were the successors to the ancient Celtic builders who signed their work with an oak leaf.

From the perspective of our investigations into the rise of

the Gothic cathedrals the third brotherhood, the Children of Solomon, are the most important. They are credited not only with the building of Chartres Cathedral but most of the other Gothic Notre Dames as well, certainly those at Rheims and Amiens. Many of the churches they built are signed with the *chrisme a l'épée* – a cross of Celtic appearance enclosed in a circle.

The Children of Solomon were instructed in sacred geometry, the "Trait," by the Cistercian monks. In this case there would have been created a fraternity of religious builders on the same lines, if you like, as the Order of the Temple, to whom their protection would have been confided. They were named after King Solomon, who commissioned the Temple in Jerusalem and buried the Ark of the Covenant within it. The Children of Solomon and those other builders of Templar churches in the south of France, the *Compagnonnage Tuscana*, traced their Mysteries back to Egypt and biblical Israel via their Roman and Greek roots, as part of a *collegia* of constructors known as *Les Tignarii*, reputedly created by the renowned initiate of the classical Roman era, Numa Pompilius.

What was the exact relationship between the Children of Solomon and the Order of the Temple? Were they within the order, affiliated to it, or just associated with it? It is a matter of record that the Knights Templar gave a rule to them in March 1145, known as the *Rule of St. Devoir de Dieu et de la Croissade*. This was a rule for life, for work, and of honor for all the initiates involved in the construction of churches. The rule was accompanied by the following words:

We the Knights of Christ and of the Temple follow the destiny that prepares us to die for Christ. We have the wish to give this rule of living, of work and of honour to the constructors of churches so that Christianity can spread throughout the earth not so that our name should be remembered, Oh Lord, but that Your Name should live.[192]

It is thus highly probable that this Masonic order was affiliated to the great Order of the Temple of Solomon in some way and it is interesting to note that, in some powerful eyes at least, they were viewed as close allies. The *Compagnonnage* who were directly involved in the building of Gothic cathedrals were certainly protected by the Order of the Knights Templar and it was probably due to the influence of the Templars that they were granted great privileges, including freedom from all taxes and protection against legal action by the constructors of other buildings. It is highly significant that, at the time of the suppression of the Templars, the Children of Solomon lost the privileges and immunities granted to Masons.

One indisputable link between the Knights Templar and the Children of Solomon that we have already referred to is their joint, massive and all-pervasive involvement in that fantastic flurry of cathedral construction so aptly called the Rise of the Gothic. The involvement of the Masons is self-evident and that of the Templars only marginally less so:

> The Knights Templar were founded ostensibly to protect the pilgrimage routes to The Holy Land, were almost openly involved in financing and lending moral support to the building of Cathedrals throughout Europe.[193]

Inevitably, questions arise from the juxtaposition of the Templars return from Jerusalem and the sudden explosion of building in the Gothic style that followed. Namely, did the Templars find the keys to this new form of building in the course of their excavations under the Temple Mount? Or were there other influences in Jerusalem that can clarify the origins of this new form of architecture? Two learned historians of note, the gifted Englishman, William Anderson, and the French scholar, Jean Boney, both claim that the Gothic arch was introduced from Islamic culture. The Scottish historian and clergyman, Gordon Strachan, has elaborated this idea in detail. Strachan's suggested origin for the Gothic arch is not only totally credible but is also consistent with what we know of cultural interchange at the time of the First Crusade and thereafter.

He is convinced that the origin of the pointed arch that is the foundation of the Gothic style of building lies outside Europe. Like William Anderson and Jean Boney he agrees that its origin is Islamic and claims that it came from the Holy Land, resulting from "A unique blending of indigenous building skills with the architectural genius of Islam." The Templars, during their early years of residence in Jerusalem, met many members of the Sufi orders who were undergoing a revival in their fortunes at that time. The Sufis were the main mystical order of Islam, devout believers in a form of inter-faith pluralism epitomized by the words of Jalaluddin Rumi: "The religion of love is apart from all religions. The lovers of God have no religion but God alone." A belief shared by the Templars and the *Rex Deus* families back in Europe, Strachan claims that it was as a result of their contact with the Sufis that the Templars learnt the geometric method used to design the Islamic *mukhammas* or "pointed arch." They put this to the test in Jerusalem by building a three-bayed doorway with pointed arches on the Temple Mount that can be seen to this day. Thus knowledge of sacred geometry gained an immense boost from contact between the initiatory Orders of both faiths, the Templars and the Sufis and resulted in the development of the pointed arch in Europe and a totally new style of sacred building.

The result of this inter-faith cooperation can still be seen and appreciated in the flowering of artistic and religious expression of the medieval Gothic cathedrals.

Both Kenneth Rayner Johnson and the modern initiate, Fulcanelli, promoted the view that the Gothic form of architecture devised under Templar influence was, in itself, a kind of code that purveyed its eloquent hidden message in a substantial and highly visible architectural form of *la langue verte*, or the "language of initiation." Even today this tangible legacy of the Templars can be detected in the influence of sacred geometry that can be discerned in all the ecclesiastical buildings of the true Gothic era. The Templars were the acknowledged experts in this field. Their use of the ancient and sacred art to build the serenely beautiful round churches, or oratories, associated with the Order, which are believed to have profound Kabbalistic or occult significance, has left us with a permanent record of that knowledge and skill.

The Templar's seminal influence on the building of the medieval Gothic cathedrals is recorded by the noted twentieth century mystical writer P. D. Ouspensky:

It is known that there existed "Schools of Builders." Of course they had to exist, for every master worked and ordinarily lived with his pupils. In this way painters worked, in this way sculptors worked. In this way, naturally, architects worked. But, behind these individual schools stood other institutions of very complex origin. And these were not merely architectural schools or schools of masons. The building of Cathedrals was part of a colossal and cleverly devised plan which permitted the existence of entirely free philosophical and spiritual or psychological schools in the rude, cruel, superstitious, bigoted and scholastic Middle Ages.

These schools have left us an immense heritage – almost all of which we have already wasted without understanding its meaning or value.[194]

Fulcanelli, who succeeded in savoring the full flavor of those distinctly different, medieval times, stated that:

A church or a Cathedral was not merely a sanctuary for the faithful, orthodox worshippers, but also was a gathering place, a sort of philosophical "stock exchange" where lingering pockets of arcana, with roots in pre-Christian systems, were practically flouted under the noses of an unsuspecting, undiscerning clergy.[195]

He, too, described how the initiated spoke in a type of argot or slang, *la langue verte*, in order to disguise their real subjects of conversation from casual eavesdroppers. He maintained that the Masons who built the cathedrals, the Templars and all other initiates were, by this simple means, able to communicate without jeopardizing their freedom or their lives. This language, which was designed as a defense against persecution, eventually became the language not only of initiates, but also of all the poor and oppressed, and in this manner became the medieval precursor for cockney rhyming slang and the "jive talk" of the American inner-city ghettos.

From the viewpoint of the spiritual or occult historian, the general sweep of history is often described as being guided by schools of initiation.[196] Even from the perspective of the more academic historian, evidence is coming to light that reinforces the view that behind the official version of the historical process lies another, the so-called "hidden hand" of history which is recorded in the secret traditions handed down over centuries by folklore, poetry, esoteric schools, and secret societies such as the Masons. Cautious, if limited, acceptance of this somewhat startling viewpoint is steadily growing.

One persistent Western esoteric tradition recounts that the excavations under the Temple of Solomon were made to locate the Ark of the Covenant, hidden there from the Roman soldiers of Titus. Another legend speaks of an hereditary group of initiatory families known as *Rex Deus*, who claimed descent from the hereditary high priests of the Temple in Jerusalem and from Jesus himself. It is assumed that information about the Temple treasure was handed down orally through these families and that Hugues de Payens, the first grand master of the Knights Templar, and Bernard of Clairvaux were part of this secret group. This may explain the speed and efficiency with which the knights completed their excavations under the Temple Mount. They certainly appeared to know what they were looking for and exactly where to dig; they must have obtained accurate information from somewhere. What is certain is that when the nine knights had finished their "dig" their return to Europe was rapid. All nine escorted their finds, whatever they might have been, back to France, after which the founders visited England and Scotland. The events within Clairvaux's family at the time he joined the Cistercian Order also tend to support the *Rex Deus* theory; the reactions of his family when he announced his vocation were a little odd, to say the least.

The Cistercian Order at that time was relatively new, weak and definitely struggling. Bernard's family appeared shocked when he first announced his intention to join it, but their reactions were quickly and completely transformed. Not only did this

noble family withdraw their opposition to his plans, but most of
his male relatives and many of his friends, over thirty in all, opted
to join him in the religious life. What strange reason lay behind
this collective outburst of religious fervor? Whatever it was, it was
compelling indeed, for the party of postulants included Bernard's
elder brother – the heir to the family estate – his two younger
brothers and his uncle, the knight Gaudri of Touillon.[197] By the
time Bernard had reached the age of twenty-four, he was appointed as abbot of the new Cistercian Abbey of Clairvaux.

At the inauguration of the new abbey, Bernard spoke eloquently of the ancient land of Palestine saying:

Hail Land of Promise; The Holy Land, which formerly flowing
with milk and honey for thy possessions, now stretchest forth
the food of life and the means of salvation for the entire world.

To what exactly was he referring? Had not Christ supposedly
brought about the salvation of mankind already? Surely Bernard,
as a senior churchman, had dedicated his life to just that doctrine?
The only means of salvation that he could possibly mean was the
discovery of supremely sacred knowledge.

The discovery in 1948 of the Dead Sea scrolls perhaps gives us
a further clue. Among these ancient documents was the so-called
Temple Scroll containing a comprehensive list of the various sites
used to hide the Temple treasure. If the *Rex Deus* legend has any
truth at all, it must be reasonable to assume that they had inherited similar information. This theory also tends to explain the many
mysterious expeditions to strange lands by the Templar Knights.
Their expedition to Ethiopia certainly cannot be dismissed as an
essential element of the Order's objective of guarding the pilgrimage routes to the Holy Land.

The warrior monks of the Knights Templar, as initiates of the Holy Grail, were bound to secrecy on pain of death if they revealed the hidden path they followed. However, whatever their hidden agenda, they did fulfill their avowed aims of protecting the pilgrimage routes and fighting to protect the Holy Land. Their military prowess became legendary. Seemingly unafraid of death, these gallant knights were both feared and respected by their enemies. They fought with great distinction throughout the entire occupation of Palestine by the Christian forces. Yet it is odd that these brave knights of the Christian cause refused point blank to fight in the bloodiest crusade of them all. They took no part in it whatsoever, despite the fact that it was fought far nearer to their European centers of power and recruitment. Apparently the Knights Templar were unwilling to engage in battle with other Christians whose only crime was that they followed an initiatory path. In the history of the Albigensian Crusade, the century long genocidal action against the Cathars, there is no record of any Templar military activity whatsoever. The question that must be asked is, "Why?"

Galileo facing the Roman Inquisition. Painting by Cristiano Banti.

CHAPTER 11

The Crusade Against Fellow Christians;
And The Founding Of The Holy Inquisition

By their fruits shall ye know them.[198]

– The Gospel according to St. Matthew

Try as it might, there was no way that the Church could ever exert total control over the hearts, minds or souls of medieval mankind, for despite the very real power of the papacy, Europe was never entirely under its absolute and unquestioned control. Pockets of independence existed and certain groups of Christians, such as the Celtic Church in Ireland and the Galician Catholics in France and Spain, refused to acknowledge the supremacy of the Bishop of Rome and yet they continued to survive. Neither of these "Christian" faiths thought that Jesus was God; for them he was the supremely inspired teacher who was sent to reveal the one, true spiritual pathway to God. Pockets of acceptance of other "heretical" faiths existed in districts that lay beyond the control of the major kingdoms of Europe, such as the Languedoc which, under the suzerainty of its *Rex Deus* nobility, demonstrated a surprising degree of toleration for other faiths and minority religions for over two centuries. In this southern oasis of peace, in contrast to the rest of Christian Europe, Jews had attained positions of wealth and power in a tolerant, but nonetheless Christian, culture. This buffer state between France and Aragon was ruled by feudal lords who were, in effect, almost completely independent of either king, and its benevolent atmosphere provided the perfect ambience for the growth of the most fascinating heresy in the entire history of the Church.

By the twelfth century a society evolved in the Languedoc of such dazzling creativity, tolerance, peace and prosperity that it became a focus of envy for the rest of Europe. The Occitan culture had developed almost democratic political and social structures founded on the values of toleration and freedom of belief – an unheard of prospect anywhere else in Western Europe.[199] The spirituality of this region shows in the songs and poems of the troubadours, which treated every aspect of daily life as well as the realms of religious practice. It was believed that the poet should be spiritually uplifted by his love and that this should then manifest itself in his behavior towards his fellows by showing greater gentleness, tolerance and consideration for all, especially his inferiors. What is of even more significance is that the troubadours were invoking the Holy Spirit in a female form, proclaiming the worship of Sophia, the goddess of wisdom.[200]

This culture reached such a level of creative development that one scholar, C. S. Lewis, claims that it could have spawned an Occitan Renaissance two centuries before the Renaissance in Italy. Sadly this flowering of courtly and civilized values is remembered more for its brutal extinction at the hands of Holy Mother the Church than for the beliefs that both created and sustained it.[201] The pope could not tolerate a rival religion in Europe, much less one that, by example rather than preaching, put his own corrupt and oppressive Church to shame. By means of a brutal crusade in the name of the gentle Jesus, he tried to erase from the memory of mankind a religion that threatened to rival and outgrow the Roman Catholic Church. One that preserved the true initiatory teachings of Jesus, a spiritual pathway followed by a people of deep and abiding spirituality, known to history as the Cathars.

The Cathars were not heathens, unbelievers or pagans, but a sect who claimed to follow the "true teachings of Jesus" as James and the original disciples in Jerusalem did; a demanding way of devotion that could only be sustained by a people of deep and abiding spirituality. For centuries, gaining an understanding of the beliefs of these god-fearing people was fraught with difficulty. Most of the source material explaining their beliefs had been destroyed and the only available contemporaneous references were those preserved by their persecutors. Even today, the Catholic Church is hardly the most credible or objective commentator on either the creeds or rituals of its theological opponents. The discoveries of the Gnostic Gospels and other scrolls in the Nag Hammadi library have given us some belated clues as to the true nature of such beliefs. These documents, taken in conjunction with more recent discoveries, do allow us to interpret the records of the Inquisition in a manner that, hopefully, allows us to gain a more accurate and truthful appreciation of the Cathar creed.

In our search, we need to discover the facts that can explain the brutal butchery that took place and to discern the motives for this act of intentional genocide: mass murder committed by those who claimed to be the earthly representatives of the "Prince of Peace." These are not questions just for scholars and theologians. They are of supreme relevance to people of every creed, race and color who wish to create a just and equitable society. When we study the crusade against the Cathars, or the more recent Holocaust against the Jews, we may be able to find the means to understand and, more importantly, prevent or combat racial and religious intolerance whatever its source, or rationale.

The highly visible history of the Cathars draws tourists in their thousands every year. Impressive Cathar castles decorate and adorn each and every hilltop, pinnacle and promontory, standing as silent symbols of their fierce desire to maintain their political independence and religious freedom. What strange reality lies behind these remains? What were the differences that divided this region from the rest of oppressive, Catholic Europe? What did the Cathars actually believe? Why were they perceived to be such a threat to church and pope?

The Cathars were Christians who founded their beliefs and practices firmly on the Gospel of John. They "knew" that Jesus came to reveal and not to redeem, for it was the gnosis inspired by the teaching of Jesus that led to the perfection of souls, and therefore to salvation.[202] Their central belief, that the soul was trapped within an earthly prison of flesh and could only be liberated by knowledge that gave access to the divine, was neither novel nor unique. They claimed that these beliefs originated long before Catharism in a form of Gnosticism that had been handed down from the Temple Mysteries of Pharaonic Egypt, through the Therapeutae, the Essenes and the revelations of John the Baptist, different in origin, but substantially the same as the Druidic gnosis that had spread westwards via the Celts into pagan Europe.[203] A divinely inspired gnosis perfected by the teachings of Jesus that spread from the original disciples in Jerusalem via the Byzantine East to the Catholic West.

The Cathars denied the validity of all the Catholic sacraments without exception. As their belief system depended on the imparting of knowledge, they had no credence at all in the idea of "grace," which was of pivotal importance to the Catholic religion. Jesus was regarded by the Cathars as the supreme hierophant or teacher rather than as the Son of God, in the traditional Christian sense. The Catholic doctrine claiming that Jesus was simply a divinely ordained human, a "sacrificial goat" sent to suffer crucifixion to redeem the sins of mankind, was the one they most emphatically denied. They dismissed veneration of the Cross with the question "Would you worship the gallows your master died on?" The only symbols which seem to have had any importance whatsoever for the Cathar communities were the Gnostic discoid cross and the dove. Even here there is considerable debate as to the precise role these played in their belief structure.

Cathars believed that sacred knowledge sent by God via Jesus had been transmitted in a continuous and unbroken initiatory stream from biblical times down to their own. The final re-union of the soul of each initiate with Almighty God could only be brought about by the gaining of this gnosis. If, by any chance, the soul did not gain this sacred knowledge before death then it had to reincarnate in another body and try again to receive the gnosis that brings salvation in its wake. The sign of the attainment of this state of "enlightenment" was demonstrated by the Cathar sacrament known as the *consolamentum*.[204] In the normal course of events each initiate had to undergo a three-year novitiate before being granted this form of spiritual baptism; alternatively it could be granted to any believer at the point of death. Whichever route was taken, the newly "consoled" Cathar was deemed to have acquired the rank of a *perfectus*.[205] The sacramental ceremony of the *consolamentum* was performed by a *perfectus* in the presence of other *perfecti* and the family of the candidate. There was one much misunderstood ritual known as the *melhorer*, given by a hearer to a *perfectus*. It was simply a formalized, respectful greeting to which the *perfectus* would respond with a blessing – unfortunately it later gave rise to the charge that the ordinary hearers worshipped the *perfecti* and not God.

The Cathar initiates lived in communities, irrespective of

their previous social background. They led a life of simple but strict discipline and, as animals might contain souls awaiting revelation, they ate no meat or animal-based foods, though fish was permitted. Complete sexual abstinence was also mandatory for the *perfecti*, as the creation of more imprisoning bodies could only delay the eventual illumination and liberation of souls. The ordinary believers, or hearers, were exempt from this demanding regime. They lived normally, ate meat, married and had children. They were, however, expected to prepare themselves to receive the *consolamentum* on their deathbed.[206]

It is recorded in the Gospel of Thomas that Christ told his disciples that they would be capable of doing everything that he himself had done. Therefore, like Jesus, the *perfecti* lived the simple life of wandering disciples: teaching, caring, preaching and healing as they went. They practiced medicine based upon a profound knowledge of medicinal plants and herbs as well as giving spiritual healing, thus following the example of the Therapeutae, the Essenes and the apostles who followed Jesus.

In the Languedoc there were five Cathar dioceses, namely Agen, Albi, Carcassonne, Toulouse and Razès.[207] There were further dioceses in Champagne, the Sees of France, Lombardy, Tuscany and the Balkans. Each was administered by a bishop assisted by a "major son" and a "minor son" elected from the ranks of the deacons.[208] When the bishop died, he was succeeded by the major son, the minor son was promoted and a new one elected. Deacons, communities of *perfecti* and the body of hearers all came under the guidance of the bishop and his assistants. The communities of *perfecti* were not simply monastic and contemplative centers; they were also workshops, communal living quarters, initiatory schools and healing centers. There was no discrimination between the sexes and women were admitted to the initiatory rank with the same ease as men.

The individual *perfectus* was subject to on-going training throughout his or her life, constantly developing skills according to their level of understanding, their talents and spiritual insight. It was like ascending a ladder of spiritual progress; at each rung a different level of esoteric knowledge was imparted. One such teaching explained Mary Magdalene was the wife of Jesus; similar teachings were current among the Knights Templar and are believed by some to have been among the "truths" rediscovered by them in the Holy Land or passed down through the *Rex Deus* teachings. What is certain is that some of these heretical traditions may have flowed westwards after the crusades and took firm root in a variety of unlikely places, such as Bulgaria and Lombardy, before penetrating deep into the consciousness of the Cathars, Templars and the Gypsies. The Cathars, Bogomils and Knights Templar were all accused of practicing sorcery, particularly on the twenty-fourth day of June, the alleged birthday of John the Baptist. This common charge may reflect the suspicion by Church authorities of close links between the Knights Templar and the Cathars.

Oddly enough the term Cathar was first applied by their critics. Its derivation is obscure, although often alleged to imply the "Pure Ones." The Cathars simply called themselves the "believers," "Christians," or in the case of the *perfecti*, "good Christians." The *perfecti* were also known as the "good men" or the "friends of God," like the pious "men of righteousness" among their Essene precursors. The name *perfecti* itself arose from the Latin phrase *hereticus perfectus* – complete heretic – a description applied by their persecuting opponents in the Church. Catharism is quite clearly of the dualist variety of Gnosticism that can be detected in early Zoroastrianism, the works of Pythagoras, the Mithraic cults, early Christianity and Manichaeism.[209] Cathar organization has also been compared to the

Druidic hierarchy of the Celts with the Druids themselves compared to the *perfecti* and the troubadours to the Druidic bards.

The Languedocian society in which the Cathars flourished was well in advance of its time. It had developed a degree of democratic moderation that was exercised by the bourgeoisie on the feudal administration of the Languedoc nobility. The bourgeoisie, professional lawyers and merchants, had been strengthened by the growing power of an emergent group of skilled tradesmen who derived their power base from the workshops set up by the *perfecti*. These stimulated the rise of specialist trades such as paper-making, leatherwork and textiles, creating a new skilled class of artisans well indoctrinated with Catharism.

The Cathar religion may have been a derivative of the Bogomil heresy that flourished in the tenth century,[210] for some tenuous links have been established between the Cathars and the Bogomils of Constantinople, Asia Minor and the Balkans. Trade routes that linked both Venice and Genoa with Byzantium after the crusades facilitated this communication with the East. Thus the crusades had, paradoxically, created the means whereby the new heresy could flow inexorably westwards. St. Bernard, who had preached the crusade to the Holy Land so effectively, had, as we shall see, signally failed to combat the Cathar heresy. New preachers and new methods were called for if the Church was to stifle its fast growing rival.

Militant papal intolerance and brutality made the people of the Cathar country pay a horrendous price in suffering and delayed the Renaissance for another two centuries. The instruments used in this truly memorable exhibition of Christian love, were the raising of a crusade, or Holy War, against fellow Christians and the creation of an organization whose infamous activities were immortalized its name, the Holy Office of the Inquisition.

This was created and employed as an official instrument of religious repression at the direct behest of the papacy – all in the name of the gentle Jesus of course! The response of the papacy was predictable in nature, although unforeseen in its brutality. By declaring a crusadę against the heretics, the pope attempted to erase all traces of the Cathar religion from history and the memory of mankind.

The saintly Bernard of Clairvaux was one of the first to try and combat the Cathar religion. He was dispatched to Toulouse to refute the teaching of an apostate monk and Cathar called Henry, who was preaching under the patronage of the Count of Toulouse. In a letter to the count, Bernard spoke of the religious situation he had discovered in his realm: "The Churches are without congregations, congregations are without priests, priests are without proper reverence, and, finally, Christians are without Christ."

Speaking of Henry, the Cistercian leader wrote that, "He revels in all his fury among the flock of Christ."[211] Yet nonetheless Bernard is on record as saying that these heretics should be persuaded of the error of their ways by reason and not by force,[212] for he had developed a great respect for the spirituality of these so-called heretics and he said of them, "No one's sermons are more Christian than theirs and their morals are pure."[213] This respect was not widely shared, for the clergy in Liège complained to the pope that this heresy seemed "To have overflowed various regions of France. One so varied and so manifold that it seems impossible to characterize it under a single name."[214] This heretical community was described as being vigorously anti-clerical in nature, consisting, apparently, of grades of listeners and believers with their own hierarchy of priests and prelates.

Rome now sent a preaching ministry to the Cathar country led by a relatively unknown but fanatical Spanish priest, Dominique

Guzman.[215] This eloquent and devout man also failed to bring the Cathars to heel, but he was made of sterner stuff than his Cistercian predecessor. In a vain attempt to terrify this aberrant flock into submission Guzman issued a highly prophetic warning:

> For years now I have brought you words of peace, I have preached, I have implored, I have wept. But, as the common people say in Spain, if a blessing will not work, then it must be the stick. Now we shall stir up princes and bishops against you, and they, alas, will call together nations and peoples, and many will perish by the sword. Towers will be destroyed, walls overturned and you will be reduced to slavery. Thus force will prevail where gentleness has failed.[216]

This brutal message failed completely. How could it be otherwise, when those who heard it could not even begin to comprehend the horrendous prospect Dominic had just described? Perhaps some of them knew that in the first century Pope Clement had stated that death should be the penalty for heresy. Others might have been aware that Priscillian and one of his companions had been executed for heresy in 385 CE. All were aware of the brutality of the crusades against the infidel, but who could even imagine the appalling reality that lay behind the venomous claims of the Spanish monk? In spite of the language used and all the threats in his tirade, the reality was that Dominique Guzman was simply one Christian priest preaching a tirade of abuse to other Christians. The Cathars could never guess that this man would found the Inquisition to stamp out the smallest trace of their culture and creed by torture, terror and the warm embrace of the stake. The tolerant, gentle people of the Languedoc lived in a land of stability, religious freedom and love. The message of the Spanish priest was not merely incredible but also completely alien to their culture. They were soon to be forcibly enlightened.

The true nature of Christian love was to be revealed in a manner that the world would never forget. Total destruction in the forthcoming religious war between the Roman Church and the Cathars was to be their loving gift from the heir of St. Peter. This war of extermination lasted for thirty-five years; the repression and torture of the unfortunate survivors by the Inquisition continued for over ninety years after that.

God's supposed representative on Earth, Pope Innocent III, declared a crusade against the Albigensian heresy in 1209. The rewards for the butchers who took part in this anti-Christian crusade were tempting indeed. An indulgence granting pardon from their past sins – and from any they might commit in the course of their holy duties – was granted to each crusader who served for forty days.[217] They also had the traditional rights to the lands, property and goods of any declared heretic, be they nobleman or peasant.[218] Every freebooter, rogue, adventurer or landless member of the minor nobility not otherwise gainfully occupied, engaged in an unholy race to take part. Truly this was a "God-given and divinely blessed" opportunity to murder, rape and pillage without remorse or punishment. Yet for reasons that have never been satisfactorily explained, the military orders created to make war against the infidel in the crusades in the Holy Land were conspicuous by their absence. Neither the Knights Templar nor the Knights Hospitaller played any significant or active part in the crusade against the Cathars. The French king, who stood to gain a great deal in land and power, simply played the part of an interested observer until near the very end of the war, when the chance arose to annex the Languedoc into the kingdom of France.

Nonetheless, thousands soon flocked to the crusade, sustained by their zealous faith and, spurred on by their new right to dis-possess the heretics of all their possessions, these holy warriors set to with a will. The crusaders gained castles, land and loot as their reward for discharging their onerous duties of murder, rape and genocide. They were closely followed by the newly formed Dominican clergy, and their secular counterparts, who tried to ex-tinguish any trace of perceived heresy with torture and the cleans-ing flames of the stake.

In July 1209, the crusading army laid siege to the prosperous city of Béziers. It soon became obvious that the city would fall to the invaders. Being aware that the majority of the inhabitants were Catholic, the leaders asked the papal legate, the Cistercian Arnold Aimery, for guidance on their attitude to the population during the attack. His response must be the most callous ever uttered by a "man of God" even in time of war: "Show mercy neither to order, nor to age, nor to sex ... Cathar or Catholic – Kill them all ... God will know his own when they get to him!"[219] The crusaders followed his advice to the letter. At least twenty thousand civilians died that day, seven thousand of which were murdered in the sacred precincts of the Catholic cathedral.[220] Most of these must have been Catholics themselves, but probably Galician Catholics and not Roman Catholics – Christians who did not acknowledge either that Jesus was God or that the pope was the supreme head of the Church.

Fierce, flesh-fueled tongues of flame soon flickered skywards to illuminate the hearts and minds of the noble crusaders. The first Cathars were burnt at the stake at Castres;[221] at Minerve one hundred and forty *perfecti* were burnt alive – this became the in-evitable fate of all *perfecti* captured by the crusading army.[222] It was not simply the heretics who suffered; all who fought alongside them ran enormous risks, for the normal rules of chivalry simply did not apply. After the successful siege of Bram, the new leader of the crusaders, Simon de Montfort, cruelly abused all the surviving defenders. He selected one hundred men, at random, and gouged out their eyes; he then ordered their lips, ears and noses to be sliced off as an example to all who opposed him. One man was at least treated relatively mercifully – he only had one eye gouged out. The one-eyed survivor was then ordered to lead his blind, bleeding and maimed companions in the direction of the Castle of Cabaret, to be a graphic and gory warning of the fate that awaited all who had the temerity to oppose the holy army.[223] The defenders of Cabaret were far from terrified by this appalling example of Christian chivalry. They resolved to fight on; Cabaret did not fall! Thereafter, the code of chivalry was completely flouted in the name of Christ, the most noteworthy example occurring after the fall of Lavour. The eighty surviving knights, who had defended the town with commendable valor, were rewarded by being sentenced to death by hanging. The hastily erected gallows collapsed under their weight. Responding to this sign from God that their fate was unjust Simon de Montfort then ordered that their throats be cut. Lady Guiraude, the chatelaine of the castle, was given to the crusaders for their sexual pleasure. When the perverse soldiery had slaked their carnal appetites she was cast into a well and stoned to death – the traditional biblical penalty for adultery.[224] The *pièce de résistance* was predictable: over four hundred Cathars were burnt alive on a huge fire. Another sixty unfortunate heretics were burnt a short time later at Les Cashes.[225]

At the Battle of Muret, the slaughter is said to have exceeded that of Béziers.[226] During the sack of Marmande, William of Tudela recounts how five thousand men, women and children were brutally hacked to pieces. As if that were not enough to terrify the population at large, an attempt was made to starve the people into submission by burning crops as a matter of routine.[227] The war lasted for thirty-five years, sometimes relatively quiescent, at others flaring up in scenes of brutality never before witnessed in Christian Europe. The war itself effectively came to an end with the surrender of Montségur in 1244.[228] For perhaps the first time the crusaders behaved, briefly at least, with some semblance of chivalry and the garrison was spared. All within Montségur were given time to recant; there was a long truce lasting a fortnight. Legend recounts that several *perfecti* were smuggled out during this period in order to secrete the Cathar treasure – whatever that may have been. The Catholic used their traditional methods of dealing with the Cathars, for as the defeated garrison marched from the scene, their way was lit by flames as more than two hundred and twenty *perfecti* were burnt alive in one enormous conflagration.

Yet despite the torture and the prospect of the ever-waiting flames, throughout the entire period of the war and the Inquisitorial terror that ensued, only three *perfecti* are known to have abjured their faith. Most were only too willing to die for their beliefs, for their souls to pass on to immediate unity with God. Horrendous though it was, even this most brutal war was not deemed sufficient to stamp out this "outrageous" heresy. The question that arises in the mind of any reader must be, "What did the Cathars actually believe that made them such a danger to the Church of Rome?"

The Church did not rely on the crusade as the sole means for eradicating the Cathar heresy. Early on in the war they created a new weapon that was to be used, with increasing skill and venom in the centuries that followed in the battle against both heresy and reform. Headed and staffed by the new Dominican Order, the "Holy Office of the Inquisition" was to become ruthlessly efficient. Founded in 1233, its first victims were the Cathars. It is still in existence today in the guise of the Congregation for the Doctrine of the Faith, which, until recently, was headed by Cardinal Ratzinger, now Pope Benedict XVI. Under the lash of the Inquisition, the Languedoc discovered that the somewhat dubious, allegedly divine "blessings" of a Christian peace were as unendurable as the cruel curse of the recent crusade. The devout Dominican fathers of the Inquisition refined the use of interrogation, trial in secret, prosecution without defense, torture, harassment of families and execution by burning at the stake. Mass burnings continued, but now as a consequence of Inquisitorial condemnation rather than as a consequence of conquest by force of arms. Two hundred and ten heretics were publicly burnt at Moissac as a matter of deliberate policy, as the Inquisition deliberately created a climate of fear within which heresy would not dare to raise its head. The Inquisition, being non-violent men of God, merely condemned the heretic; he was burnt, publicly, by the state.

If an accused heretic abjured his faith under interrogation or torture, he was not necessarily sentenced to the flames; other options could be more appropriate. Penalties were varied and included imprisonment for years or for life, automatic confiscation of property, obligatory pilgrimage to the Holy Land or the wearing of a yellow cross sewn on one's clothes (exact dimensions specified).[229] Thus anyone who aided one of those who wore this badge of infamy would be condemned for aiding and abetting heresy. The yellow cross was a sentence of lingering death by starvation to those who wore it and an invitation to join the ranks of those under interrogation for any who had pity upon the wearer.

Interrogation by the Inquisition usually meant disclosure of the intimate and most trivial details of the prisoner's life. Proof of guilt could be found among relatively minor events of days long past; association with a heretic during early childhood was sufficient proof of guilt for the Dominican friars. Relatives, and all who had associated with a known heretic, were subjected to inter-

Secrets of the Western Esoteric Tradition

rogation in their turn. In any comparison to the Inquisition, the *Gestapo* or the KGB would be considered simply as inept amateurs who were, in relative terms, benevolently disposed towards their victims. Under the Inquisition the innocent suffered as much as the guilty, for this divinely guided organization was an instrument of terror unequaled in all of mankind's violent history.[230]

Yet in spite of the efficiency of the Holy Inquisition they failed to extinguish Catharism in its entirety. Vast numbers were burned or murdered in the course of the crusade and many were forced into exile, others simply went underground and founded or joined the various dissident movements that later spawned the Protestant Reformation. Catharism, as we have described it, vanished from direct sight at the beginning of the fourteenth century. Of the Cathars who went underground, many joined the Knights Templar;[231] contemporary records disclose a large influx of knights from the Languedoc into this military order when the crusade was all but over. Others sought a similar refuge after the fall of Montségur. At a later date the corpses of these poor unfortunates were disinterred by the Inquisition, tried and convicted of heresy post-mortem and their bodies then ritually burnt.[232]

The Cathar way of life can only be judged by the way they followed the teaching of Jesus. They esteemed peace, harmony, love, and tolerance for other faiths, Christian or not. The *perfecti* lived, taught and gave healing as Jesus and his disciples did, their way of life benefiting the entire community in which they moved. Furthermore, the *perfecti* and the ordinary believers displayed immense courage in the face of brutal persecution and the terrifying certainty of death at the stake. By what standards can we judge the Church, the papacy, the Inquisition and the crusaders? Did their determined and deliberate actions benefit anyone other than themselves? Is burning at the stake the culmination of Jesus'

152   HIDDEN WISDOM

commandment to love thy neighbor as thyself? They might argue that, in the historical context, the health of the Church of Christ might demand occasional surgery – but at such a cost?

Who were the true followers of Christ? Who were the real heretics? According to St. Augustine of Hippo, heresy consists of "the distortion of a revealed truth by any believer or unbeliever." As Jesus himself is, without doubt, the greatest teacher of revealed truth, then those who distort, negate or deny his words are the true heretics. Who were the heretics in these unseemly and terrible events? The Church believed that it had succeeded in extirpating a dangerous heresy. I submit that its motives were very different in that it felt threatened by a rival organization whose behavior was perceived as a living criticism of Church wealth and corruption, which denied the Church's claims to sanctity and sole access to the sacred. What then was the fate of the Cathar refugees?

Many fled to Tuscany where they went underground. It is highly probable that their heirs gave refuge to fleeing Templars when their turn came to suffer at the hands of the Inquisition. Others fled to the St. Clair lands near Rosslyn in Scotland where they founded a paper making industry. There they too played a significant part in the survival of fleeing Templar Knights. Others just vanished. Cathar Gnostics may have apparently vanished, but Gnosticism itself continued as an underground movement that thrived and grew like a many-headed hydra. As one head was cut off, another grew and spread its tentacles unseen and in secret. There would always be recruits committed to the unswerving search for truth in an increasingly repressive and autocratic religious world. It found those recruits among the talented men who followed the Templar beliefs and whose intellectual and spiritual heirs played such a vital role in the Reformation, the Renaissance and in the founding of the democratic societies that ultimately ensued.

Mediaeval wood carving of a "Green Man," one of two almost identical figures
on a misericord in the parish church at Ludlow, Shropshire, England.

CHAPTER 12

Holy Mother the Church Eats Her Own Young!

Within a hundred years of their foundation the Knights Templar became the richest and most powerful order in Europe. They became, in effect, the first international corporation, richer than any single kingdom and rivaling in power the Church itself. To the alleged treasure they are said to have found in Jerusalem was soon added huge and numerous donations of land from the *Rex Deus* families to which they were connected. This gave the Knights a power base that they used to create a multitude of enterprises. Their role in protecting pilgrims to the Holy Land soon expanded into providing transport and shelter for all devout pilgrims, whether they journeyed to Jerusalem, Rome, Chartres, Mont Saint-Michel, Rocamadour or Santiago de Compostela.

The Knights Templar became the first effective travel agents in the world, inventing what we would now call the "Package Tour Industry"; it could easily have been called "Halo Tours Inc." Their sales brochure was an earlier, four-folio, Benedictine tract, the *Codex Calixtinus*.[233] This document gave the precise route from any part of Christian Europe to the shrine of St. Jacques at Compostela. One folio gave useful instructions on how to avoid thieves, bandits and dishonest innkeepers en route; another was devotional in content and gave the appropriate hymns and prayers for the pilgrimage. The Templars certainly acted as bankers to the whole enterprise; to the pilgrims themselves, as well as to the rest houses, monasteries and cathedrals visited by them. The pilgrimage to Compostela was second in importance only to that of

Jerusalem and far more important than any pilgrimage to Rome. It was known by several names, the "Shell Pilgrimage," or secretly as the "Alchemist's Pilgrimage," because for the members of branches of the *Compagnonnage*, or Knights Templar, it was the "Pilgrimage of Initiation,"[234] the outward form of an inner, mystical journey along the path of learning. It gives one pause for thought: why was this initiatory journey not undertaken to Rome, which was easily accessible and associated with both St. Peter and St. Paul – the supposed first leaders of the Christian Church after the death of Jesus – but instead to a small, obscure, relatively inaccessible corner of Spain and a city associated with James, the brother of Jesus?

For both military and commercial reasons, this warrior order developed and maintained the largest and most disciplined fleet the world had yet seen. Their boats were probably based on Arab designs with lateen sails, allowing them to sail far closer to the wind than the square-rigged designs common in Northern Europe. They also possessed a large number of highly manoeuvrable war galleys fitted with rams, many of which were constructed by Venetian shipbuilders. The fleet plied the Mediterranean from ports on the coasts of Italy, France and Spain, but their main base was Majorca. They also used ports on the Atlantic coast of France, especially La Rochelle from where, it is has been alleged, they conducted trade with Greenland, the North American mainland and Mexico. Be that as it may, what is beyond doubt is that by ensuring the security of all the major trade routes throughout Europe, they created a climate of peace and stability that allowed merchants to ply their trade at minimum risk and with comparative ease over greater distances than ever before. Europe began to bloom economically, enjoying a climate of commercial confidence that was unprecedented. This amazing transformation came about as a direct result of the application by the Templars of a bizarre mix of military skills and sacred gnosis. Unlike their contemporaries within the mainstream Church, the Templars' spiritual knowledge was for application in this world instead of simply being the guaranteed route to the next: an attitude that contrasted starkly with the Church's view that spiritual knowledge would only be revealed in the next world, while absolute obedience to the pope and the clergy was the rule in the present.

After a short time Europe was interlaced with a network of Templar holdings. Guarding the trade and pilgrimage routes were commandaries, churches, villages and military outposts. Their commercial interests were impressive and varied. These supposedly military men were also experts in mining, quarrying, building, viniculture and farming in every climatic zone of the Christian world.[235] Their superb fleet enabled them to extend their trade routes to the very fringes of the known world. And, largely arising from their contacts with Islam in the Holy Land, the knights gained an immense respect and a profound level of knowledge about the highly sophisticated culture the brutal crusaders had invaded.

For any Christian student of history, it is salutary to learn that the crusades were neither a liberating nor enlightening adventure for the Eastern peoples of Christian, Jewish or the Muslim faiths. The crusaders were, like those who pillaged the Cathar country a century later, an ill-disciplined horde of looters, landless nobility, robber barons, criminals, debtors, penitents, adventurers and intolerant fanatics invading an alien and far superior culture to their own. They were far from chivalrous, in fact chivalry was an alien concept that the Knights Templar acquired from the heathen Saracens and brought back to Europe. That was not the only valuable importation from the Islamic world. The Greek classics made their way back into European consciousness during the same era, being translated from Arabic – not Greek – into the major languages of the Christian world. Technology was another major import from the Islamic East. The telescope, the principles of stellar navigation, considerable advances in both medicine and surgery, mouth-to-mouth resuscitation and free access to the world of knowledge and ideas were among the many benefits brought westwards by these secret initiates of the Holy Grail.

It may come as a surprise to many students of this formative era that the Knights Templar are often slandered by later Church historians as illiterates.[236] Yet, these so-called illiterate knights devised a highly sophisticated secret alphabet to encode their records and commercial transactions. It is now known that they invented the first form of credit card and were the originator of the cheque or banker's draft.[237] They used "notes of hand" long before the Lombard bankers. The Templars used their wealth wisely and their activities soon extended into power-broking on a truly regal scale, creating the first effective, international banking system and lending vast sums to popes, princes, prelates and kings.[238] This successful knightly order spawned many imitators; after all, imitation is the sincerest form of flattery. One such, the Teutonic Knights, was covertly founded by the Knights Templar with whom they maintained secret contact until the sudden and brutal dissolution of the parent order. Similar orders that rose to prominence by modeling themselves on the Templars were the Knights of Calatrava and the Knights of Alcantara. Both were founded soon after the Knights Templar and, strangely, St. Bernard of Clairvaux is known to have played a significant, if somewhat mysterious, role in their foundation.[239]

Unlike the Roman Church, of which they were supposedly part, the Templars did not concern themselves with the salvation of individual souls, but with the transformation of entire communities and nations. Their hidden agenda was to create a new worldwide, spiritual ecumenism and restore true monotheism to the world, uniting Christianity, Judaism and Islam.[240] Their military and commercial activities created a climate of economic growth that strengthened the power of the merchant class and ultimately led to the development of capitalism.

Their wealth, power and influence aroused considerable jealousy and resentment among some state and church officials. Philip le Bel of France was heavily in debt to them and carried a deep resentment over the fact that he had been refused admission to the Order. He soon created the opportunity to destroy them. Plausible reasons for an investigation of the Templars were not hard to find or create in that age of repression and injustice. There was known contact between the Templars and Islam; links had also been maintained between the Knights and the Cathars. Witnesses were bribed or bullied to make accusations of heresy.[241] The French king prepared his case in great secrecy, browbeating the pope and suborning witnesses with venomous skill.[242] The plot came to fruition on Friday the Thirteenth of October 1307, when Jacques de Molay, grand master of the Templars, and sixty of his senior knights were arrested in Paris. Simultaneously, other leading Templars were seized throughout the realm of France. Some escaped arrest and many minor knights and officials simply fled, an episode made memorable by the aphorism "Friday the Thirteenth, unlucky for some."

The Templar high command were imprisoned and tortured for several years, with the Order being charged for their upkeep throughout that time.[243] The final act of this drama was played out on March 14, 1314, when Jacques de Molay and Geoffroy de Charney, the preceptor of Normandy, were publicly burnt on a slow fire on the Isle Louvier in Paris. One strange aspect of this bloody butchery yet defies explanation. The great treasure of the

Templars, the very cause and objective of this brutal enterprise, had vanished without trace, as had almost the entire Templar fleet. The king was foiled.

The accusation of idolatry implicit in one of the charges, the so-called worship of Baphomet, has been explained as variants around a single theme. Idries Shah states that Baphomet is a corruption of the Arabic term *abufihamet* (pronounced "bufhimat") which translates as "father of understanding." Magnus Eliphas Levi proposes a similar theory: he claims that Baphomet should be spelled backwards, which gives the term "TEM. OPH. AB." This he construes as standing for *Templi Omnium Hominum Pacis Abbas*, which he translates as "Father of the Temple of Universal Peace Among Men." This was given further credence by the work of an eminent historian of early Christianity, Hugh Schonfield, who applied the "Atbash Cipher" to the word Baphomet, which then translated as Sophia. Thus the alleged idolatry was simply the veneration of the spiritual principle of wisdom, or Sophia, usually associated with ancient Greek, Egyptian or early Mesopotamian initiation.[244] The veneration accorded to the Black Madonna, black carvings or icons of the Madonna and Child, by the Templars tends to support this view. At first this would look like a normal Catholic practice for that time. The reality is, however, a little different when we take into account that a significant proportion of Templar gnosis derived originally from Egypt. In ancient Egyptian symbolism, the color black indicates wisdom. The Templars were venerating the mother of wisdom, the ancient goddess Sophia embodied in the form of the goddess Isis, now cleverly transposed into an acceptable "Christian" context.

This rather bizarre concept finds further reinforcement from an oddly orthodox source when we study the early years of the Order. When drafting the rule for the Templars in 1128, St. Bernard of Clairvaux laid down a specific requirement on all the knights to make "obedience to Bethany and the house of Mary and Martha."[245] According to some authorities this indicates that the great Notre Dame cathedrals built by the Templars and Cistercians were not so much dedicated to Mary, the mother of Jesus, but to "Our Lady" Mary Magdalene. According to the Nazarenes, the Magdalene was garbed in black just like the priestesses of Isis. In this context the Madonna would be represented as black, surmounted by Sophia's crown of stars. Her infant, the child of Jesus, wears the golden crown of royalty. In the Gospel of Philip, Mary Magdalene was described as the "symbol of divine wisdom."

Another persistent legend associates Baphomet with the severed head of John the Baptist, a saint accorded considerable veneration by the Knights Templar. The reliquary said to contain the head was brought back from Constantinople after the crusades and now rests in the Cathedral of Amiens.[246] We must not forget that the Knights Templar were Gnostic initiates and all forms of gnosis are founded on dualism: for example, knowledge and ignorance; good and evil; life and death; spirit and matter; light and dark; the Alpha and the Omega. This duality is to be found in the Revelation of St. John with Christ and the anti-Christ, and the Virgin and the Whore of Babylon. Yet because of the Church's horror of Gnosticism, with the exception of the dualistic imagery that occurs within the Revelation, most forms of dualistic symbolism were either anathema to the Church, or at best, highly suspect and liable to investigation. Yet the Templars had found that some aspects of dualism could be presented in an acceptable form within the Christian Church. Their very role was in a real sense dualistic, for they were both warriors and monks – men of war and followers of the "Prince of Peace." This dualistic nature pervaded all their operations. They derived their wealth from their power base in Europe that then allowed them to operate in the Orient. Their symbolism is a graphic expression of their Gnostic dualism: the black and white of their battle standard, the Beauseant; the Templar seal of two brothers on one horse; the two knights behind the *escarboucle* carved above the doorways of Rheims, Chartres and Amiens cathedrals. Their terrestrial domains were "twinned" and this, like the symbolism of two brothers on one horse, is believed to represent Castor and Pollux, possibly the Holy Twins, and often the two-faced god Janus. The Abrasax, which was the seal of the grand master of the Templar Order, was pure Gnostic symbolism of such a nature that it is impossible to describe it as orthodox. They also used the ancient Gnostic symbol of wisdom, the serpent who eats his own tail.

Sculpture and the art forms used by the *Compagnonnage* in France and various Masonic guilds and brotherhoods in Scotland and England also display their clear and unequivocal Gnostic beliefs. There are the carvings of the "Green Man," found in large numbers at Chartres Cathedral and to a lesser degree in most of the Gothic churches and cathedrals of the Templar era. Another modern author described the association of the Green Man and the Masons:

> Even if one were to regard him at the lowest level, as a mascot
> of the Masons, his presence in so many regions and over so long
> a period indicates that he had a particular meaning for them.
> Did he sum up for them the energy they had to transform, the
> energy of both living nature and of the past stored in the col-
> lective unconsciousness? Did he, at the same time, express the
> spirit of inspiration, the genius hidden in created things?[247]

The beliefs that sustained the creation of so many representations of the Green Man pervaded other aspects of European life. They too refer us back directly to the Babylonian deities of Ishtar and Tammuz, which becomes clear when we study British folk tradition:

> ... the May Queen followed in a cart, or chariot, drawn by young men and women. Her partner or "consort," the Green Man, descendant of Dumuzi, Tammuz and Attis, also called the "Green One," was clothed in leaves. In some parts of Europe the couple were "married." So May Day celebrated the sacred marriage and the ritual and regeneration of life ... The face of the Green Man gazes out from the midst of carved foliage on Gothic cathedral screens, pulpits, vaulted naves and choir stalls ... invoking that more ancient knowledge of the relationship of the goddess to her son, incarnate through him as the life on earth.[248]

It is not only through the carvings of the Green Man that we can discern the importance to medieval man of this ancient initiatory stream. The same connection can often be found through other forms of artwork. In Rosslyn Chapel, near Edinburgh, erected by Earl William St. Clair as a lasting memorial to both Gnostic and Templar initiatory beliefs, there are stained-glass windows dedicated to the Saints Michael, Longinus, Mauritius and George. What is St. George, the patron saint of England, doing in a patently nationalistic Scottish chapel? A study of his history showed that the mythical personage we now call St. George was reputed to be an Armenian. According to Pope Gelasius (494 CE), he "is a Saint, venerated by man, but whose acts were known only to God." Closer examination of the legends link his origins to St. Michael and begin to give us a basis upon which we can cast new light on his esoteric importance. The earliest known mythological personage on whom

St. George is based is Tammuz. We have mentioned the seemingly incongruous connections between the Sufis and their apparent enemies, the Templars. Tammuz provides one of the clues to this. Most modern authorities now believe that El Khidir, the mystical teacher of the Sufis, Tammuz and St. George are simply one and the same person portrayed in a varying mythological guise.[249]

Tammuz is variously described as the spouse, son or brother of the goddess Ishtar and is known as the "Lord of Life and Death," a title which has deep Masonic overtones, and yet one which predates the reputed history of the Masonic movement by several millennia. One account tells that when Adam was sent to the gates of heaven, Tammuz offered him the bread and water of eternal life that Adam refused, thus losing his immortality. It is interesting to note that St. George is depicted as standing upon a rose-colored board decorated with roses or rosettes, a symbolic reference to the goddess Ishtar. The roof of Rosslyn Chapel is smothered in carvings of rosettes. In contrast, Saints Longinus and Mauritius are shown standing on a chessboard, the so-called "Checkerboard of Joy" that represents both the Templar battle flag, the Beauseant, and the mystical "hop-scotch" symbol of the deeply secretive Pilgrimage of Initiation.[250] Here it is depicted exactly as it is used in Masonic Lodges; as part of the floor design upon which people stand for ceremonies and rituals. However, such symbolism was soon to vanish from plain sight, for after the crusade against the Cathars, the founding of the Inquisition, the suppression of the Templars and the withdrawal of immunities from the Children of Solomon, the initiatory orders once more had to go underground.

Being condemned for heresy in the early fourteenth century of medieval Europe had a great deal in common with the fate of the victims of the show trials in Russia in the Stalinist era. The victims in both cases became "non-persons." Their records were destroyed and all traces of them disappeared. The Church did its best to ensure that their beliefs were completely erased. It was as if they had never existed. Modern historians studying the Templars are therefore left bereft of reliable information, for the majority of the remaining records are those of the persecutors and, Holy Mother the Church is not the most dispassionate of sources. Thus defining and understanding the realities that lie behind the romantic legends of these warrior knights is fraught with difficulty. Careful and prolonged research has, as yet, only disclosed some of the intriguing facts underpinning the history of this most mysterious of noble and chivalrous orders.

Reactions to the suppression varied from country to country. German knights of the now disbanded Order joined either the Hospitallers or the Teutonic Knights. One Scottish knight and a leading Templar, William St. Clair of Rosslyn, met his death in Lithuania, fighting for the Teutonic Knights. In Portugal, the Order simply changed its name to the Knights of Christ and carried on under royal patronage. Later, the Portuguese explorer Vasco de Gama became a member and Prince Henry the Navigator was a grand master of the re-named Order.[251] In Spain, the archbishop of Compostela wrote to the pope pleading that the Order be spared, as it was needed in the fight against the Moors.

The pressing need for the military skills, discipline and dedication to the Christian re-conquest of Spain was fulfilled in a simple way. Members of the Knights Templar were encouraged to join similar military Orders. These differed from the Templars in that they owed their allegiance to the Spanish crown rather than the pope: Orders such as the Order of St. James of the Sword, more commonly known as the Knights of Santiago, became affiliated to the Knights Hospitaller, thus ensuring its own survival. Like the Templars, the Knights of Santiago soon became immensely powerful and by the end of the fifteenth century they controlled more than two hundred commandaries throughout Spain. Thus Templar influence, both military and spiritual, survived the bloody suppression of the Order itself in mainland Europe. In France and England some members joined the Knights Hospitaller, but most simply vanished. Or did they?

We now know that many fled to Lombardy, Scotland, Portugal and the Baltic states. John J. Robinson describes how the fleeing knights were assisted in their escape by the lodges of the Craftmasons until they reached their safe havens.[252] It is, perhaps, appropriate at this time to consider whether or not these particular lodges that gave shelter and passage in this manner were of the Children of Master Jacques, or the *Compagnons Passants*. In Portugal the refugees joined the Order of the Knights of Christ; in the Baltic states they joined the Teutonic Knights; in Lombardy, aided by the Cathars who had preceded them, they used their skills to strengthen the emergent banking system; but in Scotland the story was very different.

The Knights Templar who reached Scotland fought as allies of Robert the Bruce and played a pivotal role in winning the Battle of Bannockburn. This battle won the crown for Robert the Bruce and gained royal protection for the persecuted order. Warned to go underground by the king, after an inconclusive trial on charges of heresy where the verdict was the equivocal Scottish one of "not proven," the persecuted knights shared their knowledge, insight and skills with Scottish Templar families and this led, some centuries later, to the foundation of two important branches of the underground Gnostic streams – Freemasonry and Rosicrucianism. Both, in their various forms, exerted an enormous influence on the creative people who brought about the Renaissance. This relatively small group of intellectual and spiritual giants who transformed the thinking, art, commerce and social system of a continent created the intellectual climate within which science, democracy and intellectual freedom could spread, seed themselves, take root and flourish. All the seminal thinkers, artists and philosophers of this period were initiates of one or another of the spiritual organizations that were the indirect spiritual heirs of the much maligned and persecuted Knights Templar.

Fortunately one perceptive and courageous man, Earl William St. Clair of Rosslyn in Scotland has left us with a fascinating, if somewhat puzzling, storehouse of coded Templar information. This Scottish nobleman was well aware that books, authors and even readers could be burnt for heresy, so he left us with a permanent and fireproof library of arcane and Gnostic instruction – Rosslyn Chapel, perhaps the most profusely and intricately carved church building of its age and size in Europe. It is, in fact, Earl William's legacy to all who seek spiritual enlightenment: a multi-faceted, complex exposition of the initiatory tradition of the Knights Templar; a veritable, three dimensional "teaching board" of Gnostic, late medieval initiation.

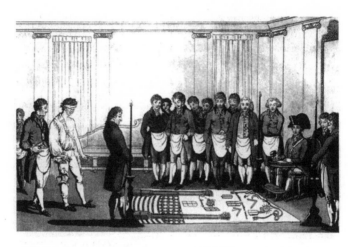

Initiation of an apprentice Freemason around 1800. This engraving is based on that of French author Léonard Gabanon on the same subject dated 1745. The costumes of the participants are changed to the English fashion at the start of the 19th century.

CHAPTER 13

The Sons Of The Widow:
Freemasonry And Rosicrucianism

Who will come to the aid of the son of a widow?[253]

-Traditional call for help from a Freemason in distress

He who is as wise as a Perfect Master will not be easily injured by his own actions. Hath a person the strength which a Senior Warden represents he will bear and overcome every obstacle in life. He who is adorned like a Junior Warden with humility of spirit approaches nearer to the similitude of God than others.[254]

– Gedricke, 18th century Masonic historian

Physical energies combine harmoniously with spiritual energies on the path of initiation, the path of awakening and awareness. By moving forward lucidly and reflectively, we help others who would like to follow the path or discover it.[255]

– Frederic Lionel, *Mirrors of Truth*

English Grand Lodge Freemasonry has always claimed that Freemasonry, as we now know it, sprang fully formed, with its core rituals fully developed, out of some mythical vacuum in the eighteenth century, a view that is only credible to those who still believe in Santa Claus and the Tooth Fairy. The truth, which is very different, has been widely known for centuries to most Freemasons and historians who have studied the matter thoroughly. Robert Graves, as I have mentioned earlier, traces the roots of Freemasonry back to the early Sufis who, he claims, were the real builders of the original Temple in Jerusalem. According to Graves, Masonry came to England during the reign of the Saxon King Athelstan. In Scotland it has long been acknowledged that the Craftmasons merged with the Templars when the latter order went underground and that the first Scottish lodge of Freemasons was founded under the guidance, leadership and protection of the St. Clair family of Rosslyn who were the hereditary grand masters of both the hard and soft guilds in Scotland as well as leading Templar Knights throughout the history of the Order. Three St. Clair knights fought at Bannockburn with their Templar confrères and led the charge that routed the English invaders, thereby saving the throne for Robert the Bruce, who was the sovereign grand master of the Templar Order and Masonic guilds. This is commemorated in the St. Clair family chapel at Rosslyn where his death mask is carved in stone.

The founder of Rosslyn Chapel was Earl William St. Clair, Lord of Rosslyn, Pentland and Cousland and the third St. Clair "Jarl" of Orkney, a nobleman with singular talents. Earl William has been variously described as "one of the Illuminati," a "nobleman with singular talents" and a "man of exceptional talents much given to policy, such as buildings of Castles, Palaces and Churches."[256] He was a grand master and an adept of the highest degree. The hereditary grand mastership of the Masonic guilds remained in the St. Clair – or more commonly – Sinclair, family until 1736 when the then grand master, yet another William Sinclair of Rosslyn, resigned his "Hereditary Patronage and Protectorship of the Masonic Craft" to effect the erection of the "Grand Lodge of Ancient, Free and Accepted Masons of Scotland." He was immediately grand master, in an election that some authorities claim was rigged, in which position he nonetheless served with distinction.[257] It is important to remember that the Sinclair family played a vital role in the preservation and continuance of not only the Order, but also the spiritual knowledge and insight of the Templars, long after the warrior knights had been brutally suppressed in most of Europe.

William's grandfather, Henry, the first Sinclair Jarl of Orkney, actually discovered mainland America nearly one hundred years before Columbus.[258] Earl Henry crossed the Atlantic, wintered in Nova Scotia among the Micmac Indians and then sailed on to present day Massachusetts and Rhode Island.[259] In Westford, Massachusetts, there is tomb carving of a Templar Knight, a member of the Clan Gunn and in Newport, Rhode Island, a round tower built of stone in the manner of the Templars. Proof of this remarkable voyage is indelibly hewn in stone on both sides of the Atlantic; at Westford, Newport and within Rosslyn Chapel in Scotland.[260] Within the confines of the chapel are carvings of maize, which were made over fifty years before Columbus set sail across the Atlantic. Maize was unknown in Europe at that time and was only found in North America.

Rosslyn Chapel was created as a superbly carved commemoration of every historic and heretical spiritual pathway known at that time. This mystical place is nothing less than the ultimate pinnacle of an initiatory pilgrimage that was sacred to the memory and beliefs of the Knights Templar, the Order of Grail initiates whose insignia and symbolism are imperishably recorded in its mystical carvings. It is the final destination of a mysterious, religious journey undertaken by the immediate spiritual heirs of the suppressed Templar Order, which became known as the Alchemist's Pilgrimage, or as the Pilgrimage of Initiation.[261] Thousands of pilgrims traveled there after completing the arduous trek to the shrine of St. Jacques of Compostela. Why? I have suggested in an earlier work that this may have been because of some relic kept at Rosslyn, a Black Madonna perhaps?[262] However, another explanation may well be more accurate.

After the suppression of the Templar Order, the initiates had once again to disguise their initiatory processes under the cloak of Christian ritual and practice. What better disguise was there than to make a series of ostensibly devout Christian pilgrimages to cathedrals constructed on sites known to the ancient Druidic initiates as the "seven chakras of the Earth." All these cathedrals contain a profusion of arcane artwork that acts as esoteric, initiatory teaching boards and their crypts could serve as initiation chambers. My first literary collaborator and teacher, the mystical writer Trevor Ravenscroft, suggested that Celtic pilgrims who worshipped the Earth goddess journeyed from Iberia to Scotland via the seven Druidic planetary oracles, associating the alignment of the spirit senses within themselves to the corresponding alignment of the Earth's energy centers.[263] The sequence of the sites corresponds to that of the seven heavenly bodies known to the ancients: the Moon, Mercury, Venus, the Sun, Mars, Jupiter and Saturn. Later the Christians built the Church of *Notre-Dame de la Dalbade* in Toulouse; the great cathedrals at Amiens, Chartres, Compostela, Paris, Orleans; and the chapel at Rosslyn on these Druidic sites. This great configuration bounded by two pillars, at Cintra and Rosslyn, with the five cathedrals and a church in between, all lie under the royal arch of the stars of the Milky Way.

This strange and secretive pilgrimage was believed to have started with a journey from Cintra to Compostela, the first of the seven Druidic sacred sites. Initiation on any spiritual pathway is a form of ritualized mysticism wherein the novice is taught and guided by a hierophant to develop the use of his organs of spiritual perception. These seven organs, or chakras, are ritually awakened in a predetermined order, from the base upwards to the Crown and at each site the novice is initiated into one of the seven degrees. Thus the Pilgrimage of Initiation is not simply one journey encompassing each of the seven sites, but a series of journeys made in a predetermined order from Compostela, representing the base chakra, northwards to Rosslyn, representing the Crown chakra, with each stage of this initiatory journey only being made after an appropriate and approved period of intense and profound spiritual preparation.

The novice making an initiatory pilgrimage from Cintra to the shrine of Santiago demonstrated that he had shown sufficient dedication and humility to qualify for the privilege of initiation by manifesting the essential qualities of humility and obedience. First degree initiation was the result that flowed spiritually from the awakening of the base chakra that connects us with the Earth and physical reality; it can only be opened after the attainment of true humility, for this is the chakra that literally keeps us rooted. The first degree of initiation is commonly symbolized by the Raven in its capacity as a messenger of the gods. In this degree, the new initiate learns to express the visual in images that could be understood at different levels by both the outside world and by the initiated. When the powers of spirit and matter combine, the seven chakras act as a single channel. This power follows a winding path as it moves between the centers and in Eastern schools of initiation is described as the raising of the serpent known as the "Kundalini." Once awakened this then raises its head through the other chakras as the initiate ascends to the higher levels of initiation. It is not surprising that the esoteric symbol associated with the "Wouivre," the telluric force described by the Druids and the Templars, is the serpent. The specific order of the awakening of the chakras from the base to the Crown explains why, in the Pilgrimage of Initiation, the ritual order of progress is a complete reversal of the normal, hierarchically approved, pilgrimage to Compostela.

When the initiate had progressed thus far along his chosen spiritual path and has shown his true worth, he would be instructed to make the pilgrimage from Compostela to *Notre-Dame de la Dalbade* in Toulouse, built on the site of the Mercury oracle. Mercury, of course, was simply the Latinization of the Greek god Hermes, the winged messenger of the gods. At Toulouse he would be initiated into the Mysteries of the second degree with the opening of the sacral or abdominal chakra, which is the doorway to the unconscious mind. The second degree of initiation is known as that of the "occultist" and is symbolized by the Peacock. The many splendored plumage of this royal bird represents the initiate's powers of moral imagination which became manifest when the aspirant discovered his own inner space and could retire whenever he so wished into the hidden isolation of his own spirit. He had become the "hidden one," or "occultist," who could now communicate directly with Hermes Trismegistos, the thrice blessed one of the Greek Mysteries whose bust adorns the eastern wall of Rosslyn Chapel and whose statue looks down over the *Place de la Trinité* in the center of Toulouse.

The Knight became the symbol of the third and warrior degree and when the aspirant had gained sufficient inner strength and moral courage to represent the good against the evil in the world, he was named the "warrior." The aspirant achieved this degree when he was initiated into the Mysteries of the Venus oracle at the sublime Cathedral of Orleans. When the aspirants were properly prepared for further advancement along their chosen spiritual path they would visit the site of the heart chakra and undergo their initiation in the mystical underground chamber of Notre Dame Sous Terre in the crypt of Chartres Cathedral, the ancient site of the Sun oracle. There they were accorded the degree of the "lion." The Swan was the sacred symbol of this degree. At this level of spiritual development the divine element has become ensouled within the initiate to the extent that he could look into the core of his own being and shrink from no toil which duty demanded of him. This degree was mirrored by the awakening of the heart chakra, often called the "abode of mercy," which represents the union between the physical and spiritual aspects of the personality.

Initiation into the fifth degree was performed in the chamber under Notre Dame de Paris, the site of the Druidic oracle of Mars, and in Grail symbolism was depicted by the Pelican. Such an initiate lived for the perpetuation of his own people, being granted their name – for instance, the Persian, the Egyptian, the Greek, or the Israelite – and dedicated his life to their service. He now worked within a conscious unity of the folk-spirit of his people – that is, he could suffer the responsibility of speaking for his own karmic community. The fifth degree was granted at the awakening of the throat chakra and is associated with communication and demands that a distinction be made between purposeful words and thought, and those that are idle and meaningless noise.

The brow chakra, known to many as the "third eye," or the eye of the mind, is connected with the pituitary gland. This center relates to the right side of the brain and to the spiritual faculties of insight and intuition; it brings a direct "knowing." When this chakra was awakened the aspirant would undergo initiation into the sublime Mysteries of the Jupiter oracle and gain advancement to the sixth and penultimate degree, denoted by the Eagle. This took place in the glorious confines of the Cathedral of Amiens. All who were privileged enough to undertake the Pilgrimage of Initiation would have been spiritually gifted men indeed and those who rose to attain any of the higher degrees of initiation would have been men of exceptional talent, humility and dedication. What can I say of those who might have attained the seventh and highest degree? Were they those awarded the gift of entry into the Order of the Golden Fleece, founded by the Duke of Burgundy on the occasion of his marriage in 1430; an exclusive knightly order, limited in number and made up of men of the highest rank and ability, the true giants of the early Renaissance? There were only twenty-four men of supreme talent in that order, of which Earl William Sinclair was one. Was this chivalric order the outward face of *Rex Deus*, those families who claimed direct descent from the twenty-four high priests of the Jerusalem Temple? Or was this perhaps the overt face of that secretive, select few who had finally achieved the highest order of them all – the Kings of the Grail – the seventh and final degree of initiation?

The Crown was the royal symbol of the "King of the Grail." It was attained with the culmination of the spiritual journey at the opening of the Crown chakra, which is mystically united with the pineal gland, known to the initiates of the Greek Mysteries as the "seat of the soul" – the seat of consciousness and the doorway to the creator. Even the supreme rationalist, René Descartes himself, claimed that the pineal linked body and soul. This chakra is sometimes regarded as a unique center of consciousness and is therefore separate from the other six. Its opening is essential for attaining complete attunement in the processes of both healing and meditation; its full flowering occurs when the head of the serpent-like Kundalini reaches the Crown chakra, for which the psychological key word is "awakening."[264] The enlightenment that flows from the opening of the Crown chakra is the supreme and total fulfillment of the Grail search. The ultimate degree of initiation, which represents this apex of mystical illumination, was awarded at the seventh site, the ancient and revered site of the Saturn oracle itself, Rosslyn. Deliberately built by Earl William Sinclair as the focal point for every known path of initiation, Rosslyn Chapel was, in truth, simply the superbly carved reliquary of the Grail. As Europe's principal Grail center it was the "omphalos," or "spiritual umbilicus," of the world.

While there is only circumstantial evidence for this theory of initiatory pilgrimage, a great deal of corroborative opinion and theory does exist. There are also many subtle pointers that indicate that we are getting a little nearer to the truth. Biblical mention of the ravens that fed Elijah is held to mark the beginning of his path of initiation. The events at Serepha where he heals the "son of the widow" show him to be a "hidden one," an occultist of the second degree. On Mount Carmel he defends the knowledge of the spirit and as a "warrior" represents good in the fight against evil. On Horeb, when he perceives Jehovah within his own soul, he achieves the fourth degree, that of the "lion."

His achievement of the final three degrees was revealed to his pupil, Elisha, who inherited his mantle on the occasion of Elijah's assumption into heaven,[265] when he saw the fiery chariot of the Sun hero drawn by horses across the heavens. Elisha describes the vision in these words: "My Father, my Father, the chariot of Israel and the horses thereof," and this sublime initiatory process was found within Israelite *masseh merkabah* mysticism, otherwise known as the "chariot mysticism" of Judaism in biblical times. Reinforcing the idea that there are Earth chakras of similar nature to the human spiritual centers, one writer records:

There seem to be strong parallels between energy in the body
and energy in the landscape and ... energy flows and sacred
centres correspond to the meridians and acupuncture points
in the human body. ... Some have taken the parallels between
the human body and the Earth much further and have postulated "chakra" points on the Earth's surface which have
specific effects in landscape terms appropriate to the nature of
the corresponding chakra. The heart chakra, for example, has
been seen in terms of a river curving around a conical hill with
a church. They are often referred to as "landscape temples."

Various axes have been suggested incorporating the
seven chakras. One is supposed to run from France
up to Scotland.[266]

One strong confirmation of the validity of the theory of the
Pilgrimage of Initiation came from a very ancient source that was
particularly revered by the medieval initiates. An Egyptologist,
Jane Sellars, found in the ancient manuscript "Book of Two Ways,"
that the topography of the roads to Rostau in the sky was replicated on water and land in the two kingdoms of Egypt. She suggested
that the path by way of the waters of the Nile was represented
in the heavens by the constellation of the Milky Way. In Celtic
mythology the silvery constellation of the Milky Way was identified with Lug's Chain, often symbolized by the silvery smear of a
snail's track. It was also known as the Ashen Path, or the "Track
of Souls." Silver became the symbolic emblem of knowledge and,
in the Dark Ages, those who left bright tracks behind them in the
form of books or learning, were called the "Snail Men." The Milky
Way thus became the esoteric symbol signifying the attainment
of great knowledge. In the Egyptian Pyramid Texts, which are the

oldest esoteric writings yet known to man, it is clear that the ancient Egyptians did indeed equate the River Nile, on which their gods were born, with the celestial river of the Milky Way. The question that arises from this is simple: Did the ancient Egyptians use the Nile, the earthly counterpart of the celestial river, as a pathway of initiation?

According to the ancient initiates, the two kingdoms of Egypt were a living Temple built by the spirit of God, where man could play his ritual part and reunite his spirit with the divine as the result of an alchemical process. The Temple of God on the Earth, Egypt itself, was patterned on an "eternal archetype" of the supreme achievement of nature, namely man. This geographical representation of the human archetype had a spine, a head in the north and a body in the south. Along the serpentine spine, represented by the River Nile, lay seven great mystical centers marked by temples, the earthly equivalent to the seven major chakras in the human body. Each of these had specific rituals and secret teachings which directly related to their function as chakras. Those who were initiated at particular temples were expected to dedicate their lives for the benefit of all who inhabited the two kingdoms of Egypt. Once again, we find the fundamental concept that the fruits of initiation, sacred knowledge and wisdom, were to be used for the benefit of the entire community, race or tribe and not just for personal spiritual or financial gain.

The root chakra was embodied by the temple on the Island of Philae near the town of Elephantine. According to some scholars this center was the "quarry" from which the stones were to be hewn in order to build the Temple of God on Earth. It was directly linked with the Earth Mother herself, "Anna the Black Virgin." Thebes was the site of the Temple functioning as the sacral chakra. This procreative center was believed to be the power center of the body, generating the force that puts thoughts into action. In *The Encyclopaedia of the Occult* we read that in 1888, excavations at the Temple of Thebes revealed a statue of the god Kabeiros with a hammer in his hand. In ancient Egypt the chakra of the solar plexus was represented by the Temple of Abydos, the center of transmutation where the energies of the lower body could be gathered up and transmuted into the higher self, whose seat was the heart chakra. This chakra had two earthly forms, one at Hermopolis and the other at Akhetaten (known today as Amarna). These dual centers of the "royal self" acted jointly as the center of inspiration, perfect love and life itself. Here all things were held to begin and end: it was the Alpha and the Omega, the center of Truth and the Will of God.

The Temple of the throat chakra was at Memphis, the center of speech and spiritual creativity. Here was born the "Word of Love" that inspired the initiate to hear God, talk to God and to know God. The brow chakra at the Temple at Heliopolis represented the third eye, the eye of the mind where the voice of God was "seen" as a thought form. The final, or Crown chakra had two Temples, Behedet and Heliopolis, where the vision of absolute truth was completed. This was the ultimate center of initiation where the initiate was granted pure knowledge and an awareness of God that is beyond all understanding. Here the initiate was spiritually connected with the *An*, the "Heavenly Father" or the "Mind of God" itself.[267] We also need to remember that the ancient Egyptian initiates of Isis called themselves the "sons of the widow."[268]

The excitement that I felt when I discovered this ancient Egyptian process of initiation at the temples built upon these sacred sites of the Earth chakras, is almost impossible to describe. Not only did this illuminate the principles of the Pilgrimage of Initiation, but there were further links that strengthened the derivation of much of medieval, initiatory practice from its roots in ancient Egyptian belief and ritual. Firstly there is the veneration of the Black Virgin mentioned earlier, with connections between medieval Knights Templar practices and Egyptian belief being reinforced, not only by the veneration of Isis, but also by the worship of the Earth Mother at the Temple at Philae. The influence of sacred geometry on the building of medieval cathedrals, on Templar round churches and their simple chapels has already been mentioned. I had puzzled over the role Cintra played in all of this: if there were seven sacred sites in Europe which had in turn been used as Druidic oracles, Earth chakras, Roman temples and Christian churches, what was the purpose of an eighth site so far to the south in Portugal?

As I began to review the evidence collected in my Egyptian research, a possible solution to this puzzle presented itself. In ancient Egypt, before being accepted as a candidate for initiation, the novice or aspirant had to undergo a prolonged and demanding period of probation and preparation. Only when he had successfully passed the tests that demonstrated his purity, obedience, his control over earthly desires and willpower, would he move on to the temple on the Island of Philae. This prerequisite of prolonged preparation took place at Buhen, on the Nile at Egypt's southern border. Now at least we had an analogous position for Cintra which, like Buhen, lay far to the south of the other centers and, furthermore, was situated in the one mainland European country where the Knights Templar had neither been tried nor suppressed. The inclusion of Cintra perhaps has another purpose; it draws our attention to the magical number eight, a number of great significance to the ancient Egyptians and the Knights Templar. Furthermore, a nineteenth century castle built specifically as a Masonic museum stands near Cintra today.

When researching the pilgrimage to Santiago de Compostela, I came across the work of Elyn Aviva, who wrote *Following the Milky Way: A Pilgrimage Across Spain*. In this thesis she recounts how, when en route to Compostela, as she rested in the shade of León Cathedral, another pilgrim limped his way towards her and greeted her. She asked if he was a *Peregrino a Santiago*? His response was strange indeed:

> No! I walk the *Camiño de las Estrellas*, the Milky Way, not the *Camiño de Santiago*. The Milky Way is the true and ancient path of spiritual death and rebirth. The *Camiño* was just a Christian attempt to camouflage the true way.[269]

The ancient center of spiritual death and rebirth mentioned by the limping pilgrim was, of course, the Moon oracle of the Druids, the present day site of the Cathedral of Santiago de Compostela. Aviva was intrigued and amused by his bizarre answer, so she enquired how could she find the "true way"? His reply confirmed the concept of the Pilgrimage of Initiation. He described the true way as one that led along a path under the vault of the Milky Way in the heavens and passed through churches marked by certain carvings of mystical birds and animals – symbols of the seven degrees of initiation perhaps? He went on to explain, in terms that rang loud bells with me, that: "The ancients left carvings on the churches, but it is hard to read them because the initiation rites were secret and carried on by word of mouth, and that he and others were trying to reconstruct them."

Aviva who, at that time, was a self-confessed agnostic, was a little confused by this encounter, but eventually she was to admit that, despite her initial perceptions, she was not simply on a physical journey to Santiago but was indeed treading a powerful and pervasive esoteric pathway: week after week along the route she was being spiritually transformed and both her sense of perspective and her values were undergoing a dramatic change. She stated: "Perhaps those who travel the Camiño are impacted with faint echoes of ancient worship, faint images of archetypical power."[270] Aviva's final sentence closely identified her with the theory of the initiatory pilgrimage: "I do not know what road I travel, except that there are many hidden beneath the one – and, perhaps beneath the many is the One."[271] It is perhaps salutary to realize that in the Sufi tradition, the "One" is the only truly indivisible, God himself. It would seem that I was not alone in believing that the Pilgrimage of Initiation started in Spain and wended its hidden way northwards, signposted by carvings of birds and animals, recognized for their true meaning only by the initiated.

It is highly probable that as Europe became riven by warfare and dispute as a consequence of the Reformation, initiatory pilgrimage for the Masonic heirs to the Templar tradition became increasingly difficult, if not impossible. At that point, I began to suspect that the initiatory rituals previously conducted in the crypts of the seven churches and cathedrals became absorbed into the rituals of emerging Freemasonry and Rosicrucianism.

The mysterious order we now know as the Rosicrucians certainly pre-existed the man usually described as their founder, the author of the *Chymical Wedding of Christian Rosenkreutz*, pastor Johann Valentin Andreae. It formed an "invisible college" of like-minded, spiritually gifted men whose enlightenment was not apparent to the rest of the world. For reasons of their absolute secrecy it has proved virtually impossible for historians to trace with any degree of certainty the true nature and extent of the Order. Its influence, even today in the twentieth century, is reckoned by many to be profound. Many of the formative figures throughout the seventeenth and eighteenth centuries admitted to Rosicrucian influences in their thinking. They became known as the "Invisibles." Their immediate spiritual ancestors were most probably the society known as the *Orden der Unzertrennlichen* or *Indissolubisten*.[272] Founded in 1577 it included among its membership mine owners and craftsmen smelters; alchemy was one of their foremost interests.

It now seems certain that the Rosicrucians sprang from, among other roots, a long tradition of contemplative mysticism in the true Germanic tradition. In continental Europe, Freemasonry developed with an innate anti-clerical and anti-Catholic foundation. In England it developed somewhat differently for there the main Church was itself part of the political and hierarchical establishment, thus the anti-clerical bias was not so pronounced. Some Masonic lodges arose in America, directly connected with the Royal Arch and Rosicrucian degrees of Scottish Masonry. It is generally believed that the Royal Arch and Rosicrucian degrees of Scottish Masonry have direct links with the premier family in Masonic History, the Sinclairs of Rosslyn.[273]

These origins of the Royal Arch and Rosicrucian degrees of American Freemasonry may explain the high quality of some of the attainments of their members, for clearly manifest among them were supremely gifted men of great spiritual insight and moral force. These perceptive and powerful men left a lasting imprint on what has become modern society. The gift of the Constitution of the United States of America – the legal foundation for all the basic values of freedom, democracy and the rights of man – is the lasting spiritual legacy that we have received from this branch of Freemasonry.

Freemasonry in all its forms, for good or ill, soon appeared to become an indispensable key to high office. For instance, a large number of prime ministers in England from Robert Walpole in the eighteenth century to Ramsey MacDonald in the twentieth were Freemasons. This pattern of power was repeated throughout Europe, and also existed in America where many presidents prior to John F. Kennedy were Freemasons of a high degree. This influence was not just restricted to the heads of state but permeated the entire power structures of the judiciary, the police, the armed services and civil administration of the Western world. In this way, spiritual initiates continue to exercise profound influence, for good or ill, on all aspects of society today.

The influence of the Masonic order has long been a matter of speculation and public concern, but the existence of the *Rex Deus* families was almost completely unknown until quite recently. However it is now known that they spread their teaching far beyond the limited confines of their bloodline, firstly by founding the Knights Templar, then by the propagation of the Grail sagas, by promoting the tarot, through their influence on early Freemasonry, and by their patronage of great artists of the Renaissance such as Botticelli and Leonardo Da Vinci. Their initiatory teaching is also recognized as having a seminal influence on scientists such as Robert Boyle and Issac Newton and esotericists such as Robert Fludd and Johann Valentin Andreae; individuals of genius and originality held by historians to be the major forces in the creation and sustaining of the new age of enlightenment we call the Renaissance.

Martin Luther in 1533. Painting by Lucas Cranach.

CHAPTER 14

The Floodgates Open: The Rising Tide Of Ideas

The medieval outlook changed radically in the sixteenth
and seventeenth centuries. The notion of an organic, living and spiritual universe was replaced by that of the world
as a machine, and the world machine became the dominant
metaphor of the modern era. This development was brought
about by revolutionary changes in physics and astronomy,
culminating in the achievements of Copernicus and Galileo,
and Newton. ... Acknowledging the crucial role of science
in bringing about these far reaching changes, historians have
called the sixteenth and seventeenth centuries the Age of the
Scientific Revolution.[274]   – Fritjof Capra, *The Turning Point*

A great change was blowing up in Europe, greater perhaps
even than the religious and political upheaval that Martin
Luther had set going. The symbolic year of destiny was ...
1543. In that year, three books were published that changed
the mind of Europe: the anatomical drawings of Andreas
Vesalius; the first translation of the Greek mathematics and
physics of Archimedes; and the book by Nicolaus Copernicus,
The Revolution of the Heavenly Orbs, which put the sun at
the centre of the heaven and created what is now called the
Scientific Revolution.[275]   – Jacob Bronowski, *The Ascent of Man*

When we consider the divine basis for the development of agriculture, handicrafts and skills of the first civilizations, the intimate links between the respect for nature and the spiritual insights of the primitive shamans, and the pivotal role that the hermetic cults of ancient Greece played in the first full-flowering of consciousness, it is not surprising to find the pattern repeated in the fifteenth century and beyond. The fact that the vast majority of the men whose courage and insight brought about the Reformation in the Church, and those who led the Renaissance in European intellectual and artistic life, were mystics, initiates or their pupils is almost self-evident. The paradox is that these deeply spiritual men began an apparently irrevocable process that was to create a complete separation between the spiritual and material worlds. After Newton and Descartes, the universe itself was perceived as being a machine, simply a resource to be understood and exploited. Spirituality, faith, all the mystery and magic that had been the central controlling force in people's lives began to disappear.

Prior to the Christian era, the vibrant, living center of religious feeling in every culture was the power and spirit of nature; the very Earth itself was regarded as a goddess and given many names. Even Christianity believed that agriculture, animal husbandry and farming were pleasing in the eyes of God. The Christian mystics had stressed the intimate relationship between God and nature, but the newly emerging rational culture of science and politics was soon to outlaw all such awareness. This tendency continued and strengthened until, being increasingly divorced from nature, we began mortgaging the future of mankind as a whole for short-term ends. Humanity's future is under threat today as a direct result of the emergence of modern scientific man. This process started to make its indelible and definitive mark with the advent of Martin Luther and Copernicus, but the Renaissance itself had started much earlier, and for very different reasons. Among the republics of Italy trade had grown considerably, which in turn stimulated production, for one had to have goods in order to trade. It was this heightened level of production and exchange which stimulated the beginnings of the Renaissance. The Italian republics were not alone in this development. The Northern ports of the Hanseatic League and the Flemish and Dutch cities had also grown, not only commercially but also in population and importance. Social relations within all of these centers were in a state of flux; the landed aristocracy was declining in importance and, at the same time, the new mercantile bourgeoisie were growing in wealth and power. As a direct consequence, the Church was clearly seen to be losing her grip on social and political activities in Northern Europe.[276] The move towards more open access to culture, literature and art, and the right to free and open debate started in Northern Italy in the late Middle Ages and spread throughout Europe. This rapidly burgeoning thirst for knowledge carried within it clear signs of change and a distinct inclination among the more inquiring and progressive elements within society to operate outside the oppressive framework of the Church. In Florence, Cosimo de' Medici embarked on a series of projects that were to transform Western culture. Medici dispatched agents all over Southern Europe to seek out ancient manuscripts lying disregarded in the monastic libraries of Christian Europe[277] and, after the Reconquista of Spain, in the Muslim libraries of Granada and Toledo where they discovered a vast amount of classical Greek texts.[278] In 1444, Medici founded Christian Europe's first public library, the Library of San Marco in Florence.[279] Renewed and reinvigorated by these events, the study of the classical literature, philosophy and science of ancient Greece flourished and became the foundation for an insatiable spirit of enquiry that triggered an artistic and intellectual Renaissance.

The Church of Rome was no longer perceived as the guardian of all knowledge, insight and progress but was, on the contrary, regarded as a very definite obstacle to progress in both the intellectual and the economic fields. The Renaissance, in intellectual and cultural endeavor, was characterized by a growing admiration for the learning of ancient Greece and Rome, which had first re-entered European consciousness through the Mystery school at Chartres and was now reinforced by the flood of Arabic manuscripts brought to Western Europe by Cosimo de' Medici and others. A positive hunger for philosophy, literature, art and learning spread through the new mercantile class hand in hand with a rise in literacy. The invention of printing is now seen as a further stimulus to the new movements that ushered in the modern world. The primary impact of printing was to extend and spread literacy and an insatiable thirst for knowledge among the new economic winners in society.

The first books to roll from the press reflected the changing thinking of the time: a Bible, considerable theology – now difficult to censor and control – many works of classical Greek and Roman philosophy, ethics and the new academic, investigative discipline of science. Classical philosophy was used in the main to refute the narrow dogmatism of the Church and also to widen the educational base of the laity. Truly, the smell of printer's ink became the incense of the Reformation.[280] The Renaissance also reclaimed numerology, astrology and the tarot from their heretical reputation, and made alchemy both the handmaiden and the rival of science.

The Church nevertheless continued desperately to try to manipulate, dominate or control the rulers of nations, not only with dogma but also by means of political chicanery, playing off nation against nation, ruler against claimant, and when necessary people against their rulers; moves that did little to increase its popularity among the princes of Northern Europe. The laity in general, pious, superstitious and ruled by the fear of eternal damnation, was increasingly sickened by the corruption that was endemic among the clergy. Protests about the overt and massive extent of venality that could be discerned at all levels of the hierarchy were many, varied and completely ineffective – as indeed they had been for centuries. Effective protest when it came was not so much against the behavior of churchmen but about the doctrine of the Church, particularly about continuing augmentations of restrictive dogma that had no scriptural foundation. The sale of indulgences was one issue that had long compounded a rather strange dogma with massive corruption. The concept of souls expiating their earthly sins in purgatory prior to eventual admission to heaven had long since gained acceptance. The opportunity to earn indulgences, seemingly the spiritual equivalent to the modern penal concept of "time off for good behavior" had been in common usage since well before the First Crusade. The idea of selling indulgences for money was relatively recent, adapted from an old German tribal custom of commuting the punishments of convicted criminals in exchange for gold. Yet paradoxically, it was in Germany that the sale of indulgences aroused the most anger.[281]

In 1517 a devout and angry monk, Martin Luther, nailed several pieces of paper to the door of Wittenberg Cathedral. The paper contained ninety-five theses of dispute with Church doctrine, dogma and practice. For this courageous and rebellious monk, mere moral reform of the Church was worse than useless; he desperately needed to get the theology right. First he had to know how man justified himself with God, and that, according to Luther, was a theological problem, not moral. Luther firmly believed that the Church's main problem was not financial corruption, but the theological distortions on which the corruption was based. To get the doctrine right meant more theology, not less. He intended to reform and purify the Church; instead he split it apart, instigating what we now call the Protestant Reformation – a movement that was to have far reaching consequences, not only in religious and political affairs but also in the development of science.

The Reformation soon acquired the two allies it needed to sweep Northern Europe away from the coattails of Rome and place it firmly center stage in world affairs, where its influence would increase and mold religious, economic and scientific thinking for centuries to come. The forces whose combined effects were to bring this about were the invention of printing and political dissatisfaction. The princes and kings of both Northern and Western Europe were far from content with continuing interference by the pope and his hierarchy. Printing created the essential environment of academic interest and criticism without which the Reformation could not have begun.

The new form of Protestant Christianity that developed was based on the flawed concept of returning the Church to the simplicity of faith and practice of the time of St. Paul. In other words, to the original foundation propounded by the "Distorter of the True Teachings of Jesus." This, somewhat dubious objective, was, however, incapable of any realistic realization for the world had changed since then and it simply was not possible to excise and reject all the complex structures of dogma and belief that had accumulated over the centuries and imprinted themselves so indelibly on the minds of men. The tolerant and perceptive scholar Erasmus had formulated the ideal conception that:

You will not be damned if you do not know whether the
Spirit proceeding from the Father and the Son had one or
two beginnings, but you will not escape damnation if you do
not cultivate the fruits of the spirit: love, joy, peace, patience,
kindness, goodness, long suffering, mercy, faith, modesty,
continence and chastity.[282]

But Protestantism, despite its differences from the Catholic
Church from which it arose, carried with it an obsession with theology and all the intolerance that flows from it; it was characterized by its doctrines of justification by grace through faith, the
concept of a priesthood of all believers and an absolute reliance on
scriptural authority. Despite this, the new Church brought with
it from its ageing and corrupt parent the guilt-inducing doctrine
of original sin, the cruel concept of the Just War, and a fanaticism
that was born of certainty. An absolute certainty of belief that was
to become the fertile spawning ground of a bitter intolerance that
led to the burning and torture of heretics as enthusiastically by
Protestants as by Catholics.

Europe was ripe for dispute, theological controversy and war.
It soon experienced all three.

Erasmus in fact, rode on the crest of the New Learning which
seemed to offer unlimited opportunities for spiritual and intellectual advancement, and which presaged a thoroughgoing
reform of society, conducted from within by a universal and
voluntary movement. This rosy prospect was obliterated in
the middle decades of the century, and what in fact happened
was quite different: a division of Christianity on a compulsory
and state basis. Two armed camps came into existence: one,
half-reformed, basing its claims exclusively on scripture; the

other, unreformed, based exclusively on authority; and between them an unbridgeable chasm, filling with the victims of war and persecution.[283]

Differences over scriptural interpretation produced within the new religion a radical wing composed of several squabbling sects, each convinced that they, and they alone, had the true message of simple, biblically based, faith. Many churches simply changed names, the priests married their mistresses and the congregations carried on much as before, almost as a "nationalized Catholicism" with a married clergy. It was, however, the influence of the radical sects that was to bring about massive change. Their opportunity to accomplish this was aided by the social pressures that had long been accumulating.

The Reformation and the conflicts that came in its train exacerbated movements of population in progress throughout Europe. Demographic change for economic reasons gained impetus from those who fled from religious persecution, war and civil commotion. Other social pressures developed as a consequence of increased trade and the accumulation of wealth that accompanied it, and a new entrepreneurial class emerged with a thirst for education and comfort. Due to the blatant corruption of the clergy and hierarchy, few people now bequeathed their estates and wealth to the Church; instead they passed it on to their families who used it to educate their children and increase their business. A new and transformative movement was beginning. Capitalism was emerging from the crumbling structures of the Middle Ages.

The Church, far from playing the role of midwife to the new trading concepts, had indeed played a reverse role, only grudgingly permitting trade but emphasizing agriculture. The only Church organization that had exerted a positive influence on trading pat-

terns, the Templars, had been ruthlessly suppressed. The fledgling capitalists of the late Middle Ages were often extremely pious
but they had, of necessity, to develop a way of life that was outside the constraints and guidance of the Church, if for no other
reason than that the Church took no interest in trade. Pious the
merchants may have been, but they were also anti-clerical, for to
them the Church represented authoritarian repression, corruption and constraint, all inseparably entwined within the unpopular role of principal tax gatherer. These independently minded
entrepreneurs were to be found in Northern Italy, Germany, the
Low Countries and the Rhineland, throughout all the centers of
trade and commerce. The concept of reformed Christianity drew
them like a magnet and the direction that most of them took was
northwards, towards the new centers of religious reformation and
away from the repressive intolerance of Rome.

The growing accumulation of wealth in private hands, allied to a rapidly increasing population, steadily augmented the
demand for goods and accelerated the growth in trade. This
led to increased profit, which created more disposable income
and, as a result, further increases in demand. This process alone
would have had a pronounced effect on both trade and production. With the opening up of trade routes to the New World this
cumulative process was irrevocably changed and accelerated,
deepened and expanded until its effects were felt throughout
Western Europe.

The question of the origins of capitalism has become a search
for the elements which encouraged the accumulation of capital at the close of the Middle Ages. ... what preceded the industrial revolution and made it possible was a socio-political
revolution in late medieval Europe: the emergence of a civil

society ... an autonomous sphere of economic activity unim-
peded by political or religious restrictions.[284]

Many scholars at first believed that the foundations of capitalism
were laid on different grounds; the Reformation itself, and the
attitudes to work of some of the more radical sects in the new
religion, were all held to be responsible for the new system. The
so-called "Protestant work ethic" while not necessarily responsible for the creation of capitalism, does carry a great deal of responsibility for the evolution of the capitalist system, especially
in the New World of America. The value attached to hard work,
thrift and efficiency in one's own "calling" was, especially in the
Calvinist view, deemed to be the sign of the individual's "election,"
or personal salvation. The introspective attitudes of St. Augustine
and his conception of predestination had been taken up by the
Calvinists with an almost indecent enthusiasm. John Calvin, a fellow student of Erasmus, rapidly became one of the most blinkered, bigoted and intolerant of the leaders of the dissident wing of
the Protestant Reformation. The German sociologist Max Weber
postulated the thesis that this "Work Ethic" was the most important factor in the success of Protestant groups in the early stages
of European capitalism.[285] Undoubtedly it had a dramatic effect,
but Weber's conception is no longer widely accepted.

The fact that economic success was held as temporal evidence
of eternal salvation, and thereby to be vigorously pursued, did
play a major role in the financial success of many non-conformist
groups profoundly influencing the direction and form that capitalism took. It was also a formative influence on the way many
colonists in the New World regarded both indigenous populations and the exploitation of natural resources, but it was not the
cause of the capitalist system. The emphasis on the religious duty

to make fruitful use of the "God-given resources" that each individual had at his disposal was enormously significant. Richard Henry Tawney argued that the political and social pressures mentioned previously were the main cause, but other factors, especially the ethic of self-help, frugality and individualism, were of greater significance.[286] Weber firmly believed that social consciousness determined social change. Marx also sought the roots of social change in changing social consciousness, but came to different conclusions. The social development that made the accumulation of capital possible by destroying the ecclesiastical-cum-feudal system of values that had stultified all inquiry and growth, intellectual or economic, were of far greater relevance to Marx, who was the true founder of modern sociology.[287]

The growing transformation of society that was taking place as a result of the religious reformation, allied to the sustained and growing thirst for knowledge that arose from the Renaissance, was all-embracing in its nature. The increasing wealth among the merchant families of Europe led to a secularization of the patronage of art, previously the sole preserve of the Church. First in Italy, centered mainly around Florence and Venice, and later in the trading nations of the Low Countries, there occurred a veritable explosion of prolific talent that laid the foundations of the artistic world of painting, sculpture and literature that we revere so much today. Michelangelo Buonarroti, Botticelli and Leonardo da Vinci in Italy were followed later by the great Dutch masters Rembrandt and Frans Hals. As the centuries passed this artistic impulse spread widely across the entire continent. Philosophy flowered again, and through its innate questioning of the world, science became a dominant field of study in its own right. In the Middle Ages man had never entertained even the remote possibility that he could understand nature in its entirety, much less become its master, for knowledge of nature was not dependent on man's intellectual abilities but depended completely on divine revelation. The Church was the sole guardian of knowledge and it discouraged, on pain of torture, any questioning of revelation.

The Renaissance had brought about the secularization of learning just as the new Protestant religion, in its quest for purity of belief and worship, had ruthlessly stripped away all the old trappings of the veneration of relics, religious statuary, iconography and all the so-called pagan rites that linked the congregation to the world of nature. Protestantism carried the desacralization of nature to its ultimate, annihilating extreme.[288] Thus it created an intellectual and religious climate wherein the spirit of scientific inquiry, allied to the new dynamism of the reformed society, could flow freely and ruthlessly, and aggressively demolish all respect for nature as a creation of God. Philosophical and scientific debate moved out of the monastery and into the laboratory and the university. Yet, paradoxically, the founding fathers of this new science, Newton, Leibniz and Descartes, all shared one objective, to show that science was compatible with theology.

Later, in the seventeenth and eighteenth centuries this attitude was completely changed. The whole function of science was questioned; new methods of empirical investigation became the norm. Many of the founding fathers of science played their part in this fundamental shift of perspective. Bacon, Descartes, Kant and Galileo all seemed to share the same goal: to devise and codify rational, investigative procedures in such a manner as to free them forever from arbitrary interference and unfounded, superstitious assumptions. Francis Bacon was in truth the founder of the empirical method. He believed that man could, should, and indeed must enlarge the range of his knowledge in order to gain control over his surroundings.

Let faith and reason each treat of their several concerns and not encroach upon each other. The only function assigned to reason in the religious sphere is to deduce consequences from principles accepted on faith ... Reality only presents itself to us when we look upon the world of the senses. The senses alone provide us with realities, the realities of empirical knowledge.[289]

Thus science, previously regarded as a search for wisdom, understanding and harmony so dear to the philosophers of ancient Greece, underwent a dramatic change into a rational, detached and empirical investigation of the means to control, dominate and subdue nature itself. The importance of mystery in life, the mystery and wonder of "God in all" so beloved of the mystics, was lost.

Isaac Newton, Francis Bacon and René Descartes all contributed to the shift in human consciousness that finally separated humanity from the ancient spiritual heritage that had linked it in an intimate and self-sustaining relationship with nature. Luther had started the religious reforms that culminated in a desacralized religion, stripped of all its mysterious epiphanies, which now bound man to a sterile faith divorced from the realities of creation.[290] The Reformation and Renaissance combined to bring to birth the alienated reality of the sense-world completely divorced from all knowledge and respect for the domain of the spirit. The stage was set for the deification of reason itself. As a direct result of the scientific revolution Western Europe became a spiritual desert; the universe and all that it contained was viewed simply as a machine, the world as a physical resource to be ruthlessly exploited. The spirituality and sense of magic that had bound mankind in mystical unity with nature had, seemingly, been obliterated.

Yet the Renaissance and even the Reformation had been started, formed and inspired by the same impulse that had created and sustained the first full-flowering of the fruits of knowledge in Greece two thousand years before: paradoxically, that very impulse that led in turn to the threefold alienation which Marx described so eloquently. Man's alienation from nature, from his own self and from the rest of humanity arose directly from the work of men who were all initiates of the very spiritual world that science now denied existed.

Throughout the Middle Ages the hidden wisdom of the secret orders of initiates had continued to irrigate the spiritual desert of the times. We have mentioned *Rex Deus*, the Mystery school at Chartres, the Rosicrucians, Templars and their heirs, and the complex way they all seem to intertwine, influence and inspire each other. The initiation cults and the mystics exerted their influence upon individuals who at first glance seem unlikely prospects for their attention. Luther himself acknowledges that the mystics, especially Meister Eckhart, had influenced him profoundly.[291] Sandro Filipepi, better known to posterity as Botticelli, was a Hermeticist and a pupil of Veruccio, a hierophant who also instructed Leonardo da Vinci; an esotericist described by some as a Rosicrucian and by contemporary Catholics as "of an heretical cast of mind," and by the twentieth century initiate, Rudolf Steiner, as one of his own precursors.

The great scholar Robert Fludd of England was not only one of Europe's leading exponents of esoteric thought, but was also the author of one of the most comprehensive compilations of ancient hermetic philosophy ever written. Reputedly a Rosicrucian, although this seems unlikely, he was fulsome in his praise of that order. He was one of the principal scholars responsible for the translation of what was later called the "Authorized Version of the Bible" – the King James Bible. The priest, alchemist and author Johann Valentin Andreae was indeed a Rosicrucian of note, and is often credited with the foundation of the Rosicrucians by historians who believe that Christian Rosenkreuz was merely a legendary figure. Andreae was almost certainly the author of the so-called "Rosicrucian Manifestos" which gained wide circulation in Europe in the mid-seventeenth century.

The scientists of the new era were mostly members of the hidden stream of initiates, all deeply involved in esoteric spirituality, for they believed that in the hidden wisdom were the buried secrets of human nature and the universe that were to be found nowhere else. Among them were Isaac Newton and Robert Boyle. They were all initiates, yet played a highly influential part in founding a new system of science and philosophy that was to alienate the mass of humanity from the spiritual world. Initiates of many orders combined in a loose network with moderate scholars in the tradition of Erasmus to form the "Third Force," a movement of moderation created to combat the excesses of both Catholics and Protestants. A group of eirenic evangelists who, in concert with the Dutch esoteric movement of the "Family of Love," formed a so-called "Invisible College"[292] who were in constant correspondence with one another and who were given a highly visible manifestation as the Royal Society in England.

The Royal Society was formed by a group of scientists of profound religious conviction, yet men who were so embarrassed by the restrictions placed upon the advance of knowledge by religion that they dedicated their meetings purely to scientific matters and banned all discussion of religion at them. It has been suggested, and with good cause, that this move was as much to protect the fledgling society from religious persecution and repression as to advance the cause of scientific debate. Ironically it was in reaction against the work of Newton and Bacon that a later esoteric and mystical stream arose in the unlikely guise of the poets Goethe and Blake, separated by nationality and language, but united in spiritual insight and vision.

Thus we can now see that the hermetic schools, mystics and initiates had a founding role in creating a system of science that, paradoxically, alienated humanity from the very nature it studied. The world at large was to be used, understood and experimented upon. The Earth itself, and all contained within its compass, became respectively both the laboratory and the guinea pigs for scientific experimentation. The results of this empirical quest were to deify reason and transform the world from a science laboratory into a growing, polluting, oppressive collection of "dark satanic mills" that spewed forth their filth unceasingly from the first Industrial Revolution to the present day. The world's progressive degeneration from Earth goddess to scientific laboratory and, ultimately, to global garbage can, was the inevitable consequence of the scientific and religious alienation from nature.

Mohandas K. Gandhi (1869–1948), political and spiritual leader of India.

CHAPTER 15

The Age Of Exploration: The Destruction Of Native Cultures And Peoples

The Spanish Conquistadores reached a conclusion that the Native peoples did not have souls and therefore it was perfectly all right to enslave or murder them. Much of the same kind of thinking is alive and well today in countries such as Paraguay, Brazil, Chile and others where the Native peoples are still hunted down and killed ... The question at this point that needs to be addressed is, what kind of theology were the institutionalised churches propagating that could lead to such a de-humanizing analysis of missions of peoples. And, is this kind of theology still functioning in the churches in the 1980s?[293]

– Fritjof Capra, *The Turning Point*

The Evil that men do, lives after them, the Good is oft interred with their bones.[294]

– Shakespeare, *Julius Caesar*

To understand the roots of the veritable explosion of exploration and the subsequent exploitation of the newly discovered lands that took place in the late fifteenth century and after, we have to examine briefly the limited, but formative, experience that preceded it. The cruelty, sheer greed and intolerance that were the characteristics of the so-called crusades are a matter of record, and, perhaps because of their cruel intolerance, the crusaders made no inroads whatsoever upon the religious beliefs of the Islamic peoples. Islam was believed by its followers to have been founded upon revelations granted by Allah to Mohammed, specifically to correct the spiritual impurities of Christianity and replace it with true monotheism. In answer to that, Christianity had nothing to offer except brutality. The behavior of the crusaders against their own co-religionists of the Eastern Empire was at least as bad as that they displayed to the Muslims. Attempts were made to convert the Africans as early as 1444, but these petered out by the mid-sixteenth century. Knowledge of Africa and its peoples, gained at this time, was later used almost exclusively to found and maintain the slave trade.

Motivated by greed, population pressures, immense curiosity and a soupcon of evangelical enthusiasm, the traders and explorers of Europe began their imperial adventure. This became a race in which the competitors took different geographical routes to seek their goals yet used remarkably similar methods to attain them. From the religious perspective it was in the territories occupied by the Spanish and the Portuguese that missionary work was taken most seriously, yet while each expedition had a clear commitment to convert the heathen; profit was always the prime motive. Missionary work was mostly undertaken by the religious orders, mainly Franciscans and Dominicans, who accompanied the explorers acting under the orders of the crown.[295] Later the Jesuits also played an important role. The motivation for evangelism itself was mixed. The clergy were inspired by religious zeal, the authorities had need of a docile and subservient labor force in all of their colonies, the settlers themselves needed the sense of security that religious uniformity could bring. Conversion was an inextricable offshoot of conquest; indigenous populations were brutally told that their own gods had failed them and that the

Christian God was superior. Why else had the Europeans won? The secular clergy's attitude is exemplified by the actions of Juan de Zumárraga, the first bishop of Mexico, who had learnt from the example set in the years of Christianity's early domination in the Roman Empire. The bishop instituted a brutally effective campaign of destruction against native cults, culture and religion by trying to erase all signs of the pre-Christian beliefs. This zealot destroyed over five hundred temples and more than twenty thousand idols, and is regarded by many historians today as the greatest destroyer of antiquities and cultural artifacts in the entire history of South America, if not the world. An enviable reputation for a man of such a superior, Christian, civilized culture.[296]

A dramatic counterpoint to this official attitude was provided by a Franciscan of the sixteenth century, Bernardino de Sahagún. This scholarly and compassionate friar spent over sixty years in Mexico and believed implicitly that it was vitally necessary to understand the "spiritual maladies" and the "vices of the country" in order to bring about not only the conversion of the entire population but also their effective absorption into the colonial system. He used highly original methodology and extraordinary insight to compile a classic study entitled *Historia general de las cosas de Nueva Espana*. This mammoth twelve-volume work was published in two languages, Nahuatal and Spanish. It covered in minute and respectful detail every aspect of the religion, customs, constitution, intellectual and political activity, flora, fauna, languages and agricultural practices of the country. This monumental work is rightly regarded by many scholars as the greatest single achievement of the literary and historic field of the entire Renaissance.[297] On completion it received the respect given to any independent and academic work in the Roman Catholic world – it was immediately suppressed by order of King Philip of

Spain in 1577 and did not see the light of day again until 1779.

A highly regulated form of agriculture based on complex and well-maintained irrigation systems was established in the Andean highlands over one thousand years before the Spanish conquest. These systems were developed by people who had a deep understanding and respect for nature, and reached their peak under the Tiahuanaco and Chuma dynasties and the Inca Empire that followed. Intensive agriculture depended entirely on a state-regulated irrigation system, which in turn allowed the production of large regular surpluses, which were then distributed at the behest of the emperor. Their distribution was used as a means of social control to reinforce his rule and authority. The Spanish conquistadors ruthlessly destroyed this well-ordered, ecologically aware society in their rapacious and relentless search for gold. The emperor was imprisoned, held to ransom for an enormous quantity of gold and then murdered. The leaderless society fragmented and scattered, the remnants being reassembled along Spanish lines. New villages and towns were founded; the native population was herded into them as unwilling servants or slaves, and European crops were introduced. Many of the survivors fled to the marginal lands of the high Andes and elsewhere at the periphery of Spanish influence. They scattered fast to avoid slavery in the mines and enforced serfdom in the farms of the new colony.

The loss of population among the Native American peoples that took place within one hundred years of the European invasion amounted to genocide – pure and simple. Before the arrival of the Europeans the total population was estimated to be in the region of seventy-five to eighty million inhabitants. Less than one hundred years after the arrival of the Christians this had fallen to between ten and twelve million. The West Indian population was almost completely wiped out; on one island the entire native population had been reduced to twenty-four households.[298] In the context of the total world population at the time, this crime far exceeds in scale, nature and brutal effect, even the Nazi Holocaust against the Jews, Gypsies and Russians in the Second World War. The eventual answer to the labor shortage created by this wave of mass murder was the reinstitution of slavery with black slaves from West Africa. As slavery had originally vanished from European society for economic and not theological reasons, this created no qualms of conscience whatsoever for Christians of any denomination, merely problems of logistics: difficulties of supply and demand that the new systems of capitalist trade would soon answer with brutal efficiency.

Luther and the early Protestants in most parts of Northern Europe at that time took no part in any form of foreign missionary enterprise. They were more concerned with converting Christians of other denominations than in evangelizing pagans, a habit that has more than a residual influence on many fundamentalist sects to this day. In England however, the situation was somewhat different. Many seamen and traders were pious and even fanatical Protestants who felt a strong compulsion to proselytize. In North America such missionary efforts were almost always left in their secular hands. Thus conversions had a distinct tendency to serve the interests and objectives of commerce, as they were the result of individual effort and conviction. Little or no support was provided by either the state or the Anglican Church.

The early European ideal of the fully Christian state founded absolutely on religious principles and ideals came to fruition in the Northeast of what is now the United States. The birth of Protestant America was an act of deliberate policy, an institution of church-state perfectionism. The attitude of Protestants towards slavery, however, was no different from that of the Spanish

Catholic colonists further south. In 1667, Virginia laid down that "Baptism does not alter the condition of the person as to his bondage and freedom." In 1743, George Armstrong claimed that American slave owners held the blacks in "an irrational contempt ... as creatures of another species, who had no right to be instructed or admitted to the sacraments." This statement mirrored almost exactly the view of the Spaniards quoted in the introduction to this chapter, and was soon reinforced by many other biblical defenses of slavery.[299] Thus the reformed Church was clearly little different from its parent. It was not until the nineteenth century that concerted efforts were made by European or American Protestants to organize large-scale missionary work. Even then natives from whatever country or culture were held in contempt and their cultural values derided as inferior. Such evangelical efforts were inevitably entwined with colonialism and, as such, viewed with great suspicion by the native populations, especially the Africans and Indians.

The Puritans, whose search for religious freedom and a state founded on Christian principles created the beginnings of the United States, were, in their fanatical religious certainty, singularly ill-equipped to create an ambience either of tolerance or effective evangelism.

Of themselves they could initiate nothing of significance. Indeed, we now know they did not. Their brief and bitter hour here ... is but a sad, microcosmic recapitulation of the history that Christianity had already enacted in the Old World ... repeating helplessly its negative achievements: the suppression of dissenters, the search for and the destruction of alien enemies; and the costly self repression that would finally sunder the very sect itself. To have been genuine reformers, they would have had to accept the New World. But nothing in their history told them how this might be done.[300]

There can be no attempt in the context of this book even to begin to describe the slow, systematic destruction of the North American Indian population by their European, civilized colonizers, except to list the theft of their lands; the ritual betrayal that followed each treaty with the white man; the use of war; deliberate infection with smallpox; the herding into reservations – which after all are nothing more nor less than large concentration camps – or any of the other means of destruction, persecution and genocide that were used against these people. They were described by white, Christian contemporaries as "bloodthirsty savages." Yet what of the morality of the actions of those who employed such perverse descriptions?

The Native American people were, and in their surviving descendants still are, people of intense and deep spirituality who had always instinctively, deliberately and consciously sought spiritual guidance in all they did and who lived in vibrant harmony with the land and all the creatures who inhabited it, perceiving through their natural insight the truly spiritual nature of each and every aspect of creation. This form of spirituality, as mentioned in an earlier chapter, is common to all hunter-gatherer societies and that can now be heard in their own words:

> Every part of this earth is sacred to my people … The sap
> which courses through the trees carries the memories of the
> red man. … Our dead never forget this beautiful earth, for it
> is the mother of the red man. We are part of the earth, and
> it is part of us. … The water's murmur is the voice of my
> father's father. The rivers are our brothers, they quench our
> thirst … the air is precious to the red man, for all the things

share the same breath. ... We know that the white man does not understand our ways. ... The earth is not his brother, but his enemy, and when he conquered it, he moves on. His appetite will devour the earth and leave behind only a desert. ... Perhaps it is because I am a savage I do not understand. What is man without the beasts? If all the beasts were gone, man would die from a great loneliness of spirit. For whatever happens to the beasts soon happens to man.[301]

Crazy Horse dreamed and went into the world
where there is nothing but the spirits of
all things. That is the real world that is
behind this one, and everything we see here is
something like a shadow from that world.[302]

All things are the work of the Great Spirit. We should all know that he is within all things: the trees, the grasses, the rivers, the mountains, and all four legged animals, and the winged people: and even more important, we should understand that he is above all these things and peoples.[303]

The white colonizers, imbued with the Christian precepts of love, truth and charity, persecuted and betrayed the native Indians whom they described as painted, heathen savages. Yet any true picture of the Indian's intense spirituality reveals that they had a love and respect for God's gift of nature that is still signally lacking in their white brethren's life even today.

The rapacious greed of the European invader and his intellectual and racial arrogance might have been enough on their own to trigger the genocide and cultural destruction that followed the invasion of the Americas. Religious certainty and fanaticism, injudiciously mixed with the new concepts of science and the Protestant work ethic deeply embedded in the new creed, combined effectively to desacralize all of creation in the minds of the colonists.

The slave trade which was to be the foundation of the economies of Spanish America, the West Indies, and the Southern states of the U. S. also played its part in the creation of wealth and industry in England. The newly emerging economies of the colonies required a constant supply of cheap and reliable labor. To some extent, this was supplied by colonists themselves, by indentured labor or by the use of convicts from the founding states of empire, but it was mainly met by the institution of slavery. A triangular trade was rapidly established which not only sustained the growing needs of the new states, but also became the foundation stone for many an English fortune. Cheap goods were exported to Africa, exchanged for slaves who were then dispatched in conditions of extreme brutality to the Americas. The slaves were sold and cotton, tobacco and other goods exported in their turn to England. The fortunes of Bristol grew and prospered mightily from this vile commerce in human misery. The full exploration and development of Africa had to wait for several centuries, but the West Coast was readily exploited as a source of slaves.

The colonization of Africa, and its eventual domination by the economic, military and cultural might of Europe, led once more to the destruction of native cultures and spirituality. The lifestyle of the African natives varied widely across the extent of this immense continent with all its variation in climate and topography. A few brief examples must suffice to indicate some of the spiritual and cultural aspects of life of the wide range of peoples who inhabited this vast land. The Bantu, who were the main ethnic group in what is now South Africa, were conversant with the solar system and knew that the Earth revolved around the Sun – a concept that they had held long before Galileo was persecuted for promulgating such an heretical belief.[304] How they knew this is difficult to assess; perhaps in the spiritual humility, which was central to their religion, they simply assumed that their planet was not the center of the universe. This same humility enabled them to learn from the animals the secrets of herbal medicines that can cure ills for which the white man today still has no effective answers. They knew the secret of drugs that can rid people of gallstones and kidney stones with no difficulty at all. The initiates of a religious cult at Kariba commonly used surgery of a high degree of skill. The seemingly most primitive people of all, the Bushmen of the Kalahari, had much they could have taught the European invaders, if the arrogant Christians had had the wit to listen.

The Bushmen, though still living by force of circumstances in the ways of pre-historic man, were, and still are, the most intelligent and talented race in Africa. With their paintings in caves and shelters they have made the most profound contribution to the "documented" history of Africa. The Bushmen have recorded with their pictographic writing, events that took place many thousands of years ago. ... The Bushmen are the most scientific race in the whole of Southern Africa. They were the first to have a proper calendar ... With their knowledge of the seasons and weather conditions they regulated their migrations and, but for their supreme knowledge of nature they would long since have become extinct in the very areas in which they thrive today. ... Their knowledge of herbal medicines, poisons and antidotes still baffle white scientists today.[305]

By the time the "Dark Continent" was fully opened to the Europeans, scientific knowledge in the Western world had reached a high level of development. The colonists made no attempt to understand the culture, religion or history of their subject peoples and the African was simply regarded as either a savage to be subdued, or at best as an illiterate and recalcitrant child to be disciplined in the name of civilization. The entire continent was viewed as a source of raw materials for the ever-hungry factories of Europe, a market for European goods and the political plaything of empire. Few major European countries did not at one time or another play the exploitative colonial game. Britain, France, Holland, Germany, Portugal, Spain and eventually, Italy, all indulged in the cruel and brutal exploitation of both peoples and countries which gave us the full flower of European Christian colonial idealism – apartheid. Even after the "winds of change" blew over Africa in the era of liberation, political and economic domination not merely continued but intensified: economic aid and the international credit system still holds the ex-colonies in their restrictive grip.

Africa and the Americas were not the sole recipients of the dubious, alienating gifts of European Christian culture. From the sixteenth century, Christian attempts to evangelize the world were continuous in one theater or another, and were at times extremely vigorous. But they never set off a chain-reaction; instead they tended to require constant reinforcement and stimulation. Christianity took firm hold in South America, but in Asia where the missionaries had to compete with well-established and well-organized sophisticated religions, the result was very different, especially as the missionaries lacked the vital support of a colonial government. Where Islam was already established, Christianity made little or no progress. This is still apparent in Western Asia,

Northern India, Malaya and Java, despite the fact that in these areas the Christians wielded immense political and economic power. It was, broadly speaking, the same with the other great Eastern religions – Hinduism, Buddhism and Confucianism. Wherever they were established and mature, and associated with the racial consciousness of the locality, Christianity could not penetrate in depth,[306] a fact that, sadly, did not prevent the spread of political and economic domination by the colonial powers.

Trade, conquest and exploitation were the means by which European ideas and culture made their devastating impact. While it is true to say that for the majority of the population in the colonized countries of Asia the invaders made little impact on their spiritual lives, European standards of trade, work, land use and post-colonial industrialization have had a devastating effect not only on the temporal lives of the native populations of Asia, but also of the world.

The deep and profound gifts of Eastern spirituality, derided as they were in the colonial era, have survived strong and intact and have now come full circle to nourish the spiritually starved peoples of present-day Europe and America. Many of the themes and ideas that have come to us from the East have a familiar ring. Richard Wilhelm speaking of the Tao path shows clearly that embedded deeply within it is the concept "That humanity participates in all cosmic events, and is inwardly as well as outwardly interwoven within them."[307] The contrast between the hidden nature of Western initiates living in a repressive, Christian society and the open reverence given to their Eastern counterparts is stressed by the French philosopher Gabriel Marcel, who also asserts that the benefits of sacred knowledge are to be shared within the wider community:

The true function of the sage is surely the function of linking together, of bringing into harmony. I am not thinking only or even chiefly of the Greeks, but of classical China, of the China of Lao Tse, and what here strikes me in a really marvellous light is that the sage is truly linked with the universe. The texts are unmistakable and revealing: the order to be established in life – whether of the individual or the city or of the empire – is in no way separable from the cosmic order.[308]

The modern scholar Fritjof Capra has discovered many points of validation of modern science by the ancient Eastern mystics who were so derided by the colonists. Here he relates ancient Taoist wisdom to the conceptions of the modern Nobel Laureate Ilya Prigogine:

The concepts of process, change, and fluctuation, which play such a crucial role in the systems view of living organisms, are emphasized in the Eastern mystical traditions, especially in Taoism. The idea of fluctuations as the basis of order, which Prigogine introduced into modern science, is one of the major themes in all Taoist texts. ... Among the Eastern traditions Taoism is the one with the most explicit ecological perspective, but the mutual interdependence of all aspects of reality and the nonlinear nature of its interconnections are emphasized throughout Eastern mysticism.[309]

Before the first century CE Chinese civilization had achieved a stability, order and competence that far exceeded that of the Europe of the Renaissance. Founded on the "wisdom of the sages" – the same "hidden wisdom" of the Western initiates – working through the Confucian concepts of family, fidelity and order, the Chinese

Empire developed an agrarian way of life that combined efficiency, prosperity and stability. The Taoist initiates brought to it the blessings of philosophy, medicine, science and technology, and were revered by the people for so doing. The vast population was supported by an intensive agrarian development that in turn sprang from complex irrigation systems dependent on accurate calendars, intimate knowledge of the seasons, and an efficient technology that allowed one man aided by simple machines to raise water from the rivers to the fields. Scientific knowledge of plants and crops were spread throughout this vast land by the invention of printing; agrarian and medical knowledge were disseminated in encyclopaedias that were in circulation long before Christianity became the official religion of the Roman Empire. Scholarship, literacy and investigative science were encouraged and revered. Law, civil order, taxation and the dissemination of knowledge were all aided and upheld by an efficient and highly respected bureaucracy; entry to that privileged class was by written examination that required at least six years' intensive study before the first qualifying test. All this was achieved at a time when Europe was in the dark ages of imposed and dogmatic ignorance.[310] The Sung dynasty did not fall due to internal weakness, but because of external pressures brought about by the invasion of the Mongols. This occupation by the wild horsemen from the Steppes lasted less than ninety years. The reestablishment of the wider empire of the Ming dynasty maintained its stability by once more returning to the ancient sacred wisdom of the past, strengthened by the deliberate refusal to trade abroad. The Chinese knew that culturally they were the center of the world. Foreign traders had to come to China to obtain the fruits of their culture – China would not go out to the world. From China came not only exotic goods such as silk and porcelain, but knowledge of medicine that reached Europe via the Arabs, and inventions such as printing and gunpowder that were in turn to totally transform the face not only of Europe, but of the entire world.

The wisdom of Taoism, the entire cultural heritage of Chinese civilization and the well-established, orderly nature of the Chinese imperial system all combined to form an impenetrable bulwark, not only against the inroads of Christian evangelical missions but against European culture itself.[311] In the early days of Christian contact with the imperial court, the Christians had to dramatically change their attitudes, for they were not regarded as teachers of a superior wisdom, but as pupils from an inferior culture – a bitter pill for the arrogant Europeans to swallow. European infiltration into China came very late, and when it came it was brought by war not by conversion, and by the deliberate creation of a trade that was sternly resisted by the Chinese authorities. It was the introduction of the opium habit and its deliberate encouragement as an act of British policy and trade that sparked off the so-called "Opium Wars."[312] As a result of these conflicts China was laid wide open to the corrupting, political, economic and scientific influence of the West.

When the early colonists found themselves in conflict with peoples and cultures that were intrinsically resistant to the Christian message, other means were soon found to bolster the twin aims of conquest and economic exploitation that were the real motive for expansion. The Christian nations of Europe became masters of the art of "divide and rule." Any inherent conflicts within the subject nation, whether they originated in ethnic, racial or religious differences and rivalries, were ruthlessly exploited to the advantage of the colonial power. In Africa, tribal rivalries and, later the tensions between the Indian merchant classes and the native Africans were often the keys to power; in India, it was the conflict between the Muslim and Hindu populations; in Asia, the rivalry between the indigenous peoples and the ubiquitous Chinese entrepreneurs; in Palestine, the Arab-Jewish divisions not only gave easy access to power and manipulation to the colonists, but also sowed the seeds for later conflicts.

It is not surprising that the spiritual and political leader responsible above all others for the independence of India, Mahatma Gandhi, spoke not only in spiritual but also in political terms when he pronounced on sin. Gandhi, from his enlightened spiritual perspective, was of the firm conviction that all sins are modifications of *himsa*, the basic sin. For him, the only sin, in the ultimate analysis, is this variation of *attavada* or the "sin of separateness": from nature; from one's fellow man; and ultimately, from God.[313] According to the Jain maxim, he who conquers this sin conquers all others. The mahatma also said that "I am part and parcel of the whole and cannot find God apart from the rest of humanity," consciously or unconsciously echoing John Donne, Dean of St. Paul's, who had exhorted England's merchants to evangelize the natives and who wrote: "No man is an island whole and entire in himself, each man is part of the main."

No one can change history, for good or ill, all we can do is learn from it. In this time of global crisis it is necessary to look back critically, so that we may understand the formative influences, the deliberate repression of initiatory spirituality that led to the institutionalization of inequity and injustice. Those who do not learn from history are condemned to repeat it. We do not have the time or the resources that allow for a wide margin of error; for the Industrial Revolution and all that flowed from it put the final seal of approval on both man's complete alienation from nature and the destructive thrust of the development of a scientific system, denuded of all moral perspective.

Newton by William Blake (1795).

CHAPTER 16

Two Revolutions That Changed The World

In investigating the roots of our current environmental dilemma and its connections to science, technology and the economy, we must re-examine the formation of a world-view and a science which, by re-conceptualizing reality as a machine rather than a living organism, sanctioned the domination of both nature and women. The contributions of such founding "fathers" of modern science as Francis Bacon, William Harvey, René Descartes, Thomas Hobbes and Isaac Newton must be re-evaluated.[314]

– Carolyn Marchant of Berkeley University, cited by Fritjof Capra in *The Turning Point*

The Italian Renaissance was one clear, tangible and highly dramatic manifestation of the fruits of hidden wisdom. This sudden flow of changed perceptions soon turned into a questing flood of intellectual endeavor that burst upon the world like a tidal wave of new consciousness sweeping old ideas aside with brutal, irresistible force and fertilizing the minds of the "new scientific man" with conceptions that continued to change and remold the entire world from that time to the present. The leaders of the newly emerging society were not, as in the past, the noble and the highborn. Like the cardinals and artists of the Renaissance, the prime movers of the Industrial Revolution, the philosophers, economists, inventors and captains of industry were proud to claim that they were born in humble circumstances.[315]

The Industrial and French Revolutions put an end to man's blind acceptance of inherited position, authority or subservience. In the minds of industrialists, scientists and philosophers, it would also lead to the mastery of nature that would free men from the tyranny of all the old superstitious ways. The twin revolutions now began to succeed where evangelism and conquest had failed; their influence permeated, undermined and finally destroyed all resistance to the European domination of rival cultures, nations and empires. Change began to march masterfully and violently throughout the entire world, benefiting some, bringing untold misery to others, transforming all before it. An unstoppable, irreversible, paradoxical melange of technological advance, philosophical and political liberality, pauperization, pollution and institutionalized brutality created the emergent political and economic structures whose actions threaten the very existence of the world we live in today.

England was both the cradle and the first nursery of the Industrial Revolution. Starting in the late eighteenth century, it was slow to develop at first, but its diffusion soon became rapid. By 1850 it had penetrated into Belgium, France, Germany and the United States of America. By the early twentieth century it had reached Northern Italy, the Baltic states and Russia. Japan was the first Asian country to enthusiastically adopt its advances. By the middle of the twentieth century the Industrial Revolution had spread into India, China, South America and Africa,[316] into the very areas previously deliberately deindustrialized by the Western imperialist powers, or kept as mere providers of raw materials for the manufacturing bases in Europe and as markets for their products. In less than two hundred years, the tentacles of the Industrial Revolution – which arose from changing conceptions of man's relationship with God and nature – had penetrated nations, continents and cultures which had previously been impervious to the blandishments of European evangelism, trade and ideas. Gunpowder, industrial "goodies," and wage economies had triumphed where the "Word of God" had apparently failed.

World development from the eighteenth century onwards became irretrievably influenced, formed and sustained by the conceptions arising from the two revolutions, both of which were completely European in origin and philosophy. Political and economic systems which were structured and motivated by European self-interest began to challenge, change or destroy the previously strong and apparently stable cultures of the Middle East, Africa and Asia. The Industrial and French Revolutions so influenced world economic, political and philosophical development that the broad European perspective narrowed down for a considerable period, to a Franco-Britannic one. The historical roots of the Industrial Revolution, the very thinking that informed it and the results brought in its train, are succinctly described by Carlo Cipolla:

> The Industrial Revolution can be regarded as the process
> whereby the large scale exploitation of new sources of energy
> by means of inanimate converters was set on foot. ... In the
> North Western part of Europe, the sixteenth and seventeenth
> centuries witnessed also a most remarkable mercantile development which favoured the accumulation of physical wealth
> and entrepreneurial skills.[317]

This revolutionary development was brought about by pioneering industrialists who took the very substance of the Earth and bent it to their will. In fact three revolutions occurred in swift succession, each influencing, sustaining and strengthening the long-term effects of its predecessor. The fruits of the American, the French and the Industrial Revolutions created a complex web that first enveloped and then re-structured the Christian world and subsequently the entire planet.

It was soon apparent that a high price had to be paid for this so-called "progress": the destruction of craft-based cottage industries, the pollution that arose from the factories and new manufacturing centers, massive overcrowding and the deliberate creation of a new underclass – the urban proletariat. The growth of cities accelerated at an alarming rate. The new urban patterns that began to emerge provided a large, ready-made labor force as well as accessible markets. Factories situated on the outer fringes of large cities were able to take advantage of both of these factors and in addition had ready access to raw materials from the hinterland. The poverty and desperate overcrowding of the new industrial towns and cities was intensified by the very principles on which the new captains of industry operated. Labor costs, like all others, were held to a minimum.

The theoretical basis for much of what occurred in the formative period of the Industrial Revolution was firmly based on the new science of economics. The most influential of the new economists, and the man who became in many ways the "guru" of the new entrepreneurial classes, was Adam Smith. His *An Enquiry Into the Nature and Causes of the Wealth of Nations*, published in 1776, is described by Eric Hobsbawm as "one of the most important works ever published."[318] Founded largely on his theories, the emerging industrial system produced sustained growth, massive wealth and social advancement for the capitalists and entrepreneurs and at the same time, created conditions of immense squalor and deprivation for the workers. Yet it was the same Adam Smith who claimed, "No society can surely be flourishing and happy, of which the far greater part of the members of that society are poor and miserable." Violent and philosophical reactions to the contradictions between this basic principle and the social realities experienced by the poor would not be long in coming, though strangely they did not reach their most violent peak in the industrial heartland of England.[319]

The new industrialists shared Smith's contempt for the old system. Protestant entrepreneurs of Baptist, Unitarian, Quaker and other persuasions were hard, realistic men who were possessed by spiritual certainty. They not only held the old aristocracy in contempt and felt neither pity nor compassion for their own workers, they knew with absolute certainty that God was in charge of the new "clockwork universe" and under his guidance, it was obvious that God's elect would prosper.

The Church, previously the traditional route to position and education, now provided fewer opportunities, for except for a few Protestant sects it was, in proportion to the rapidly expanding population, in comparative decline. Political factors hastened this; anti-clerical zeal closed many abbeys and convents on the Continent; and respect for the established clergy, long perceived by the public as an arm of the state or as the ally of the aristocracy in Britain, was waning. The major route to position, power and comfort was thus through the exercise of the entrepreneurial spirit. Opportunities for the new inventors and captains of industry expanded, not merely with the population, but also with the new developments of industry itself. Yet all these factors were in turn molded, changed or otherwise affected by another revolution that took place in a foreign country, for different reasons and in a more openly disruptive manner. While the economy of the nineteenth century world was largely formed by the British Industrial Revolution, the politics, ideology and aspirations of that same world were largely formed by the events of 1789 in France.

France gave the world its most vibrant conception and stereotype of mass revolution, and exported political ideas that were imitated worldwide, to the point where a tricolor of some kind became the flag of nearly every emerging nation. Not only European politics, but world politics between the years of 1789 and 1917 were the direct result of struggles for or against the principles of the French Revolution.[320] Yet its background, despite the public perception of it as a populist rising, was as bourgeois as the Industrial Revolution in Britain. The "Declaration of the Rights of Man" states that "The source of all sovereignty resides essentially in the nation." This simple-seeming statement was clarified by the cynical and talented Abbé Sieyes who stated that, "The nation recognized no interest on earth above its own, and accepted no law or authority other than its own – neither that of humanity at large nor of any other nations."

As the French Revolution was a direct challenge to inherited authority, and also had the avowed intention of exporting its explosive and seditious doctrines, the feudal rulers of Europe could not be expected to stand idly by and allow it to proceed unchecked. Aided and abetted by émigré French nobility, a massive invasion began to try and restore the "status quo." An invasion that, like a trail of gunpowder to a barrel, smoldering and spluttering at first, looked relatively manageable and harmless from a distance. But once the main charge was ignited, it was to initiate a series of wars which would engulf not only Europe, but most of the known world, and spread ideals worldwide that even now exert an almost mystical effect on the hearts and minds of oppressed people everywhere – *Liberté, Égalité, Fraternité!*

One of the most enduring concepts to arise out of this revolutionary period is the invention of "total war," which Napoleon perfected: the complete, total, single minded mobilization of all of a nation's resources, through conscription, rationing and a rigidly controlled war economy: the almost complete abolition of any distinction between civilian and soldier, at home or on the battlefield.[321] In countries old or new, feudalism, once officially abolished, was nowhere reinstated. No important continental state west of Russia and Turkey, or south of Scandinavia emerged from these violent decades with its domestic institutions or political borders completely immune to the influences of the French Revolution. More importantly, it was now clearly perceived by the rulers of all European nations that revolution could never again be regarded as purely a national phenomenon. Revolution had affected them all; scarred them all; threatened them all. Revolutionary doctrines respected frontiers no more than revolutionary armies respected the "divine right of kings" or the rights of occupied populations.

The entire period was summed up by Edmund Burke, who wrote: "But the age of chivalry is gone. That of the sophisters, economists and calculators, has succeeded; and the glory of Europe is extinguished forever."[322] As a result of her success in the wars of 1793–1815, Britain found herself without a serious rival in her exploitation of the non-European world, other than the emergent United States. Britain consolidated her hold on the trade routes of the world, not so much by occupying vast tracts of territory, but by fortifying all points crucial to the command of the seas by the Royal Navy. This gave this tiny island a degree of control in political and economic spheres quite disproportionate to her size. By the 1840s the inherent problems of the Industrial Revolution: the new proletariat; the unplanned, slum-like, breakneck expansion of cities; the poverty and injustice of the new order, were almost the sole items on the domestic political agenda of all industrialized nations. The essentially bourgeois nature of the effects of the twin revolutions that occurred in Europe at the end of the eighteenth century were given graphic illustration by the contempt of the middle classes for the working class in Europe. Henri Baudrillart postulated in his inaugural lecture to the College of France in 1853 that, "Human society had three pillars supporting it, inequality among people, property and inheritance."

The new industrial, "enlightened" society, the child of the revolution based on *Liberté, Égalité, Fraternité*, matured into an hierarchical, elitist society based on inequality, property and greed with all the attendant ills of institutionalized poverty, repression and trade wars. The new industrial elite founded their commercial activities on a system that had been rudely stripped of the moral and spiritual basis that had inspired its founding fathers. What was also new was the secularization of the masses. The gentry had long been indifferent to all but the outward, ritualistic observance of religion, often indulging in it only to encourage the "lower orders." Even among those polite and educated gentlemen to whom religion still had some meaning it appeared to relate to a God who performed no discernible function and who certainly did not interfere in the affairs of man or the state. All God seemed to require was polite acknowledgement and occasional thanks.

The Emperor Napoleon once asked the mathematician Pierre-Simon Laplace where God fitted into his scheme of celestial mechanics. Laplace replied, "Sire, I have no need of such a hypothesis." Agnosticism or atheism seemed perfectly compatible with the strong morality, discipline and organization needed by the emerging bourgeoisie in their battles with the new working class. Christianity was deemed unnecessary for this, indeed the new enlightened philosophers were proud that they could demonstrate that a natural morality deriving from "free thinking" was in many ways superior to Christianity. Yet they were shrewd enough to see a clear advantage in maintaining some form of "divine sanction"

HIDDEN WISDOM

in matters of strict morality founded firmly on old-fashioned religious precepts – for the lower orders only, of course!

It is against this complex background that we must examine the spiritual reaction against both the Industrial and the French Revolutions that sprang from the vibrant and dynamic artistic community. The arts not only flourished, they underwent an extraordinary period of development. In the midst of this artistic explosion, which mirrored the first full-flowering of the fruits of Gnosticism in ancient Greece, was embedded a vigorous and dynamic spiritual reaction to both the individual thinkers who sustained the new age and to the material nature of the science they had promulgated. During the twin revolutions, and for well over a century after them, there flourished artists who included Beethoven, Schubert, Goethe, Dickens, Dostoyevsky, Verdi, Wagner, Mozart, Goya, Pushkin and Balzac. There is no doubt that these men were involved in and inspired by the spiritual, political and material realities of the time.[323]

Mozart wrote of Freemasonry in his opera *The Magic Flute*, and it is rumored that he was murdered by the Freemasons of Vienna for disclosing the secrets of initiation. Dickens wrote to expose the squalor, injustice and social abuse that flowed from the new industrial system. Beethoven originally dedicated *The Eroica* to Napoleon, as the heir to the French Revolution. Dostoyevsky was given the death sentence in 1849 for revolutionary activities. Both Wagner and Goya suffered periods of political exile. Balzac's *Comedie Humaine* is a monumental work of immense social awareness. Pushkin was sentenced for involvement with the Decembrists. The great Goethe was, at one and the same time: poet, civil servant, scientist and statesman. All were, in modern parlance, "committed," creative artists. No longer was great art the result of patronage by the Church or the aristocracy; it was in a new and vibrant phase of development. Operas were written as, or understood to be, political in nature; political manifestos that in fact triggered off revolutions.

The philosopher Georg Wilhelm Friedrich Hegel rightly perceived the root cause of the new direction art was taking when he stated: "The essence of romantic art lies in the artistic objects being free, concrete and the spiritual idea in its very essence – all that is revealed to the inner rather than to the outer eye." Giving visible form to this spiritual ideal brought the artists into direct conflict with the men and the systems they most distrusted. Issac Newton was correctly viewed as the father of the society and of the system they knew was unjust, atheistic and inhumane. It was from this artistic and spiritual perspective that reaction against the new materialistic science sprang most fiercely, notably from two great poets, William Blake in England, and Johann Wolfgang von Goethe in Weimar.

It is ironic that Blake's spiritual roots had much in common with the understanding gained by his arch-opponent Newton, for both were sustained by a strong vein of mysticism – direct links can be discerned which lead back directly and inevitably to the "old gnosis." In Blake's case the influences which brought about his particular insight are known to be derived from varied strands, including Jacob Boehme, Emanuel Swedenborg, the Gnostics, the Kabbala and, above all, from the Revelation of St. John. To Blake, poet and mystic, all these separate influences were perceived as aspects of one unity: they were all shadows of the same mystery and each separate strand was both part of the whole, and the whole of which the others were part.

Blake's understanding was founded firmly on a harsh appreciation of the brutal material reality of his time. According to Joseph Priestley, following closely in Blake's steps, "Christ was thwarted by religion." Benjamin Franklin, following the same logic, proposed the idea that "Law thwarts Desire gratified." Blake himself claimed that "man-made famine thwarts the plenty that man himself makes." This was the evil against which he fought all his life. Over 150 years later the psychologist Carl Jung came to a similar disturbing conclusion: "Religion is a defence against the experience of God."[324] To all his readers it is soon apparent that Blake took an informed, insightful and apt interest in the events occurring in the world around him, yet, according to Julius Bronowski at least, "Unless we see the revolutionary in his politics and the gnosis in his religion, we simply do not see Blake as he really was."[325]

When Blake attacked the society he lived in, it was to act as a stimulus towards a divinely ordered system of justice and equity.[326] He attacked the institutions that supported the injustices inherent in society as well as the individuals who had developed its new thinking. He wrote: "Prisons are built with the stones of Law, Brothels with the bricks of Religion." He had little tolerance for those who thought as he did but who remained inactive, saying: "He who desires but acts not, breeds pestilence."

Similar views formed an integral component of the artistic insight of William Wordsworth. Condemned, or merely critically described by many commentators, as "pagan," he was far from that. His insightful genius sprang from the old gnosis, which, with the clarity of spiritual vision, spoke movingly of "higher minds" or "higher consciousness." His mystical conception of the infusion of the spirit which is within all created things, is the same insight shared by all the Christian mystics, to say nothing of the native peoples so abused and harried by their civilized colonizers.

The truly outstanding genius among the ranks of those gifted and perceptive men who reacted against the new "scientific rationalism" was undoubtedly Goethe. Theodore Roszak wrote, "In Goethe, the best of Blake and Wordsworth meet: Blake's transcendent symbolism drawn from the esoteric tradition – Gnosticism, Christian cabbalism, the Hermetica; Wordsworth's sacramental vision of nature."[327] The wide, all-embracing scope and inclusive nature of Goethe's interest is well documented, for it is as a scientist in the true Gnostic tradition that his pre-eminent position is most startlingly revealed. Goethe believed that scientific phenomena could not be explained purely in physical terms, that reductionism told an incomplete and misleading "truth." For this genius there was only one source of knowledge – the world of experience within which the world of ideas is only one part of a far greater whole. For him it was impossible to say "experience and idea" because for him the idea lies through spiritual experience before the inner spiritual eye, in the same way that the sense-world lies before the physical eye.[328] Newton and his followers had fallen into the trap of detaching the idea from the sense-world and viewing it as a separate entity, thus viewing nature as devoid of ideas. Goethe himself determined to use his perception as an instrument of scientific investigation at the level of higher consciousness: a form of Gnosticism he used to transcend the boundaries of the sense-world and arrive at an objective understanding of the spiritual forces which sustain and inform the temporal reality we see before us.

Goethe sought for expressions of spiritual reality for the organic union between all of nature, echoing Boehme and earlier Gnostic occultists. These conceptions were precisely those which resisted Cartesian, rational, reductionist analysis. This was not surprising as Goethe and those who followed him were in a state of outright rebellion against just this materialistic reductionism. Thus we can see how the inevitable conflict arises between spiritual perception, which stresses the interconnectedness of the whole, and the reductionist approach which attempts to explain the whole by an analysis of its separate material parts. The thinking, investigative world was now apparently irretrievably split between the majority of Cartesian scientists and the minority of spiritually gifted initiates. This divisive situation was highlighted by the effects of applying the newly dominant rationalist system in all walks of life. Man was now separated from his previous religious certainties, alienated from nature and, for the vast majority of people, living in grinding poverty, injustice and squalor.

Economic inequalities were not the only ones to become apparent. There were differences in educational standards too. Cultural and religious elements played their part in the value accorded to education. There was a notably greater emphasis given to mass education among Protestants and Western Jews than among Catholics, Muslims or Hindus. Enlightened, middle class England raised hypocrisy to new heights. The bourgeoisie could attain "enlightenment"; the poor had need of "socially useful superstition" – as indeed had less talented members of the middle classes themselves. Post-revolutionary France provided the most fertile nursery bed for attempts to create a bourgeois non-Christian system of morality using the Rousseauist idea of a "cult of the supreme being." There was even an attempt to deify "reason" itself and erect an altar to it in the Cathedral of Notre Dame in Paris.

While the middle classes remained divided between increasingly frank freethinkers and a majority of adherents to all form of organized religion, the freethinking segment, though small, was immeasurably more dynamic and productive. In Britain, pious Protestants were in the overwhelming majority, yet freethinkers such as Jeremy Bentham had more impact on the age than Christians such as William Wilberforce. One dominant and pervasive result of this triumph of the "enlightened" over the "religious" ideologies was that, flowing from the democratic revolutions in

America and France, all major social and political movements had become secularized. In the worldwide context, comparative to rapidly increasing populations with the notable exceptions of Islam in the East and radical Protestantism in Europe – organized, formal religion was in decline, if not in actual retreat.

Shortly after the beginning of the nineteenth century the intellectual and spiritual climate of Western Europe had completely changed among the literate classes, from one wherein religion played an important, almost supreme, role to an atheistic society whose intellectual elite fell over themselves to dissociate from the "superstitious practices" of the Middle Ages. F. Schaubach, writing on popular literature in 1863, remarked, "It is almost as though people want to show how intelligent they think they are by the degree of their emancipation from the Bible and the Catechism." The strange thing was that even among so-called freethinkers, a strong nostalgia remained for at least the outward forms of religion. For the middle class of course, religion was regarded as a useful institution that helped to maintain the poor in a suitable state of modesty, obedience and acceptance of authority. The intellectual domination exerted by atheists and agnostics was such that all the mainstream churches could do was to retire within their powerful fortifications and prepare for a long siege. The mid-nineteenth century became full of invented secular ritual – some of which harked back directly to earlier esoteric movements in outward form at least. The Catholic Church, in a vain attempt to regain its authority, distanced itself even further from reality. The dogma of "papal infallibility" – carefully worded so as to appear retrospective – was, self-evidently, ludicrous, especially in the light of the historical records of the brutal activities of the popes. Catholicism, like the papacy that ran it, was increasingly becoming a prisoner of its own desperate pronouncements.

The rising tide of scientific and rational triumphalism had almost overwhelmed the remaining bastions of entrenched, traditional religion. Not so much in terms of the numbers of their adherents, but in the pervasive and powerful influence they exerted in everyday life. By the early 1900s, both intellectually and politically, Western religion was in full retreat, metaphorically, in a state of siege: barricaded, like the papal prisoner in the Vatican, against the world; imprisoned in fortress-like enclaves, set to resist or at least outlast, the continuing assaults its ideology received from the new thinking.

Science, now freed from its mystical ballast and no longer fettered in its thinking by religious dogma, raced ahead at breathtaking speed, promising knowledge and power beyond the layman's wildest dreams. In less than two centuries it had transformed the outlook and physical life of ordinary men, and completely changed the face of the Earth itself. It has brought mankind untold benefits – but at the price of imminent self-destruction on a planet that will outlive us, at the cost of spiritual starvation, alienation and inner emptiness. Sailing without ballast, reality itself seemed to have dissolved between the physicists' hands; spirituality had seemingly disappeared, and matter itself seemed set to vanish from the material universe.

Elena Petrovna Gan (H. P. Blavatsky), founder of the Theosophical Society, 1877.

CHAPTER 17

Nationalism, Imperialism And The Esoteric Revival

By 1880 the "developed" world consisted overwhelmingly of countries or regions in which the majority of the male and increasingly the female population was literate, in which politics, economics and intellectual life in general had emancipated themselves from the tutelage of the ancient religions, bulwarks of traditionalism and superstition, and which virtually monopolized the sort of science which was increasingly essential for modern technology.[329]   –Eric Hobsbawm, *The Age of Empire*

The rise of the modern imperial ideal was a phenomenon of the nineteenth century, building on foundations laid down far earlier and fueled by the new thinking that arose from the dual revolutions. History from 1776 until 1914 traces the global transformation that resulted from the ongoing development and triumph of "liberal bourgeois society."[330] The Industrial Revolution showed the way to apparently limitless growth and the consequent prosperity for the few at the expense of the new class of landless workers. This callous exploitation was replicated in the brutality, hypocrisy and sheer greed that were intrinsic factors in all the imperial adventures of the Christian nations of Europe that followed. As industrialization spread across Northern Europe, Marx and Engels were far from being the only critics of its results or philosophy.

The philosophy that fueled and underpinned the Industrial Revolution provided both a new impetus and the effective means for global penetration by the trade and thinking of the West. Above all, it strengthened the motivation for this new imperial age: the institutionalization of pure greed for new markets allied with further greed for cheap raw materials and the immense profits that could accrue from trade. The avaricious rush for markets was outwardly clothed with the desire to transform the world with the benefits of the new theoretical systems that arose from the twin revolutions, classical political economy and its twin concomitant, utilitarian philosophy. Thus the confident conquest of the globe went arm in arm with the ideologies and concepts of liberal, bourgeois democracy.

The difficulties and conflicts that were integral factors within the developing capitalist system were apparently to be overcome simply by the creation of new markets in the colonies. The downward spread of growing prosperity from the booming factories through fuller employment for the workers certainly helped to diffuse the simmering discontent that existed among the laboring classes throughout Europe. For a short time it appeared as if all the major obstacles to capitalist growth, progress and development had magically been removed. This resulted, for some years at least, in a lessening of political reaction. This was also an unprecedented era of "world peace." Diversions such as the Crimean War, colonial conflicts and skirmishes were considered relatively minor and either ignored or taken as the inevitable price that had to be paid for the twin benefits of "peace" and "prosperity." The question arising naturally from this view of history is "How did this time of stability, prosperity and peace between nations lead to the era of world war?" It was the very contradictions inherent in Europe itself, rather than continuous capitalist growth in a limited world or the rebellious and revolutionary actions at the periphery of empire, that were to provide the fertile seedbeds of further conflict – worldwide conflict that would remodel the world in a very different mold.

The concepts of freedom founded on the French revolutionary ideals of *Liberté, Égalité, Fraternité* continued to spread beyond Europe and affect the globe. Slavery was officially abolished from its final strongholds in Brazil and Cuba by the late 1880s. Nonetheless, legalized freedom and so-called equality soon proved to be entirely compatible with massive deprivation for the many and conspicuous wealth for the few. It fell to Anatole France to express this unpleasant reality in the following terms: "The Law in its majestic equality gives every man the same right to dine at the Ritz and to sleep under a bridge." Money, or the lack of it, now became the single most important arbiter of social status, privilege and above all, power.

The inexorable march to "imperial glory" flowed directly from the massive change in understanding of the universe that occurred as a result of the triumph of Cartesian and scientific philosophies. This was given further emphasis by feedback from its psychological consequences. The bourgeoisie, by re-structuring their intellectual forces, deleted all influences derived from the old religious theology from their new understanding of the world and all its works. Religion and the miraculous no longer had a place in their view of nature, and their philosophy tended to spring from a scientific view of nature rather than from religious belief. Nature itself became, in effect, both less natural and more scientific – and increasingly more incomprehensible. Technical processes were of immense advantage, but how many who came to use and take for granted new advances such as electricity, could actually understand the theories upon which it was based? So began an ever-accelerating alienation for the bourgeoisie. This took many forms, none so strange perhaps as that among the reactionaries of the political Right, such as Friedrich Nietzsche, who used pseudo-science to justify their racial and class theories, and yet at the same time both suspected and distrusted science itself.

The great changes brought about by industrialization have, with the exception of a few scattered and aberrant countries such as Poland, been generally associated with a decline in religious tradition. In the industrially dominant countries of the West the so-called, mainly Protestant "liberal democratic" states, the cultural prescription was simple: the individual himself is alone responsible for his salvation, he should think for himself on all questions regarding the ultimate.

Was there no place in this new materialistic world for spiritual matters? Who then were the legatees on whom would fall the mantle of Blake and Goethe? Were the emasculated and embattled churches to be the sole repositories of the last failing vestiges of spirituality in the nineteenth century? They did mount an impressive effort to evangelize the inferior natives of the colonies at that time, showing that they still had some strength and commitment left. Some might claim that the orders of Freemasons carried the spiritual torch forward into the modern era, and it is arguable that in some form they did indeed do so. Coming more into the open in the seventeenth century, they proliferated in Germany, France, England and throughout the new empires. But they were not alone in this spiritual resurgence. From the one corner of the globe that had staunchly resisted all efforts at Christian evangelism arose an impulse that was to have a lasting effect. From the unlikely country of Tibet came one spiritual vision that sustained the knowledge of the super sensible in the materialistic age of empire. It came not through a Tibetan national, who would have been derided as an "inferior" and a heathen, but through the efforts of an unlikely, eccentric and talented Russian lady. Her name was Helena Petrovna Blavatsky.

This remarkable woman was born in Southern Russia in 1831, the daughter of Peter von Hahn and Helena de Fadeef. She showed precocious talents for a girl of that time and place, and became an exceptionally gifted linguist, fluent in modern and classical languages. From early childhood she had exhibited strong psychic powers and became convinced that she had some great, yet unexplained, purpose in life.[331] After a brief and disastrous marriage, now supported financially by her father, Helena began a lifetime of travel in the belief that she was destined to help stem the rising tide of materialism which was sweeping the West and spreading over the entire globe, breaking down the old entrenched bastions of Christianity. She was to rebut the rising domination of the new scientific thinking and replace it with the esoteric knowledge that, until then, had been the sole preserve of initiates and masters of the ancient wisdom. Her purpose was to teach altruism and display to mankind nobler and more ancient ideas than those of the current materialism.

She founded the Theosophical Society in New York in 1875, naming it with the Greek term *theosophia*, a word apparently coined by Ammonius Saccas of Alexandria in the third century CE, meaning the "wisdom of the gods." The co-founders of this society were both lawyers, Colonel H. S. Olcott and W. Q. Judge.[332] The stated aims were both "to study psychic phenomena" and also "to investigate the unexplained laws in nature and the powers latent in man." In New York she became a figure of controversy, accused of a variety of fraudulent practices as part of a violent campaign of denunciation by fundamentalist Christians. There was also a bitter and antagonistic response to much of her teaching from the same quarters. Doubt also surrounds her reputed travels; she herself claims that she took great pains to cover all traces of her many voyages, and it has indeed proved difficult, if not impossible, to trace her movements over many years. Colin Wilson casts great doubt over many of her claims.[333] Be that as it may, it must be remembered that her two co-founders were both lawyers of repute and experienced in the evaluation of evidence and witnesses. They, unlike Wilson, met "HPB" as she was now known, and worked closely with her for many years. The modern English judge and commentator, Christmas Humphreys, another independent man of considerable forensic skill, accepted without question that HPB's accounts are valid.

Blavatsky's written works include the two monumental volumes entitled *Isis Unveiled*, which were written in a great hurry early in her Theosophical career and which the authoress herself admits contain many errors. She reformed the society on her arrival in India in 1879 with the simplified aim: "To form the nucleus of the universal brotherhood of humanity." The total acceptance there of her basic thinking caused a transformation in her attitudes. Gone was the psychic trickery and mediumship, to be replaced by a strong reinforcement of her teaching. Apparent proof of validity of the origins of her spiritual message came with the publication of correspondence between one of her pupils, A. P. Sinnet, the editor of *The Pioneer* of Allahabad, and her spiritual masters. This was published as the *Mahatma Letters to A. P. Sinnet* in London in 1929. This work, taken with HPB's own monumental legacy *The Secret Doctrine*, now forms the principal source of early Theosophy. The Theosophical Society spread widely, especially in the English-speaking world. German branches took longer to get established, yet one of these became the springboard into public life for the greatest modern esotericist of the Western tradition, Rudolf Steiner.

Steiner, a graduate in the new scientific thinking, had read Theosophical books as early as 1884, although he claims not to have been unduly influenced by them.[334] He became interested in Goethe's imaginative, holistic science, which he perceived as the true bridge between the material world so extolled by his contemporaries, and the spiritual world he so firmly believed sustained it. At the age of twenty-two he edited Goethe's writings on natural science for a new edition of *Deutschen Nationalliteratur*. Steiner moved to Weimar in 1890, and his doctoral thesis was accepted by the University of Rostock in 1891. He remained in Weimar until 1897 and completed seven years of intensive work in the Goethian archives, at that time a point of intersection for scientific, artistic and courtly circles. The dilemma that beset this brilliant and exceptional man in regard to his spiritual vision was "how could he remain silent."[335] Yet if he spoke openly of his growing and persistent spiritual perceptions, who would listen? He broke his silence at meetings organized by the Berlin branch of the Theosophical Society, the very organization he had previously dismissed so casually. This was to be the launch pad for his first public declamation of belief. By 1902 he had become the effective leader of the German Theosophists, progressing to establish his own movement, "Anthroposophy," prior to the First World War.

The spread of Theosophy in Europe was facilitated by the spiritual climate that pervaded the intellectual elite. The decline of religion among the educated bourgeoisie and the artistic community stimulated a veritable explosion of interest in esoteric matters. The old gnosis was undergoing one of its periodic, public revivals, but now in a climate where the Inquisition no longer held sway and intellectual and spiritual freedom were the norm. In England,

Germany and especially France, esoteric orders were revived or established with baffling speed. Templar orders were reinstituted, many claiming some form of spurious or illusory descent from the original Knights, others as offshoots of Freemasonry. The Order of the Golden Dawn derived from one of them. In response to this growing climate of spiritual inquiry, a vast number of books on Templarism, magic and the occult began to flood the markets in France, Germany and England. Theosophy found ready acceptance among the bohemian fraternity of artists and intellectuals right across Europe. Anthroposophy, with its emphasis on Goethian themes, took easy root in Germany and then spread steadily, apparently impervious to man-made frontiers. Goethian beliefs also played a formative role in the thinking and perception of a technical genius of immense influence and creative ability. This gifted and original man was possessed of instinctive powers and perception that had a strangely practical and scientific application. This mysterious figure was Nikola Tesla.

Tesla had an innately spiritual conception of the world. His belief system conceived that nature did not break down at all into separate and fully describable systems that could then be fitted together again to make a fully describable whole. He knew that institutional science was inadequate, narrow and self-limiting and that it produced biased descriptions of reality which only fitted the scientific method with all its limitations, and therefore could not describe nature as a whole, vibrant entity. He questioned the concept of scientific objectivity and proposed that there were alternative frameworks of reality, which are dependent upon the attitude and perception of the individual.[336] Tesla saw with an inward eye, much as Goethe described – almost clairvoyantly – the machines and concepts he designed. His stimulating and provocative spiritual viewpoint and the productive results that ensued provoked more controversy than almost any other scientist, living or dead. He was responsible for the conception, design and construction of a prodigious series of inventions. Kit Pedler describes Tesla in the following terms:

> Throughout his life he was constantly driven to struggle free from his ordinary human state – to soar on a wing away from the soil perhaps. He possessed a quite superhuman urge to see into the unknown fabric of the universe, which was quite different from the more prosaic and codified enquiry of the ordinary scientists ... From his earliest days as a child right up to the time of his death, he seems to have had a consistent view of how we could take the energy we needed from the earth without damaging its fabric ... I do not at all mean that he was subject to great visions of God who spoke to him, but that he was able occasionally to understand, or have revealed to him, aspects of a living integrated whole ... He seemed to go into some sort of resonance with the forces of nature, much as a tuned receiver goes into resonance with incoming waves.[337]

Tesla discovered the principles of alternating current, designing the machines to generate and transmit it. He did original work on the principles of cosmic rays, the detailed structure of X-rays and the fundamentals of radio transmission, well before the scientists who are usually credited with their discovery. As a result of his capacity to visualize, Tesla could produce answers to the most complex technological problems almost instantaneously. He stated that he was able to see calculations actually occurring before him stage by stage, the solution appearing as if he were watching someone else perform in front of him upon a blackboard. He was possessed of an innate capacity to visualize three-dimensional images of new machinery in his mind's eye, in such a way as to be able to move it around in order to perceive it from different perspectives. Tesla seemed to embody the conception phrased by the scientist and philosopher Arthur Eddington: "The universe looks less and less like a machine, and more like a great thought." It was from the spiritual perceptions of Tesla, and not from the methods of science, that one of mankind's most universally applicable benefits came to fruition. Tesla, more than any other individual, made possible the entire electrical-generating system that we take for granted today. Towards the end of his life, he began to conceive of the entire substance of the planet as a manageable system, and began to draw up plans for the global transmission of energy and intelligence.

Tesla, unique among the innovators and inventors of the new technological age because of the spiritual basis of his perceptions, was far from alone in being spiritually or clairvoyantly motivated in his thinking. Goethian themes and conclusions were echoed from another Christian source, this time from the East. The nineteenth century Russian philosopher Vladimir Solovyov wrote in his *Philosophy of the Organic* that the Earth behaves like a living organism.[338] This apparently bizarre theory might have been dismissed at that time as the wild imaginings of yet another mystic from the Eastern Church were it not for the other intriguing insights that he disclosed. *The Philosophy of the Organic* was undoubtedly inspired by a conception of cosmic Christianity that forms a bridge between science and spirituality in a truly prophetic manner predating much of the later, more scientific, work of Pierre Teilhard de Chardin in the mid-twentieth century and the formulation of the "Gaia hypothesis" by James Lovelock in the space age. It was out of this same spiritual vision, inspired by the "Revelation of St. John" that Solovyov wrote a further book,

The Anti-Christ, that foretold with uncanny accuracy the rise to power of Adolf Hitler and the destruction that would be wreaked upon the world by that evil genius.[339] It is particularly ironic that such works were published at a time when the intellectual world was largely dominated by a philosophy that ruthlessly excluded the spiritual from all debate and concentrated almost exclusively on the materialist sciences.

Scientific advances continued to exert their all-pervasive influence upon the Western world. The way in which the general public perceived scientific and technological thinking had changed dramatically. Even the deprived classes in the liberal bourgeois states benefited, albeit indirectly, from science. Public health, a scandal for so long in the early years of the Industrial Revolution, was revolutionized by two simple measures. The construction of public sewage systems in the Victorian era, and the delivery of potable, piped water, thus eliminating in one fell swoop the terrors of cholera, enteric fevers and other epidemics resulting from mankind's more insanitary habits. Growing prosperity; an ever-more stable and literate bourgeoisie; the spreading of material benefits via full employment; patriotism for the new concepts of nation; increased trade and prosperity; utopian visions of the emergence of a better society; growing literacy as a result of mass education – all these interlinked and complex factors combined to create a highly seductive illusion that misled millions. This entrancing vision was of a stable, peaceful world that would continue to enjoy peace, prosperity and constant improvement in living standards as a direct result of man's inventiveness, industry and growing mastery of the clockwork universe.

The partition of the globe among a handful of nations with imperial ambitions was perhaps the most striking example of the increasing division between the "strong" and the "weak"; "developed and "undeveloped." The word "imperial" itself gained a distinctly economic dimension that it has never lost. The economic consequences of imperialism had obvious benefits for the ruling classes and the bourgeoisie, not only because of the direct and personal financial profits that ensued, but also because of the social reforms that could be financed from them. Imperialism began to seem, for a while at least, like a perfect ideological cement to bind the nation together.[340]

The new functionaries of the colonized countries, native born and therefore despised, were nonetheless deemed useful and became increasingly relied upon to keep the wheels of empire turning. For these new servants of the colonial regimes, as for their ancient and traditional masters, the lesson was simple – westernize or lose all position and power. It is perhaps inevitable that those who learned this enforced lesson should also learn to apply the ideals of "Western Enlightenment" and use their elite status allied to older, more traditional concepts, to foment rebellion and reaction against their colonial masters. Gandhi saw his mobilization of the Indian masses as a fusion between the ideas of John Ruskin and Leo Tolstoy married together with Eastern spiritual tradition. This for him was the sole means by which Western imperialism could be overcome. His movement was staffed by an elite corps of men who were all the direct beneficiaries of the systematic westernization imposed by the very conquerors they fought against. While the possibility of global conflict was viewed as a possible consequence of continued economic competition, the general public romanticized war itself. The first-hand experience of the terrible devastation war could bring had faded from the folk memory of the people. Rising nationalism gave vent to feelings of intense patriotism. No longer did Samuel Johnson's dictum that "Patriotism is the last refuge of a scoundrel" gain uncritical acceptance. Patriotism, like imperialism, was now one of the essential constituents of the cement that bound the nation together.

Throughout the later part of the nineteenth century, industrial development continued its almost exponential expansion in the Western developed countries. Conflicts that arose from the rival imperial ambitions of the European powers were settled largely by diplomatic means. Europe itself enjoyed for the most part an unprecedented era of unbroken peace. The only European war of note was the Franco-Prussian War of 1870, which proved to be a triumph for the German military and industrial establishment and an intensely humiliating episode for the French, who lost the provinces of Alsace and Lorraine as a result. Large-scale war, although always planned for, was considered a rather remote possibility.

Many explanations have been offered for the breakdown in this peaceful balance between the European powers, each tainted with the bias endemic in the political perspective and distortions inherent in the beliefs of their proponents. To later socialists the simplistic explanation was the economic rivalries between the major belligerents. Others blamed imperial tensions. Right-wing extremists placed the responsibility squarely at the feet of the socialists and their allies. None of these explanations are even remotely adequate. The sudden transition from prolonged peace to total war – one that was greeted with such patriotic fervor by the ordinary people of each of the belligerent countries – cannot be explained away so simplistically. And yet the most likely explanation seems at first glance to be even less plausible.

The tensions arising from the grandiose rearmament schemes of Britain, Germany and France acting within the unlikely alliances that developed as a result of France's fear of German militarism and Britain's perceptions of her declining naval might, created a political time bomb whose fuse was set ticking, not by foreign colonial rivalries nor by competition for trade, industrial unrest or socialist agitation, but from the actions of a small group of conspirators within the tottering Austro-Hungarian Empire. One man, Gavrilo Princip, a Serbian nationalist, lit the fuse that was to lead to Austria's declaration of war. Because of the complex and antagonistic alliances that existed this act led inevitably and irrevocably to worldwide conflict. The world can be said to have slid into war just as a careless mountaineer can slide off a precipice. All the ingredients of nationalistic pride, military planning, mass mobilization, patriotism and the full might of the military-industrial complex came together as the inevitable result of Austria's reaction to the assassination of the archduke at Sarajevo. Neither the assassination nor the war that followed were truly inevitable. The attempt at assassination almost failed, and people of greater power had been assassinated before without world conflict ensuing. This time, however, once one country – Austria – panicked and declared war, the other countries of Europe, yoked together by their alliances, inevitably and catastrophically followed suit. The *Belle Époque* was over with a vengeance. The nightmare scenario of worldwide destruction that ensued changed the world forever. Nothing would ever be the same again for the old rulers, the nations and empires they ruled, or for the ordinary citizens who went to the slaughter with such misplaced enthusiasm for the glories of war.

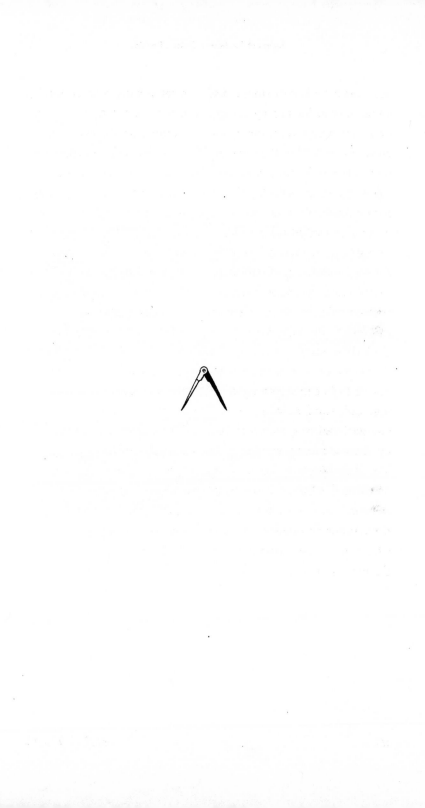

Atomic bombing of Nagasaki on August 9, 1945.

CHAPTER 18

The War To End All War;
And Some Of The Wars That Followed It

War is a series of catastrophes which result in victory.[341]

– Georges Clemanceau

Vladimir Solovyov was not the only spiritually inspired Russian intellectual with prophetic vision in the nineteenth century. His unlikely companion was the Jewish financier Ivan Bloch, whose six-volume treatise entitled *Technical, Economic and Political Aspects of the Coming War* was published in St. Petersburg in 1898. This predicted with uncanny accuracy both the stalemate of prolonged trench warfare and the intolerable economic, military and human costs that would exhaust the belligerents or plunge them into social revolution. Despite translation into many languages, the vivid warnings within its pages failed to make any impact whatsoever on either the generals or politicians of Europe.[342] The so-called civilized world, the continent which contained all the "mother countries" of the various empires, slid inexorably towards the very horrifying reality he predicted.

More has been written about the First World War than about any other conflict in history, and little needs to be recounted here. The patriotic and enthusiastic armies who met in conflict faced four years of mortal, soul destroying battle in the shell-pitted wastes of no-man's land; death amid the leafless stumps of Flanders; mutilation, death, disease and destruction in the gory, ghastly, pointless struggle for Gallipoli; intense suffering in the snow-filled wastes of Russia; or the loneliness of a last resting place in the vast, cold, watery grave that stretched from the Falkland Islands to Jutland. Millions of men confronted one another in a prolonged nightmare of death and mechanized destruction in the veritable hades of trench warfare. As all knew their "divinely ordered place" in society, they were each absolutely convinced that "God was with them!" The unprecedented magnitude of this suffering was perhaps the only means by which mankind could shatter the delusions, values and ideologies of the days of empire, while at the same time destroying the very ruling classes and systems that had propagated them.

Socialist reaction to the war was minimal. Marxist theorists condemned it, yet their followers in the hundreds of thousands joined in the mad, demented scramble for glory with the same mindless enthusiasm as their bourgeois fellow countrymen. In only one country did the working class strike their blow for freedom, and that was but a feeble blow, however courageous it may have been. These men took on the mightiest empire the world had ever known, and by their glorious failure lit the torch of freedom that was to signal the eventual demise of an entire empire. The Irish Citizen Army, in alliance with the Irish Republican Brotherhood, rose in active rebellion at the Easter weekend of 1916. Britain then made the classic mistake of making martyrs of the leaders of this bloody but abortive putsch, and thus provoked a guerrilla war that eventually resulted in a measure of freedom for much of Ireland. The poet William Butler Yeats described this armed rising as one wherein "A terrible beauty has been born."[343] These armed members of the Irish Transport Union were later described by Vladimir Lenin as the "First Red Army in Europe."

The second Red Army was not long in coming, for another empire, the Russian, was deliberately placed in peril by its own revolutionary people with the active connivance of the aristocratic leaders of its mortal enemy, the Germans.

The German General Staff and government arranged for the transportation of Lenin and his fellow revolutionaries from Switzerland, through Germany and on to Russia, by means of the so-called "sealed train."[344] Thus the German aristocracy were prepared to assist in the destruction of the Russian czar and his nobility in order to remove the threat posed by the failing Russian armies on the German's Eastern Front. The Russian Revolution, which took place in 1917, was an attempt by a materialist and atheistic ideology to impose the concepts of equality of opportunity and human rights from above. In the aftermath of the Great War it became apparent that this effort was as doomed, fundamentally flawed and even more tyrannical than the autocratic, aristocratic system it had replaced. Ideologies started to replace royal bloodlines in the nations and empires of Europe, and the supposed cure was soon to prove more fatal than the disease it purported to treat.

The immediate aftermath of the so-called "Great War" – the "War To End All Wars" – was the re-drawing of the map of Europe by the Treaty of Versailles and the various other treaties that signaled the end of conflict. Arbitrary boundaries were drawn delineating states that had no realistic justification in geography, but founded more in myth and folk memory than on any rational appreciation of the needs and aspirations of the people whose interests they claimed to serve. Shaky and untried democratic regimes were instituted in nations and states that lacked defensible and justifiable boundaries; new countries that had no experience whatsoever of the democratic process. Germany was blamed as the aggressor in the conflict and penal reparations were imposed upon her truncated remnants that bore as little regard to her capacity to pay them as they did upon the spurious justification invoked to impose them. America, after initiating the League of Nations, retreated into isolationism once more and Europe was left to her own devices. Despoiled by four years of conflict, riven by new divisions and discontent arising out of the peace treaties, and with the great bear of Russia, now an avowedly Marxist state, surrounding her Eastern borders and preaching international revolution, the "War To End All Wars" was over. Sadly, war itself, was not.

The demobilized armies returned to their homes. Having fought a war to make the world fit for heroes to live in, for many the prospect was bleak indeed. Unemployment, recession, wage cuts for the employed, hyperinflation, political chaos and a violent struggle for political power were common in many states. Whole populations had been decimated. Casualties were reckoned in millions and few families, if any, in the belligerent countries were short of dead to mourn. For those who survived, the abject terror to which they had been subjected, would distort and disfigure the rest of their lives. In Russia the long drawn-out agony continued. World war was replaced with a civil war of such ferocity that it is truly unimaginable. The proponents of capitalism were not prepared to stand idly by and see the creation of a state dedicated to the downfall of their own system, so they took part with unholy gusto. The new Russian leadership and the armies of the new socialist state were faced by a determined military challenge mounted by a host of invading forces. Not only had they to fight their own countrymen – the White Russian Army – they had to combat the combined might of the British, the Poles, the Japanese, the Americans, the French, the Italians and the Czech legion under Aleksandr Kolchak, which ruled more of Russia than Lenin's army. Peasant armies eager for loot also joined in.

Winston Churchill and Ferdinand Foch urged a full-scale invasion to stop communism in its tracks, but the various expeditionary forces were all that were sent. The Red Army, under the leadership of Leon Trotsky, fought them all – and won, but at horrendous cost.[345] The Union of Soviet Socialist Republics was established. The true cost of Western intervention was to be paid for decades to come. World history ever since has been shaped and formed from twin fears: that revolution spreading from Russia on the one hand, and Russian distrust and justifiable fear of invasion on the other. Contrary to common public perception, the "Cold War" started thirty years earlier than it is generally thought. It was rooted in the aftermath of the First World War, not the Second.

After the defeat of the White Russian Army and the withdrawal of the foreign interventionists, Russia retreated behind her borders to begin the process of reconstruction. After the death of Lenin, power was seized by Joseph Stalin, who used it with ruthless ferocity. Stalin dragged Russia from its feudal, inefficient past into the process of twentieth century industrialization by fear, brutality and repression. His means were murder, genocide, forced collectivization and the creation of a police state whose main weapons were terror and betrayal. The full extent of his crimes against humanity will, in all probability, never be fully known. Even today his crimes are still coming to light, and the legacy of fear that he bequeathed, not merely to Russia but to the world, still distorts international relations. At the very beginning of the Stalinist era however, the rest of the world took little or no notice, for capitalism had its own deep-seated problems to contend with.

The spiritually bereft world of the post-1918 era was irretrievably malformed, politically and economically, by the collapse of stability that this inconclusive war brought in its train. The collapse of the "Age of Empire," and the failed ideology that had appeared so stable in the years before the worldwide conflict, heralded a massive crisis within the free-market capitalist system. After a period of recession and some recovery, came the Great Slump of the 1930s. This was probably the only system-endangering crisis that capitalism has suffered so far in its history.[346] The market economy, by its very nature, operates through cyclical fluctuations, but in the chaotic conditions that prevailed in many European countries in the aftermath of the Great War, the need for a rethink on the very principles of capitalism was all too apparent. In Italy, fascism, an undemocratic right-wing dictatorship unifying the capitalists and the government, appeared to provide the answers. In Germany, there was a period of prolonged civil disorder as the forces of the political Right and Left struggled for supremacy. It was only after the Great Slump that the true prophet of capitalist reformation began to make his voice heard.

John Maynard Keynes, an Old Etonian, a student at Kings College and a member of what he himself described as the "educated bourgeoisie," was to be the new savior of the capitalist system. Faced with the irrevocable end of the *Belle Époque* he had lived through and enjoyed, Keynes began to devote all his brilliance, intellectual skill and ingenuity to devising the means by which capitalism could reform itself and survive, thus ensuring the survival of his class, his family and his ideals. The basis of his argument was that capitalism could only survive if the states controlled, managed and planned the general shape of their economies and, in certain circumstances, were prepared to turn them into mixed economies, a combination of both public and private ownership of key industries.[347] This message, although understood, was not to be fully acted upon until after a further world war which resulted directly from the inequities of the peace treaty that had ended the first.

In the strife-ridden atmosphere of post-war Germany, there were still some oases of peace and calm to be found. In the '20s, the "groves of academe" were as yet untroubled by the winds of change that were a portent of troubled times to come. The focal point of study and research into pure physics was at Göttingen. These were the halcyon days of Göttingen's post-war period, so much so that the unofficial motto of the university was *Extra Gottingam Non Est Vita* ("Outside of Göttingen there is no life"). Both the student body and the faculty members knew that they were the intellectual elite in the vanguard of the prince of sciences: theoretical physics. The pursuit of pure knowledge by a whole sequence of young geniuses in the totally abstract field of physics delved into a sub-stratum of nature that appeared to be completely divorced from the realities of everyday life. The development of mathematical formulae, the apparently limitless search for knowledge, new and fascinating theoretical structures, were all pursued for their own sakes. The physicists hoped to discover the secrets that would unveil the fundamental building blocks of ultimate reality, giving little thought to the eventual application for mankind that would result from their study of the minute particles of matter and how the nucleus of the atom could be artificially disintegrated.

It is not within the competence of this work to recount the history of the development of theoretical physics. The leading figures in this field are now known to the general public as a result of the public horror and revulsion which was the direct consequence of the unveiling of the fruits of their labors. Ernest Rutherford working in Cambridge; Neils Bohr in Copenhagen; Frédéric and Irène Joliot-Curie in Paris; Enrico Fermi in Italy; Max Planck, Felix Klein, Max Born, James Franck, and David Hibbert from Göttingen; Arnold Sommerfeld from Munich; and the partnership of Otto Hahn and Lise Meitner from Berlin, all played their part in the ascent of the new dominance of science in the inter-war years. Göttingen was the epicenter of this hive of intellectual enquiry. Among the many foreign students who attended *Georg-August-Universität* in this ancient city was the American Robert J. Oppenheimer. Other young men of brilliance who were present near this time were Werner Heisenberg, Leó Szilárd and Edward Teller. Such was their brilliance that Nobel prizes, honorary de-grees and memberships of foreign scientific societies seemed to be theirs by right. The brief days of glory for "Georgia Augusta" were soon to be over however, for outside the hallowed walls of such oases of peace and harmony, events were moving apace that would soon disperse this brilliant clutch of scientists to other countries and another continent where they would fulfill their terrifying destiny.[348]

The advancing march of proletarian values in Russia had been replaced by a massive genocidal dictatorship under the iron fist of Joseph Stalin, and in an almost mirror-like lateral inver-sion of this callous creed, fascism reared its head and reached for power in Italy. Under the leadership of Benito Mussolini – *Il Duce* – the black-shirted thugs of the National Fascist Party marched on Rome and brought into being Europe's first fascist government. In Germany, Adolf Hitler led an even more deter-mined and evil force on its march to national and eventual world domination. Supported by the military and the industrialists, the Nazi Party gained power in a Germany weakened by the imposi-tion of punitive war reparations and by the effects of the Great Slump. Many reasons have been suggested to attempt to explain Hitler's astounding success. Some blame the economic circum-stances of the time; others place the responsibility squarely on the brutal methods used by the Nazis themselves. One modern scholar, Trevor Ravenscroft, explained it even more simply, making a convincing case by arguing that only Hitler's deliberate use of demonic powers can explain both his success and the appalling reality of Nazi rule. The brutal nature of the fascist dictators soon became apparent. Not content with simply bringing to their countries the benefits of full employment, or building new autobahns in Germany or even making the Italian trains run on time, they created police states founded on terrorism and brutality. In the annals of modern infamy, Stalin was no longer alone. Italy's imperial ambitions were all too apparent to the oppressed populations of Tunisia and Ethiopia. The advanced state of preparation of both countries for war was given graphic demonstration in the contribution they both made to the civil war in Spain, which was soon seen for what it was. Not merely a struggle for supremacy between the extremes of the political Left and Right in Spain itself, but the full dress rehearsal for a wider conflict to come – a useful laboratory to test the machines and strategies of new forms of mechanized warfare. Political repression in Italy was common knowledge. In Germany this was allied to a form of racism that plumbed new depths in the history of man's inhumanity to man: genocide against the Jews. At first this appeared in the form of institutionalized and legalized anti-Semitism, and a mass exodus of Jews began from the German Reich.

The exclusion of Jews from all professional positions, especially in the educational establishment, sounded the death knell for the so-called "beautiful days" at the University of Göttingen. A large number of the physicists were Jewish and had little option but to flee. They were assisted by the international community of physicists and many followed the example of Albert Einstein and sought refuge in the United States.[349] Many non-Jewish scientists also fled as Hitler extended his hold first on Austria and later on

Czechoslovakia. Political interference with their work had become intolerable. Few of them had any personal views on political matters and until the advent of the Hitler regime they had innocently believed that politics was separate and distinct from science, and therefore had no bearing on what they did. During the years immediately preceding the Second World War, theoretical physics was entering one of its most critical stages, during which the nucleus of the atom was accidentally ruptured by the newly discovered neutrons, showing a potentiality for the release of immense quantities of energy.[350] Eighteen years earlier, Nobel Laureate Walther Nernst had been the only scientist to see the dangers that lay ahead. He wrote that: "We may say that we are living on an island of gun cotton," when he read of Rutherford's suggestion that the atom could be artificially disintegrated, "but thank God we have not yet found the match that will ignite it." Later, in an attempt to prevent Hitler from achieving world power, the search for just that match began in earnest.[351]

For the majority of ordinary people in Western Europe during the mid- to late '30s, political and international tensions apart, life began its slow climb back to some semblance of stable normality. The technological advances, the benefits of cheap travel by means of the motorcar and more efficient public transport, and the slow but steady increase in employment levels all had their effects. The beginnings of social security schemes, poor though they may have been initially, radio and talking films, all helped foster the feeling that mankind was undergoing some form of progress towards a brighter future as a result of the benefits of science. Living standards slowly began to improve, but the dark cloud of oppression was beginning to cast its shadow over a still weakened continent.

Medical advances also accrued as a result of scientific and technological progress. Drugs of the sulphonamide group allowed massive strides to be made against infections – although they did not derive from medical research but were an almost accidental by-product of the aniline dye industry. Despite the triumph of the scientific method, beneficial discoveries were being made when the hunt was after very different hares. For the middle classes the even tenor of their life was apparently about to be re-established and there was some slight but discernible improvement for the poor. Yet living standards in the countryside of many of the new states in Eastern Europe was still abysmally low. Of these countries, only Czechoslovakia had attained any realistic level of industrialization, and with her proximity to Austria this made her particularly vulnerable to the ambitions of Adolf Hitler.

Hitler was preparing for war, constantly provoking reaction from the Western powers, seeing how far he could go without having to use force. The *Anschluss* with Austria passed virtually unopposed. The betrayal of Czechoslovakia by the British government under Neville Chamberlain was an act of calculated infamy that made war inevitable. The cry of "peace in our time" was a hollow mockery of the true state of affairs. The advances in science had been noted with methodical efficiency by the German General Staff whose interest extended far beyond the mere development of tanks, aircraft and explosives. The research division of the German Army in Berlin held a special meeting in April 1939 to consider the new advances in physics and their possible application to war. The possibility of a chain reaction in uranium fascinated them. The German War Office became deeply interested and soon placed an embargo on the export of uranium ore from Czechoslovakia that the Third Reich had recently occupied. When this news reached the exiled physicists in America, they knew that the time had come to persuade the American government to enter the race to create an atomic bomb before the

German scientific community could create one for Hitler. Leo Szilard and Edward Teller aided by the international status of their respected colleague Albert Einstein, sought, and eventually gained, an audience with President Franklin Delano Roosevelt. The difficult task of persuading the American president to authorize such action took time. In the end however, the race was on under the innocuous title of the "Manhattan Project."[352]

The conflict that started in late 1939 quickly became global in its effects, more so than any previous war had ever done. It not only involved the belligerents, but every nation in the world including those who remained neutral. No one was exempt from its reach. Entire civilian populations were subjected not only to the terrors of aerial bombardment and the firestorms that ensued, such as that at Dresden, but also suffered military occupation, repression and calculated, methodical genocide. The casualties were beyond human credibility. Over twenty-six million Russians killed. Between six and twelve million Jewish people, almost the entire Jewish population of a continent, were deliberately and methodically exterminated. All who dissented from Nazi orthodoxy, or whose racial origins were held to be offensive to the Nazi creed, were systematically wiped off the face of the Earth. Gypsies, communists, socialists, religious leaders and followers, Jehovah's Witnesses, Jews, Russian prisoners of war, German political opponents, liberal and democratic politicians – all were sent to the ubiquitous concentration camps and extermination centers. This ghastly and demonic scenario was played out against the background of the most brutal and mechanized war in history.

Mankind as a whole was stunned when the appalling reality of this genocide was revealed at the war's end in 1945. Belsen, Auschwitz, Birkenau, Treblinka, Theresienstadt, Dachau – the litany of terror feels almost endless. Few among the civilized world were equipped, intellectually or spiritually, to understand the deliberate, satanic abuse of power that had made the Holocaust possible. How could any rational, educated member of European Christian culture even conceive of the appalling reality that lay behind the euphemistic phrase the "Final Solution," much less come to terms with its horrendous completion. The concept of "crimes against humanity" was the only possible response by the victors and the Nuremberg trials resulted. Trevor Ravenscroft, carrying on the work of Walter Johannes Stein, wrote *The Spear of Destiny* in the early 1970s to place on record the fact that the nature of the Nazi regime was truly demonic; that Hitler had deliberately invoked the use of satanic powers in his attempt to conquer and dominate the world. All we can do is thank God that Hitler's Germany did not gain the atom bomb to add to his hellish arsenal. As it turned out the fear of Adolf Hitler developing an atomic bomb, which had in the first place led to America's entry into the race, was completely unfounded. At the war's end it was discovered that the leading atomic physicists in Germany had succeeded in doing their utmost to delay the manufacture of the ultimate weapon and that, in fact, their efforts were over two years behind those of the Americans. Otto Hahn who had been involved in the fragmentation of the nucleus by electrons, had stated to his German colleagues, "I only hope that you will never construct a uranium bomb. If Hitler ever gets a weapon like that I'll commit suicide."[353] Werner Heisenberg, the genius who had formulated the uncertainty principle of quantum mechanics, made sure that this never came about. He called all attempts to apply nuclear physics to destructive purposes the "service of the devil."

It was in the form of an atomic fireball of truly hellish and demonic proportions that the world came to know that human consciousness had descended to the realms of cold, inhuman abstraction. Not merely science, but the very philosophy on which both the military and political machines depended, were now clearly and demonstrably stripped of all moral foundation. The waiting world, so hungry for peace and justice, had unwittingly crossed the threshold into a truly apocalyptic age. The radioactive, still lethal ruins of the civilian cities of Hiroshima and Nagasaki gave mute witness to the dawn of a new and terrible age – the age of "mutually assured destruction" known aptly by the acronym MAD.

By the time the Second World War had reached its apocalyptic climax, the once great nations and empires that had appeared so stable less than forty years before were all virtually emasculated. Japan and Germany lay in ruins, their political and economic systems as devastated as their factories and their cities. France and Britain, who still retained all the trappings of empire, were economically and politically bankrupt. In world affairs the so-called "Four Power" conferences were in fact confrontations between Russia and America. Compared to these two great superpowers, Britain and France had little significance. As early as 1947 it became apparent that Russia too held the secret of the weapons of terror and soon developed their own atomic bomb.[354] The apparent parity of strength, and the intrinsic opposition of the two antagonistic ideologies of capitalism and communism represented by the superpowers of America and Russia, was given a tangible geographic dimension by the division that emerged between them – the so-called "Iron Curtain" that divided East and West in Europe.

The feeling of helpless impotence in the face of the atomic threat felt by the ordinary people across the world, was exacerbated by the news that not only had Russia developed its own atomic weapons but that it now led the Americans in the race to create an even more terrible and destructive bomb – the thermonuclear or "super" bomb. Now a further dimension was to be added to the forces of terror. Rockets, developed by both superpowers using the scientific and engineering expertise of their recent enemies, the Germans, were now to be used to deliver the "improved" weapons. Nowhere was safe from their reach. The balance of terror that was supposed to protect world peace had escalated into the phase of pseudo-peace, or perpetual small scale wars, under the "protection" of mutually assured destruction.

The thinking that lay behind this comforting strategy was that neither side would strike against the other as long as each knew with absolute certainty that the aggressors themselves would suffer atomic annihilation irrespective of the outcome of the first strike. Did the policy of mutually assured destruction truly maintain world peace? In fact it has been used for the very opposite purpose, to legitimise a whole series of wars since 1945 whose appalling human cost exceeds the total casualty list of the Second World War many times over.[355] Without the ever-present nightmare of a thermonuclear holocaust it is unthinkable that humanity would have allowed this non-stop chain of violence to continue unchecked for more than four decades. The true obscenity of nuclear weapons lies in the legitimization of the acceptability of conflict using so-called "conventional" weapons, any war irrespective of its cause or motivation being deemed preferable to an atomic Armageddon.

The era of post-war development that took place under the shadow of the nuclear umbrella has, by its concentration on the struggle for global supremacy between the two superpowers, masked an almost complete absence of any realistic initiative to remove the root causes of war from the world of man. Atomic strategy had replaced spiritual principle as the main criterion of international statesmanship. The chaotic conditions of the modern world have led to an almost continuous series of armed conflicts. Wars fought not with atomic weapons, though that was threatened from time to time, but with so-called conventional armaments that included the barbarous chemical weapons not used since the first global conflict, and also, it is often alleged, biological means of warfare. These are the ultimate results accruing from a system that has denied the real benefits of spirituality for nearly two thousand years – the products of a philosophy that has spawned a political system and a form of science stripped of all moral guidance. Surely by now the world has had enough, and it began to seem as though it had. But, sadly even now, at the beginning of the twenty-first century with the Cold War long over, it would seem not. Wars based upon greed, pride and the lust for power, or simply waged to keep the armaments manufacturers in business, are now apparently often waged in the name of religion in the age-old manner of the medieval era. Northern Ireland, Palestine, Israel, Iran, Iraq, Bosnia, Croatia, Afghanistan and potentially, war in the Korean Peninsula, again – the list seems as endless as the lies purveyed as justification for these conflicts. In the light of this catalogue of man-made disasters, the thought that occupies the minds of millions is simply: "Surely there must be a better way of doing things?"

Johann Wolfgang von Goethe at age 69, painted in 1828 by Joseph Karl Stieler.

CHAPTER 19

The Modern Wellsprings Of Spirituality

Our consciousness, rising above the growing (but still much too limited) circles of family, country and race, shall finally discover that the only truly natural and real human unity is the spirit of the earth.[356]   – Pierre Teilhard de Chardin, *The Phenomenon of Man*

Magic was not the "science" of the past. It is the science of the future. I believe that the human mind has reached a point in evolution where it is about to develop new powers – powers that would once have been considered magical. ... His unconscious powers have not atrophied; but they have "gone underground." Now the wheel has come full circle; intellect has reached certain limits, and it cannot advance beyond them until it recovers some of the lost powers.[357]   – Colin Wilson, *The Occult*

The modern spiritual resurgence that is now beginning to bloom first became apparent in the later part of the nineteenth and early part of the twentieth century. Esoteric thinking and gnosis were no longer hidden from plain view for fear of persecution but were open to all who sought it. Helena Petrovna Blavatsky and her followers had opened the Western mind to the truth and beauty contained within Eastern religious and philosophical tradition at a time of renewed interest in all occult matters. Since the time that the "theory of evolution" became accepted, the search into both the nature and origin of consciousness has become a matter of scientific investigation. The intellectual life of man and his culture, science, spirituality and religion is different from anything else we know of in the universe. This leads to the conclusion that there has to be more to human evolution than the operation of blind chance upon matter.

It may be considered laughable to introduce the concept of destiny into the evolutionary process, yet that is precisely what two respected spiritual thinkers did earlier in this century. These two men, both scientists who came from very different spiritual traditions, were Rudolf Steiner and Pierre Teilhard de Chardin. These two great men, each speaking from his own distinctive and individual understanding and perception, accepted evolutionary theory and extended it in spiritual terms. They developed their perceptions independently, yet reached broadly similar conclusions. Both lectured and wrote prolifically concerning the evolution of consciousness, each speaking of the operation of destiny and the "divine will."

Rudolf Steiner was one of the first modern scientists to choose a spiritual basis for his work. It is largely as a result of this that the scientific community has, grudgingly, begun to accept spiritual concepts and ideas that, until very recently, would have been viewed with derision. Steiner spent nearly ten years developing his own profound esoteric thesis. He maintained that it was not sufficient to reveal the facts and theories of spiritual reality by merely recounting the great spiritual teachings of the past, although he had great respect for them. He knew that the time had come when mankind as a whole would begin its predestined advance to a direct knowledge of the spiritual world, by developing the spiritual faculties that lie dormant in each and every individual. As he himself clearly demonstrated, these could be developed in full, rational consciousness. He believed that the critical point in the development of man's scepticism regarding spiritual reality dated from the Council of Hagia Sophia[358] in the sixth century, which abolished the conception of the human spirit from the entelechy of man. Steiner was therefore not surprised that fifteenth century man completely misunderstood the thinking, literature, art and science of ancient Greece when this knowledge was re-discovered during the Renaissance. The thinking that arose from the Renaissance quickened man's desires for mastery over the material world – for supremacy over nature. The despiritualized intellect now appeared to reign supreme. Steiner foresaw that the ever-widening gap between spirit and matter would continue to pervade the thinking for most of the twentieth century and would bring mankind to the very brink of extinction. He realized that even this process was in accord with the divine will and an integral part of man's continuing development, and believed that only in total, rational and spiritual isolation from the divine could mankind develop the self-consciousness and the true "freedom" which are the absolute prerequisites for the appearance of "love" on Earth.[359] Steiner knew that, ultimately, man's willing union with the divine would inevitably flow from the coming reunification of the powers of the spirit and the mind within each individual who sought it.

Steiner saw himself as an integral part not only of that physical world but also of the spiritual reality that sustained and informed it, and it was from this cosmic consciousness that he spoke so movingly. As a consequence of his prolonged study in the Goethean archives in Weimar he became immersed in the poet's imaginative system of holistic science, which he saw as the true bridge between the natural and the spiritual world. He became the solitary herald, at that time, of the significance of the "spiritual self" that seeks to come to birth in the souls of all humanity in our age.[360] His studies enabled him to develop a new form of initiation that was open to all who earnestly sought it. In the early '20s Steiner was occupied in lecturing and teaching, as well as in the massive work involved in completing the Goetheanum in Dornach. This building was to be a free university for the teaching of "occult science" where students could undergo the moral, artistic, scientific and spiritual preparation for initiation into the Mysteries of esoteric Christianity.[361] Steiner was not a dogmatist; he described his own spiritual perceptions to stimulate all who heard him to seek their own destiny, and cross the threshold of the spiritual world themselves. He made clear the conditions which the novice should try to fulfill before initiation: conditions that mirrored those which had always been required to strengthen the humility, piety and moral development of students of destiny throughout the ages.

Steiner attracted many followers who were dedicated to the same tasks that he felt that destiny had demanded of him. The Anthroposophical Society continued to thrive after his death, spreading knowledge not only of the visions that Steiner had derived from a state of higher consciousness but also the methodology of spiritual science. Steiner's interest in this spiritual approach to science literally knew no bounds. Investigations he initiated into educational matters, agriculture, homoeopathy and other branches of medicine are still being actively explored and developed. Anthroposophy is now a worldwide phenomenon that exerts a far greater influence than the numbers on its membership rolls suggest. Giant strides in education have been made using the Steiner system. The agricultural methods, known as biodynamic farming, have proved so effective that many who would not necessarily count themselves as Anthroposophists are now adopting them. The homoeopathic therapies, founded firmly on the basic principles of "spiritual science," are now widely used for the treatment of previously incurable cancers – in the Royal Homoeopathic Hospital in London, for example.

Goethe also conceived of a truly holistic world and sought to bridge the gap between physical reality and the spiritual powers that informed and sustained it. Steiner proved to be the highly gifted visionary who translated Goethe's conception into a vibrant reality that is gaining acceptance by the world at large. However, it is as a spiritual thinker and a perceptive historian of the evolution of consciousness that Steiner may yet be deemed to have made his greatest contribution to the world's spiritual development. He undoubtedly enabled his followers to appreciate the realities of their past spiritual history. More importantly, he showed them that all mankind can lay themselves open to the realities of the spiritual world both now and in the future – this was probably Steiner's greatest gift to the world.

Both Steiner and Goethe knew beyond all doubt that evolution was a fact, not just a theory. They were perhaps the first spiritually inspired thinkers to reach this conclusion, which is in itself somewhat startling, for prior to Goethe evolutionary theory was promulgated by many of its adherents to very different ends. The main supporters of the philosophical view that mankind, at least, was evolving, were G. W. F. Hegel and Auguste Compte. These two philosophers, more than any others, facilitated the acceptance of evolutionary theory by the enlightened bourgeoisie. This idea of the evolutionary progress of man was used in a twofold way. On the one hand it was brought into play to suggest that Christianity and the Church represented a completely outmoded stage in mankind's development; on the other it was used by many, including Marx, who viewed organized religion as the "opium of the masses," in order to propagate materialistic atheism. Evolution was viewed as substantive proof that the idea of a divinely inspired creation was now superfluous, and that reality as a whole was nothing other than matter.[362] This in turn stimulated a particularly blinkered and bigoted response by the fundamentalist churches in the United States, who have spent millions, and founded universities, to produce twisted and specious arguments that they hope and pray will "prove" the apparent falsity of evolutionary theory. Happily the view that evolution disproved the existence of God is now in a state of complete retreat. This is not solely due to the work of Steiner but also to the teaching of another spiritually gifted thinker, Pierre Teilhard de Chardin.

Teilhard was a Jesuit priest, a leading theologian, a teacher of extraordinary ability and also a palaeontologist of international repute. He conceived that mankind was the unfinished product of past evolutionary processes, and would continue to develop and reach higher states as a result. He proceeded to deal with the entire human phenomenon as a transcendence of the biological by psychic and psychological evolution.[363] In this he had much in common with Steiner. One of the enigmas that Teilhard examined was that, despite the tremendous increase in scientific knowledge that has occurred, mankind seems to lack both the ability and the systematic method by which such knowledge could be used to construct a realistic vision of life. This "knowledgeable impotence" has left mankind bereft of any bearings, either intellectual or spiritual; scientific, modern man now seems completely deprived of any coherent sense of direction. Before the eighteenth century Enlightenment, man had always derived his worldview, indeed his very way of life, from religious sources, but in the modern era this has become increasingly difficult. Pierre Teilhard de Chardin saw the root cause of this spiritual and intellectual impotence in the growing dissociation between the church and science. He was well aware of the dangers inherent in the perceptions of those scientists who stick rigidly to the facts of their own discipline, and yet see no connection between the posture they adopt within that discipline and the actual reality of the world they inhabit.[364]

It is, perhaps, surprising that there are certain points of agreement between the thinking of Pierre Teilhard de Chardin and the views promulgated by the founder of communism, Karl Marx.[365] As each took an historical perspective in their analysis of the development of man, there is an evident similarity between their views as to the nature of what constituted the turning points of history. Both laid great emphasis upon the first agricultural revolution that marked the transformation between nomadic man and the rise of civilization; they laid similar stress on the importance of the Industrial Revolution, which marked the transition from a primarily agrarian existence to an industrial way of life. Neither saw this period solely as a matter of socio-economic eventuality, but recognized that it caused mankind to see itself in a completely different way. Teilhard was more inclined to look for the primary cause of this changing situation in the mind and spirit of man – and especially in science – rather than as simply the inevitable consequence of a change in the means of production. The principles of justice, politics, science, art, religion and philosophy are necessarily involved in his vision of these momentous times. Thus his appeal to the principle of "personal responsibility," which is also echoed by Marx, is all the more cogent. For the Frenchman, the whole evolution of mankind is a growth toward "freedom," in which conception he has more in common with Steiner than with Marx.

Teilhard perceived all "life" as the result of an increase in the complexity of all evolving organisms. He went further than Steiner in explaining this and suggested that the "spiritual will" ultimately take precedence over the psychological and biological processes. Furthermore, he maintained that mankind's previous failure to achieve this spiritual perfection is the real manifestation of "original sin," from which state of imperfect development mankind can be redeemed by the merits of Christ.[366] Like so many Catholic theologians before him, Teilhard was forbidden to teach theology for his insolence in questioning the "infallible" dogma of original sin.

When we consider the principle of freedom as understood by Teilhard, we begin to perceive that all progress prior to the advent of man is a growth toward freedom, and all progress since man's arrival on Earth can be characterized as a growth of freedom itself. With the advent of human freedom evolution can be said to have acquired a new dimension; it has been transformed from an unconscious process into a conscious one. According to Teilhard this gives us a sound basis for expecting a speeding up of the pace of progress, rather than a reversal or a relapse. Even the briefest study of the history of man clearly confirms this and demonstrates that indeed the progress of man is constantly accelerating. Most moral theologians or philosophers pair the concepts of responsibility and freedom as intimately as nature entwines Siamese twins. Therefore it is not surprising that Teilhard, like Steiner, links these two concepts together. He claims that as soon as evolution reached the human stage, the original key to evolution – its character as a determined process – was replaced by a new key, that of human responsibility. Mankind has now gained the ability to interfere with the so-called blind processes of nature. For Teilhard, and for all who are concerned for the ecology and the very future of humanity, the theory of evolution is in itself a call upon human freedom and responsibility. He believed that growing spiritualization would enable Christian and non-Christian alike to find one another in a calculated effort to work for progress in the world.[367] Thus the possible foundation for the new spiritual ethic so badly needed at this moment of global crisis.

This hopeful prognosis should not blind us to the fact that mankind is still capable of intervention in nature in a destructive way. For man has, in a sense, taken evolution into his own hands and so is in a position to nullify it, by destroying all human life on Earth. Yet Teilhard believed that mankind will not resort to self-destruction but, on the contrary, will resolve upon constructive efforts rooted in growing human spiritualization, responsibility and the mature and reasoned use of the supreme gift of freedom of choice, to make the essential choices that must be made to save our planet from ultimate disaster.

Pierre Teilhard de Chardin was probably the most outstanding spiritual philosopher of the twentieth century. His vision being that the purpose of God is implanted in the universe and a constantly evolving mankind. In consequence, humanity is uniquely capable of consciously allying itself with the divine evolutionary purpose. The sweeping symbolism contained within Teilhard's conception of "cosmogenesis" is probably the most beautiful revelation of a divine purpose so far conceived by man. It is perhaps no accident, ironic though it may seem, that this visionary analysis was conceived by a man who was a professional scientist using scientific methods that had previously been regarded as anti-religious in nature. What Teilhard is indicating, in a somewhat different manner to Steiner, is that we are now in an age when man can reunite all his intellectual and spiritual capacities and attain full spiritual development, so that human freedom becomes capable of use with complete and total responsibility. The works of men such as Steiner and Teilhard give to all who choose to understand them, the key to realistic hope for the future. Julian Huxley wrote, of Teilhard's new synthesis, that the final curtain can soon be drawn over the total separation between science and spirituality in Western thought.

The religiously minded can no longer turn their backs upon
the natural world, or seek to escape from its imperfections in a
super-natural world; nor can the materialistically minded deny
importance to spiritual experience and religious feeling.[368]

Alvin Toffler wrote of the emergence of a "third wave" of civilization; Fritjof Capra of a "turning point" towards a holistic, de-
centralized and spiritual society; and many others have echoed
these themes, which are all developments of Teilhard's thinking.
Another aspect of the same truth has been perceived by a number
of concerned individuals and groups worldwide, that no small ad-
justment, or "more of the same," will serve to answer the problems
that now hurl all humanity against the threshold of the spiritual
world. Theodore Roszak placed this in the context of the spiritual
renewal of the late twentieth century:

I believe it means we have arrived, after long journeying, at an
historical vantage point from which we can at last see where the
wasteland ends and where a culture of human wholeness and ful-
filment begins. We can now recognize that the fate of the soul is
the fate of the social order; that if the spirit within us withers, so
too will all the world we build about us. Literally so.[369]

Finally, let us allow Pierre Teilhard de Chardin himself to sum-
marize his objectives:

My principle objective is not to convert you to ideas which are
still fluid, but to open horizons for you, to make you think.[370]

This task before us now, if we would not perish, is to shake
our ancient prejudices, and to build the earth.[371]

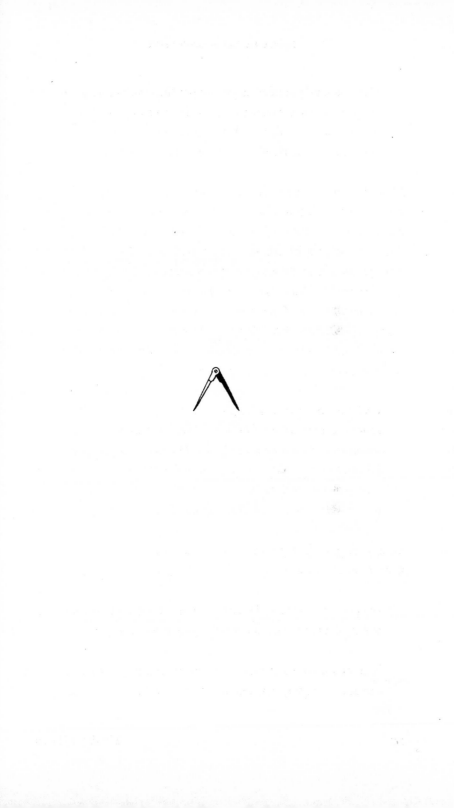

Detail from Hildegard of Bingen's *Scivias Codex*, The Mystical Body, c. 1165.

CHAPTER 20

Standing At The Threshold Of The Spiritual World

The evolution of consciousness has given us not only the
Cheops Pyramid, the Brandenburg Concertos, and the
Theory of Relativity, but also the burning of witches, the
Holocaust, and the bombing of Hiroshima. But that same
evolution of consciousness gives us the potential to live
peacefully and in harmony with the natural world in the future. Our evolution continues to offer us freedom of choice.
We can consciously alter our behaviour by changing our
values and attitudes to regain the spirituality and ecological
awareness we have lost.[372]   – Fritjof Capra, *The Turning Point*

Under the pressures of the many crises that confront mankind at the beginning of the twenty-first century, people are
thinking deeply, re-evaluating old conceptions and looking
at the world with new eyes. Neither Teilhard nor Steiner would
have claimed to be the only progenitors of this growing tide of
intellectual and spiritual transformation; they simply played their
formative and provocative parts in a cosmic process that was as
old as man himself and that has come more and more into the
open during the last hundred years or so. Following on from
Blake and Swedenborg, the group of American writers known
as the Transcendentalists continued the process during the mid-
nineteenth century. Helena Petrovna Blavatsky strengthened and

enlarged upon it. The esoteric revival in Europe, the teachings of G. I. Gurdjieff and J. Krishnamurti, strengthened the rising tide of perception that had at its core the knowledge that mysticism and spirituality had real validity and a vital relevance to the modern age. P. W. Martin predicted in the 1950s that:

> For the first time in history, the scientific spirit of inquiry is being turned upon the other side of consciousness. There is a good prospect that the discoveries can be held this time and so become no longer the lost secret, but the living heritage of man.[373]

The "hippy" culture of the '60s demonstrated, albeit in a colorful and sometimes uncomfortable way, that the seeds of a "consciousness revolution" had been planted – however unlikely that may have seemed at the time. Psychedelic drugs, abused though they were, brought to public notice in a dramatic way the exciting possibility of a change in consciousness. The "mystical type" experiences resulting from uncontrolled drug abuse were highly dangerous and transitory, tending to produce effects which were psychologically overwhelming and impossible to integrate into normal life. Non-drug transformative methods have long since taken their place; the spiritually based, therapeutic twelve-step programs and the increasing use of ancient systems of meditation have become a worldwide phenomenon: prolonged study and spiritual discipline in the initiatory tradition have reappeared once more. Now all these are available to all who seek them. Many more people became engaged in this stimulating search than had indulged themselves in the illusory attractions of the drug culture. An ever-spreading nucleus of individuals has been created who have personally experienced a visionary self-transcendence and who, taking up the ideas of Steiner, Teilhard and others, know that they might be playing an essential role in the future of all human development.

William McLoughlin, the historian, claimed that the 1960s marked the beginning of America's fourth "great awakening" and that it represented a time of cultural dislocation and revitalization that would extend for three or more decades. It is not surprising that it was in America that this movement first established firm roots, for in the words of Leslie Fiedler, "To be American is precisely to imagine a destiny rather than inherit one." He also claimed that, "Americans have always been inhabitants of myth rather than of history."[374] The counterculture that began to emerge during the 1960s was not restricted to the United States however; it spread rapidly through the new and vibrant, international "pop" culture to Europe, to countries such as France, Germany and England where there was already a growing, thinking, questioning, emergent group of middle class people, disenchanted and ill-at-ease with the emotional and spiritual desert that was the inevitable end product of the consumer society. Protest at the paucity of the spiritual rewards of an apparently successful capitalist society began to manifest itself as either a violent, destructive and unwelcome experiment that solved nothing, or as an intellectual and spiritual transformation that can bridge the gap between the old and the new.

The social activism of the 1960s and the consciousness revolution of the early 1970s moved towards a new and possibly historic synthesis: a revolutionary and outward transformation of society which actually results from an individual and spiritual form of internal transformation – change from the inside out. This can provide the means to achieve the more harmonious way of life that these troubled times demand of us: to gain the power to tell the greater from the lesser reality; to tell the eternally true from the false and illusory; and to be able to discern the sacred paradigm from the secular and purely material. This new sensibility is already manifest within an ever-expanding group of spiritually inspired seekers who create a growing pool of consciousness, which contains within it, an immense potential for the ultimate benefit of all mankind. While the spiritual quest is still developing the discrimination and discernment that is necessary, it is growing and flourishing so that we can indeed perceive that a genuine evolutionary transformation of human personality is already well underway.

This change in consciousness is as startling and epoch making as all those that preceded it. It has already created an intellectual climate characterized by a high moral idealism and a deep spiritual thirst, a growing sense of a truly global community and a new cultural synthesis that is in harmony with nature and with the Earth itself. The great task that now confronts us all as we stand upon the so-called "Aquarian frontier" is quite simply to seek a new ecology of the spirit. In this spiritual search it is not surprising that we have had to embark upon an historical and archaeological investigation into the origins and effects of mystical awareness itself in order to re-utilise spiritual perspectives effectively.

This new awakening of higher consciousness among a growing and influential segment of the population is being used to strike a distinctly new note in local, national and international political life, so that a climate is being created wherein the "old gnosis" – that ancient spiritual perception known as "hidden wisdom" – can be used like a warrior's sword against the aggression of destructive technologies. To assist in this process we each need to develop our own inherent spiritual faculties, for these are the keys not only to occult experience but also to the whole future evolution of the human race. Archbishop Desmond Tutu outlined the deceptively simple standards we need to achieve.

> We find that we are placed in a delicate framework of vital relationships with the divine, with fellow human beings, and with the rest of creation. We violate nature only at our peril, and are meant to live as members of one family. This is the law of our being, and when we break this law things go disastrously wrong.[375]

Revelation of this nature lies within all the great religious traditions, such as Buddhism:

> We are in pursuit of an extensive and perfect freedom at its highest level. Perfect freedom is what we seek now – not in the future. Civilization is neither to have electric lights nor aeroplanes, nor to produce nuclear bombs. Civilization is to hold mutual affection and to respect each other.[376]

To recover the common spiritual wisdom that lies at the heart of all the great religious traditions of East and West we need to let go of our dogmatic attitudes in religion, politics, economics, philosophy and the complex web of human relationships that these disciplines sustain. In the words of Meister Eckhart: "only those who dare to let go can dare to re-enter."[377] A simple, yet demanding, precept that contains within it the vital key to our survival. Yet we need to do more than simply survive, we need to relate to one another and to the planet we all inhabit, according to the spiritual principles that sustained the first great civilizations that lasted for so long. If, as a result of our new spiritual awareness, we can return to the age-old spiritual tradition that understands humility as "earthiness" and respect for all of nature, then we have within us the living promise of a sustainable and balanced future. Albert Einstein once said "The most important function of art and science is to awaken the cosmic religious feeling and keep it alive." The new counterculture of the transformation of consciousness accomplishes precisely that function. Western thought, as a result of political imperialism acting in conjunction with religious, economic and intellectual domination, masked but did not destroy the "hidden wisdom" preserved by the initiates and Gnostics in Europe. Nor did it affect the spiritually based thinking that had sustained the great religions of the Far East.

In the last century Britain was given a rude awakening from her dreams of intellectual, political and spiritual superiority when the military might of the entire British Empire was irretrievably shaken by a small, insignificant looking man in a dhoti – a spiritually perceptive politician and leader who gained his objective, the independence of India, by peaceful, non-violent protest. Peaceful methods that he knew were both moral and effective. He was justly called the *Mahatma* – the great soul. In contrast to Western thought, which as a result of ignoring a "theology of blessing" has very few tactics for effecting peaceful social change, Eastern religious philosophies gave Gandhi all he needed.

> For Gandhi *Ji*, to become divine is to become attuned in thought, feeling and act to the whole of creation ... Dharma or morality cannot be ultimately divorced from *Rta* or cosmic order.[378]

The effectiveness of Gandhi's spiritually based system of protest stimulated many in the Western world to similar action. The various civil rights movements in many Western countries adopted and modified his techniques. One such movement, led by Martin Luther King, Jr. in the United States, started from the proposition that "We have flown the air like birds and swum the sea like fishes, but have yet to learn the simple act of walking the earth as brothers." Now when we stand at the threshold of a new era of higher consciousness, how much more effective will be the impulse for change? The early roots of change, indeed the very process itself can often be difficult to discern in its early stages:

> Time, events, or the unaided individual action of the mind will sometimes undermine or destroy an opinion without any sign of outward change … No conspiracy has been formed to make war on it, but its followers, one by one, noiselessly secede. As its opponents remain mute or only interchange their thoughts by stealth, they are themselves unaware for a long period that a great revolution has actually been effected.[379]

The necessary conditions for change are the creation of a coherent minority who are profoundly committed to it; who firmly believe in their own distinctive principles, whether or not they are in error; and who operate in an era of sufficient perturbation and dissent to create the climate of change. Now open and widespread access to the literature and techniques of spiritual change of consciousness, is there for all to use at will. The full richness of many religious cultures, the whole spectrum of worldwide mystical experience has become available to entire populations, both in their original form and in contemporary commentaries. Mystical literature is available in bookshops, at airport news stands, in hardback erudite editions and in paperback. Courses are easily accessible offering instruction in a wide range of meditative and contemplative techniques; university extension courses, weekend seminars, Buddhist centers and Hindu ashrams abound; Theosophists and Anthroposophists thrive, lecture and publish. Highly effective and valid initiatory schools and colleges such the Beshara School, Ramtha's School of Enlightenment and the Sufi Centre in Scotland, offer pathways that help people connect to new sources of spiritual change, personal transformation, integration and growing harmony and unity. The modern information age itself is playing a vital role in this expanding process, which has accelerated exponentially with the development of the Internet.

A global constituency has arisen, formed of the spiritually aware among us who seek peace, non-violent change, justice and harmony within mankind and between man and the planet he inhabits. But before these voices can be heard, we must liberate ourselves from the tyranny of our own history. A history that is not only a record of those peaks of cultural achievement that Jacob Bronowski called the "Ascent of Man" – although they are contained within it – but one that is more accurately described as an ongoing catalogue of cumulative and ever-more destructive human errors that mankind has committed, driven by Western philosophy, to create the false ideals of the consumer society and the illusion of limitless growth. We have to unlearn fear, greed and distrust and abandon our overweening pride. That this is not merely possible but is in fact already underway, albeit in its early stages, has long been the subject of scholarly comment.

> Human consciousness is crossing a threshold as mighty as
> the one from the Middle Ages to the Renaissance. People
> are hungering and thirsting after experience that feels true
> to them on the inside, after so much hard work mapping the
> outer spaces of the physical world. They are gaining courage
> to ask for what they need; living interconnections, a sense

of individual worth, shared opportunities ... New symbols are rising: pictures of wholeness. Freedom sings within us as well as outside us ... Sages seem to have foretold this "second coming." People don't want to feel stuck, they want to be able to change.[380]

We have already progressed beyond the mere point of faith in the reality of spiritual experience, and are beginning to enter into an ever-widening spectrum of the hardheaded scientific validation of the essential truth of mystical vision. Mystical experience is in many ways the mirror image of science, providing a glimpse of what Teilhard described as the "withiness of things," the internal force of the mysteries that science vainly tries to examine from the outside. It is only since science became completely divorced from its essentially spiritual basis that mankind has abused it to the point of world destruction. For example, ancient mystics had correctly described the function of the pineal gland many centuries before modern medical science was in a position to confirm it. This puzzled the modern neuropsychologist, Karl Pibram, who asked, "How could ideas like this arise before we had the tools to understand them?"[381] Other modern physicists were also puzzled by inexplicable strange and mysterious parallels between their findings and the age-old mystical descriptions of ultimate reality.

The startling similarities between modern quantum physics and the writings of the ancient Chinese mystics of the Tao and Buddhist traditions have fascinated a growing number of dedicated researchers. Fritjof Capra gave extensive and detailed elaboration of these strange "coincidental" parallels in his important work *The Tao of Physics*. He was not alone. Gary Zukav, in *The Dancing Wu Li Masters*, reinforced this growing awareness of the essential relationship between Eastern mystical philosophy and the emerging paradigm in late twentieth century physics. This search for truth was aided by further exploration along similar lines by David Ashe and Peter Hewitt of England who, in their book *The Science of the Gods*, explored various aspects of atomic theory derived from the work of Lord Kelvin. They developed it in a manner that tends to explain the basis of the flow of energy described by Chinese acupuncturists, but in acceptable modern scientific terms. They also offer a series of provocative hypotheses which may clarify the basis of the previously inexplicable phenomena known as the "paranormal." How can this be? In the twenty-first century when we appear to be reaching a peak of development of scientifically based technology is it possible, or even probable, that Teilhard, Steiner and Goethe were far more correct in their holistic, spiritual approach than the much vaunted, reductionist, Cartesian scientific community? The answer, which is becoming more obvious every day, is simply – Yes!

Goethe was not alone in his perception of the reality of the spiritual world that stands behind and upholds the physical reality we all live in. The Persian mystic Aziz Nasafi speaks of fundamentally the same perception, despite coming from a distinctly different religious and cultural tradition.

> The spiritual world is one great single spirit who stands like
> unto a light behind the bodily world and who, when any
> single creature comes into being, shines through it as through
> a window. According to the kind and size of the window, less
> or more light enters the world.[382]

Colin Wilson speaks of another approach that unifies the spiritual and scientific research. He describes how one scientist, David Foster who, unlike Goethe, worked from a scientific perspective rather than a spiritual one, arrived at the conception of the "intelligent universe."

> It is interesting that Dr. Foster arrives at this Intelligent Universe not by starting from the idea of purpose or God, as religious thinkers do, but simply by considering the facts we now know about the cybernetic programming of living matter. What emerges is a picture of the universe that fits in with the theories of other scientists and psychologists during the past twenty years: Teilhard de Chardin, Sir Julian Huxley, C. H. Waddington, Abraham Maslow, Victor Frankl, Michael Polanyi, Noam Chomsky. What all these men have in common is an opposition to "reductionism," the attempt to explain man and the universe in terms of the laws of physics or the behaviour of laboratory rats.[383]

The British scientist, James Lovelock, was employed by the American space program as a result of his work on atmospheres. Lovelock had devised a methodology which, when applied to atmospheric analysis of other planets from outer space, could be used to detect the presence of organic life. He did not restrict either his observations or his analysis to other planets however; he also looked back at the atmospheric conditions of his own world. He found that the atmosphere of the Earth was so "improbable" in geochemical terms that only some innate regulatory process could explain it. After further study, the only regulator that he could seriously propose which would explain the atmospheric conditions he had described was life itself. He suggested that the Earth's atmosphere was the visible and life-sustaining result of a complex inter-reaction between all life forms – plant, animal, human and bacteriological – who inhabit the planet. The very planet itself, the biosphere, or ecosphere to use the current term, behaves as though it is a single, living, self-regulating organism, echoing the perceptions of the Russian mystic, Vladimir Solovyov. The Earth acted, according to Lovelock, as though "alive" and in such a manner that if life continued with each species living in harmony with this living entity, the entity as a whole would regulate itself so as to ensure the survival of all life. He named this entity "Gaia" after the pre-Hellenic goddess of the Earth.[384]

Lovelock recounts in *The Ages of Gaia* the somewhat ambivalent attitudes his fellow scientists expressed in reaction to the Gaia hypothesis. Privately many told him that they were in agreement with it, but that publicly they could not risk their professional reputations by endorsing it. Yet despite this hypocritical attitude the Gaia hypothesis has gained almost universal acceptance. Goethe's conception of nature as the "living garment of God" and Solovyov's perception of Christ as the "spirit of the Earth" are now supported not only by the works of Steiner, but by scientists of the rank of Pierre Teilhard de Chardin, David Foster and James Lovelock. The Gaia hypothesis, and the manner in which it has been increasingly validated by research, has now been accepted as a basis for action by men and women of international renown such as Javier Pérez de Cuéllar, former general secretary of the United Nations; Gro Harlem Brundtland, previously prime minister of Norway and author of the Brundtland Report on Global Warming; as well as the leaders of the two great super powers.

Another scientific discovery that reinforces the interdependence of all things, the idea that lies at the very heart of the Gaia hypothesis and of all true mystical insight, was the promulgation of the theory of perspectivism, or "general systems theory" as it is now called. This concept, first postulated by the German biologist Ludwig von Bertalanffy, has grown steadily in its influence in many disciplines and sees all of nature, including human behavior, as being interconnected. According to general systems theory, nothing can be truly understood if it is regarded in isolation; each species, each life form must be studied and examined as part of an interrelated system. The relevance of this understanding to scientific enquiry and its relationship to both the Gaia hypothesis and to the insights of the medieval mystics, can hardly be overstated. All species other than mankind have adapted both their form and behavior to the pressures of the environment. *Homo sapiens* on the other hand, has achieved the apparently "god-like" ability to adapt the environment instead, seemingly overcoming natural barriers and limitations by the development of modern scientific technologies and cultures. While no sane person would contest the fact that this has brought in its train many benefits and advances, few would argue that it has been beneficial to all the other forms of life that form an essential part of the Earth's self-regulatory mechanism.

The ever-spiraling growth of knowledge: the scientific and industrial development that has fueled the constant race towards sustained growth, has brought in its wake an unparalleled level of pollution which now threatens to destroy all human life on Earth by the twin evils of global warming and nuclear contamination. To counteract this threat, we have to develop technologies and behaviors that are truly and globally holistic. Our own species is, in comparative terms, very young – very much an experiment and experiments can fail; species can, and do, die out. All evolving forms of life have to reach an equilibrium within which they strike a harmonious balance with nature. Evolutionary developments always cause changes in the environment that surrounds them until a new balance is achieved. Man must now strive for this balance, for in the last eighty years the human population has trebled and our consumption of natural resources has increased twentyfold. The Earth is out of balance and its self-regulating mechanism can bring all into order simply by removing mankind from it. The medieval mystic, Hildegard of Bingen, noted just this point over five hundred years ago: "All of creation God gives to humanity to use. If this privilege is misused, God's justice permits creation to punish humanity."

The search for holistic answers to the problems that beset us is not restricted to the way in which mankind needs to harmonize with its environment, but must also include, as a natural and an integral part of that process, a commitment to the principles of justice and truth which regulate relationships between all humanity. The search for peace to which we have referred earlier must translate into positive action. The spiritual basis for this action can be found within the traditions of all the great religions, yet the history of man is a constant catalogue of religious wars! Religion, when used as a political tool rather than as a source of spirituality, reinforces not the interrelatedness of all mankind, but the apparent differences between races and cultures.

If we examine the uniformity of principle to be found within all the great religious traditions, we see that they share a common spiritual source for all their great teachings. There is a surprising unanimity between them on the main moral issues and, more importantly, how to apply these principles in everyday life. Religious moral principles have not been tried and found wanting, they have, sadly, usually been perceived as too difficult or idealistic and simply not tried. If we then examine the spiritual truths that lie at the heart of man's innate desire to live in peace with his fellow man, we will see with simple clarity the similarities and not the differences between the various religious traditions. In the Talmud of Judaism we find the simple instruction "What is hateful to you, do not to your fellow men. That is the entire law, all the rest is commentary." Central to the Buddhist way of life is this precept, "Hurt not others with that which pains yourself." In the earlier scriptures of the Zoroastrian religion we find "That nature only is good when it shall not do unto another whatever is not good for its own self." It is hardly surprising that in the Christian Gospel of Matthew this theme is echoed strongly once again, "All things whatsoever ye would that men should do to you, do ye even so unto them; for this is the law and the prophets." Islam, the religion of obedience to God, teaches simply "No one of you is a believer until he desires for his brother that which he desires for himself." And in the Hindu Mahabhárata it is written "This is the sum of duty: do naught to others which if done to thee would cause thee pain." This unanimity of ideals is the living embodiment of the hidden wisdom that arises naturally from the spirituality that sustains and transcends all the major religions. Yet, the sad commentary by Aristotle on the condition of humanity, "It is more difficult to organize peace than to win a war" – written more than two thousand years ago – rings just as true today. This merely reinforces the urgency with which we must learn to live on spiritual principles. The urgent need is to go beyond ritual observance to then access the world of the spirit that underlies and transcends all the great religions. This is now happening, for the Catholic theologian Anthony Padovano in his address to a conference on meditation in 1976 spoke of this changing spiritual perspective:

> The religious response that has occurred in the Western world
> – a revolution that has made us more sensitive to the religions
> of the Orient – is an understanding that whatever answers
> there are must come from ourselves. The great turmoil in the

religions is caused by the spirit demanding interiority. Faith is not dying in the West, it is merely moving inside.[385]

This statement stressed yet again the interiorization of which Teilhard spoke so movingly, the search for what he called the "Christ Within": the interconnectedness of all in all. It also gives us pause to consider what may be gained from a closer examination of the full richness of the differing cultures of the major religious traditions. The different cultural values embodied within them provide some useful ideas as to how a future global society might operate. Western economists regard human labor as little more than a necessary evil to be purchased at the cheapest cost or replaced by robotics; Buddhists view work as an opportunity to develop their faculties, to overcome egocentricity or self-centeredness. Yet both cultures expect work in the widest sense to bring forth the goods and services needed for a comfortable existence. The Western view is at present sustained by a scientific system devoid of all spiritual influences, but that of the Buddhist is firmly founded on spiritual values.

With the new and growing appreciation of the reality of spiritual perception, humanity, at this new stage of the evolution of consciousness, has within its grasp the levers of global change at all levels of activity. The American psychologist Marilyn Ferguson in her remarkable book, *The Aquarian Conspiracy*, outlines the early development of New Age thinking based firmly on the spiritually inspired, higher consciousness and argued that its spreading influence has already caused change within modern society. She claims that non-hierarchical, interconnected society is evolving within our own by means of informal networks of people with similar interests: ecological, medical, spiritual, political or any other description. Ever-growing, ever-reaching inward within each individual being who is then impelled to spread its influence outwards, permeating all of society. She claims, with some truth, that whether the rationale for our previous social structures was capitalist, socialist or Marxist, the centralization of power that was their common feature was unnatural, inflexible and insufficiently dynamic to respond to the real needs of the people they claimed to serve. The newly aligned minority, knowing that change of heart and not rational argument alone sways people, are finding ways of relating to others at the most intimate and human level.

Joseph Campbell argued as early as 1968 that, "The only possibility for our time is the free association of men and women of like spirit ... not a handful but a thousand heroes, ten thousand heroes, who will create a future image of what humankind will be."[386] The spiritually aware members of the networks that Marilyn Ferguson describes as the "Aquarian Conspiracy" know that people can be seduced into their own direct experience, that such a transformative and mystical experience changes all who have it into the living embodiment of freedom and aliveness so that they act as a living example that will convince others when rational arguments fail. Henry David Thoreau, writing more than one hundred and forty years ago stated simply, "Live your beliefs and you can turn the world around."

The greenhouse effect, allied to the widespread injustice, belligerence, strife and the political chaos of the modern world, provides the motivation for change that will impel mankind to completely reassess the very basis of its thinking and justify a radical transformation of political and philosophical values. The root cause of such a fundamental change in values, actions and attitudes is simple: the stress and perturbation that are the inevitable end product of our present way of life. The Nobel Laureate Ilya Prigogine believes that: "We are in a very exiting moment in history, perhaps a turning point. Stress and perturbation can thrust us into a new and higher order ... Science is proving the reality of a deep cultural vision."[387]

Living systems have always reacted to stress and pressure. Now at the beginning of the twenty-first century the entire planet is facing the most stressful situation in the entire history of humanity. This immense challenge will force change upon us, for good or ill. The reality is brutally simple: either we change our actions and our attitudes or we fail to survive as a species. The major threat to our continued existence comes from the global warming that has come about as a result of the greenhouse effect. An innocuous term that masks a grim reality, one that threatens all mankind and renders *Homo sapiens* a truly endangered species. Yet even here, the mystics and initiates from a variety of cultures prophesied some form of apocalyptic crisis in the early years of this century.

One prophecy originates with a little known German mystic Mühlhiasl, a simple miller whose life spanned the end of the eighteenth century and the beginning of the nineteenth. In Andreas Zeitler's *Die Prophezeiungen des Mühlhiasl*, we learn that nearly two hundred years ago this simple man predicted with remarkable accuracy the rise of mechanical transport by road, iron track and air. He also gave warning about both world wars. His final prophecy was that there would be an era of world disaster in or about the month of May 2038.

Then there are the predictions from the Marian apparitions at the tiny mountainside village of San Sebastian de Garabandal in June 1961 which stated that a great cataclysmic event would occur unless mankind as a whole changed its ways and turned to peace. Further visions listed the events that would precede the coming cataclysm. The first would be three days and nights of darkness and, as normality seemed to return, there would be "an event of light" during which everything in this world would emit light for a short period of time. This was to be regarded as a portent of immanent disaster, a call to the world to repent. As all of these events are predicted to occur within the lifetime of one of the visionaries. So, the day of reckoning cannot be far off.

Across the Atlantic, the ancient Maya suggested that a world disaster will mark the end of the present Great Cycle of the Mayan Long Count Calendar, which most scholars say corresponds to December 21, 2012 in our Gregorian calendar. The Aztecs predicted the end of civilization on December 24, 2012, due to violent earthquakes. The Druidic prophecy is for July 28, 2019. Thus between the ancient Druidic initiates of the Celtic peoples of Europe, those of the Mayan and Aztec civilizations of Central America, and at least two Christian sources, there is truly a "concurrence of the oracles." At my last meeting with the French mystic and initiate, Frédéric Lionel in Paris in 1997, he made the following statement: "As a master, you are writing of matters that are known to very few. You have a sacred duty, you must continue, there is not much time."

Many fundamentalist Christians as well as a large proportion of the general public believe that these apocalyptic prophesies herald the end of the world. However, the visions conveyed by biblical sources, esoteric tradition and teachings from all the great religions tell a very different story. There is a startling similarity between the Essene, Christian and Hindu beliefs concerning the cataclysmic events usually associated with the Apocalypse. These traumatic times are believed to herald not the end of civilization but, more importantly, the dawn of a new era where life will be transformed into "heaven on earth." While many people today may be uncomfortable with the biblical idea of the New

Jerusalem, they, nonetheless, willingly accept the concept of the new "Aquarian Age."

According to astrologers, under the influence of this sign, there will be a strong emphasis on science used not for its own sake, but in the service of humanity. It is believed to be a time of growing international co-operation and possible world government when mankind can apply warm-hearted generosity to practical ends. We have our part to play in this process: Live our beliefs and turn our world around. For if our world cannot be transformed into a global, just and equitable society, stripped of violence, greed and poverty, why *should* it survive? We have the spiritual answers to our problems in the hidden wisdom of the ancient sages and mystics. The real question is: Have we the wit, the humility and the courage to apply them?

And *in the beginning* ...

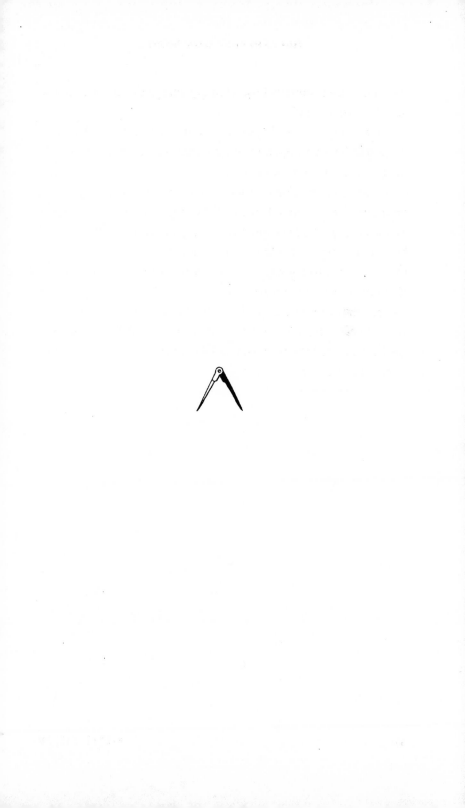

SELECTED BIBLIOGRAPHY

A.

Ahern, G. *Sun At Midnight: The Rudolf Steiner Movement and the Western Esoteric Tradition.* Aquarian Press: Northampton, 1984.

Alder, Vera Stanley. *When Humanity Comes of Age.* Rider & Co.: London, 1972.

Anderson, William. *The Rise of the Gothic.* Hutchinson: London, 1985.

Armstrong, Edward A. *St. Francis: Nature Mystic.* University of California Press, 1973.

Ashe, Geoffrey. *The Ancient Wisdom.* MacMillan: London, 1977.

Aue, Michele and Juliette Freyche. *Cathar Country.* MSM, 2004.

Avineri, Shlomo. *The Social and Political Thought of Karl Marx.* Cambridge University Press, 1968.

B.

Baigent, Michael, Richard Leigh and Henry Lincoln. *The Holy Blood and The Holy Grail.* Jonathan Cape: London, 1982.

Baigent, Michael and Richard Leigh. *The Temple and The Lodge.* Jonathan Cape: London, 1989.

Barber, Malcolm. *The Trial of the Templars.* Cambridge University Press, 2006.

Barnaby, Frank, ed. *The Gaia Peace Atlas.* Pan Books: London, 1988.

Bateson, Gregory and Mary. *Angels Fear: Towards an Epistemology of the Sacred.* Macmillan, 1987.

Bateson, Gregory. *Mind and Nature.* Bantam Books, 1980.

Bauval, Robert and Adrian Gilbert. *The Orion Mystery.* Heinemann, 1994.

Begg, Ean. *The Cult Of The Black Virgin.* Arkana, 1985.

Bock, Emil. *Moses.* Inner Traditions: Rochester, VT, 2006.

Boehme, Jacob. *Signatura Rerum.* James Clarke: Cambridge, 1981.

Bronowski, Jacob. *The Ascent of Man.* Little, Brown and Co.: Toronto, 1973.

Bronowski, Jacob. *Science and Human Values.* Harcourt Torchbooks: New York, 1965.

Bronowski, Julius. *William Blake and the Age of Revolution.* Routledge & Kegan Paul, 1972.

Brown, Joseph Epes. *The Spiritual Legacy of the American Indian.* Crossroad, 1986.

Burke, Edmund. *Reflections on the Revolution in France.* Penguin Classics, 1982.

Burman, Edward. *The Templars, Knights of God.* Inner Traditions: Rochester, VT, 1988.

Bynner, Witter. *Lao-Tsu, The Way of Life.* Capricorn Books, 1962.

C.

Campbell, Joseph. *The Masks of God, Vol. 3: Occidental Mythology.* Penguin, 1991.

Campbell, Joseph and Bill Moyers. *The Power of Myth.* Doubleday, 1990.

Capra, Fritjof. *The Tao of Physics.* Fontana,1983.

Capra, Fritjof. *The Turning Point.* Simon & Schuster, 1982.

Charpentier, Louis. *Mysteries of Chartres Cathedral.* Thorsons, 1972.

Christie-Murray, David. *The History of Heresy.* Oxford University Press, 1989.

Cipolla, Carlo M. *The Economic History of World Population.* Penguin, 1962.

Collier, John. *Indians of the Americas.* Mentor, 1947.

D.

Darwin, Charles. *The Origin of Species.* Cambridge University Press, 2009.

Davidson, H. R. Ellis. *Gods and Myths of Northern Europe.* Penguin, 1981.

Davy, John. *On Hope, Evolution and Change.* Hawthorn Press, 1985.

Dawkins, Peter. *Arcadia.* The Francis Bacon Research Trust, 1988.

Delfgaauw, Bernard. *Evolution, The Theory of Pierre Teilhard de Chardin.* Fontana: London, 1969.

Denton, William. *The Soul of Things.* The Aquarian Press, 1988.

Doresse, Jean. *Les Livres Secrets des Gnostiques d'Egpte Librairie.* Plon: Paris, 1958.

Dowley, Tim, ed. *The History of Christianity.* Lion Publishing: Herts, 1977.

Doyle, Brendan. *Meditations with Julian of Norwich.* Bear & Co., 1983.

Dubos, Rene. *A God Within.* Abacus/Sphere, 1976.

E.

Edwards, I. E. S. *The Pyramids of Egypt.* Penguin, 1975.

Eisenman, Robert. *James the Brother of Jesus.* Penguin, 1988.

Eisenman, Robert. *Maccabees, Zadokites, Christians and Qumran.* Brill, 1970.

Eisenman, Robert and Michael Wise. *The Dead Sea Scrolls Uncovered.* Penguin, 1993.

HIDDEN WISDOM

Ellis, Peter Berresford. *The Druids*. Eerdmans, 1995.

Epstein, Isadore. *Judaism*. Penguin, 1959.

Erikson, Erik. *Gandhi's Truth*. W. W. Norton: New York, 1968.

Evans, Hilary. *Alternate States of Consciousness*. The Aquarian Press, 1989.

F.

Faulkner, Robert. *The Ancient Egyptian Pyramid Texts*. Clarendon Press, 1969.

Ferguson, Marilyn. *The Aquarian Conspiracy*. Paladin Books, 1982.

Fortune, Dion. *The Esoteric Orders*. Aquarian Books, 1982.

Fox, Matthew. *Breakthrough: Meister Eckhart's Creation Spirituality in New Translation*. Doubleday & Co., 1980.

Fox, Mathew. *Hildegard of Bingen's Book of Divine Works*. Bear & Co., 1987.

Fox, Matthew. *The Coming of The Cosmic Christ*. Harper and Row, 1988.

Fox, Matthew. *The Original Blessing*. Bear & Co., 1983.

Fox, Robin Lane. *Pagans and Christians*. Penguin, 2006.

Fulcanelli. *Le Mystere des Cathedrals*. Neville Spearman, 1971.

Fulcanelli. *Les Demeures Philosophales*, 2 vols. Jean-Jacques Pauvert: Paris, 1964.

G.

Gardner, Laurence. *Bloodline of the Holy Grail*. Element Books, 1995.

Gawain, Shakti. *Living in the Light*. Whatever Publishing, 1986.

Gettings, Fred. *The Secret Zodiac*. Routledge & Kegan Paul, 1987.

Gimbutas, Marija. *Goddesses and Gods Of Old Europe, 6500–3500 BC*. University of California Press, 1982.

Gimpel, Jean. *The Cathedral Builders*. Grove Press, 1961.

Glover, T. R. *The Conflict of Religions in the early Roman Empire*. Methuen, 1909.

Graves, Robert. *The White Goddess*. Faber & Faber, 1952.

Guirdham, Arthur. *The Great Heresy*. C. W. Daniel: Saffron Walden, 1993.

H.

Haag, Herbert. *Is Original Sin in The Scripture?* Sheed & Ward, 1969.

Hamilton, Bernard. *The Albigensian Crusade*. The Historical Association, 1974.

Hancock, Graham. *The Sign and the Seal*. Mandarin, 1993.

Heschal, Abraham J. *The Earth is The Lord's.* Farrar, Straus, Giroux, 1978.

Higgins, Ronald. *The Seventh Enemy.* Hodder & Stoughton, 1982.

Hobsbawm, Eric. *The Age of Revolution, 1789–1848.* Weidenfeld & Nicolson, 1962.

Hobsbawm, Eric. *The Age of Capital, 1848–1875.* Weidenfeld & Nicolson, 1975.

Hobsbawm, Eric. *The Age of Empire 1875–1914.* Weidenfeld & Nicolson, 1987.

I.

Illich, Ivan. *Tools for Conviviality.* Calder & Bowyers, 1973.

Iyer, Raghavan. *The Moral and Political Thought of Mahatma Gandhi.* Oxford University Press, 1973.

J.

James, Bruno S. *St. Bernard of Clairvaux.* Hodder and Stoughton: London, 1957.

James, William. *The Varieties of Religious Experience.* Longman, Green, and Co., 1902.

Jaynes, Julian. *The Origin Of Consciousness In The Breakdown Of The Bicameral Mind.* Houghton Mifflin: Boston, 1976.

Jedin, Hubert. *History of the Church Vol. 1.* Herder & Herder, 1982.

Jennings, Hargrave. *The Rosicrucians: Their Rites and Mysteries.* Chatto & Windus: London, 1879.

Johnson, Kenneth Rayner. *The Fulcanelli Phenomenon.* Neville Spearman: London, 1980.

Johnson, Paul. *A History of Christianity.* Weidenfeld & Nicolson: London, 1976.

Jungk, Robert. *Brighter Than A Thousand Suns.* Penguin Books, 1970.

K.

Koestler, Arthur. *The Sleepwalkers.* Hutchinson and Co., 1959.

King, Martin Luther, Jr. *Why Can't We Wait.* New American Library, 1964.

Kroeber, Alfred. *Anthropology.* Harcourt Brace, 1948.

L.

Levertov, Denise. *The Poet In The World.* W. W. Norton, 1974.

Levi, Eliphas. *The Key of The Mysteries.* Rider & Co., 1969.

Levi-Strauss, Claude. *Le Totemism Aujourd'hui*. Presses Universitaires de France, 2002.

Lipnack, Jessica and Jeffrey Stamps. *The Networking Book*. Routledge & Kegan Paul, 1986.

Lovelock, James. *Gaia The Practical Science of Planetary Medicine*. Gaia Books, 1991.

Lovelock, James. *The Ages of Gaia*. Bantam, 1990.

Luther, Martin. *Theologia Germanica*. Paulist Press, 1980.

Lutyens, Mary, ed. *The Krishnamurti Reader*. Penguin, 1970.

M.

MacKie, E. W. *Science and Society in Pre-Historic Britain*. Elek Books: London, 1977.

Marcel, Gabriel. *The Decline of Wisdom*. Philosophical Library, 1955.

Matrasso, Pauline, trans. *The Quest of The Holy Grail*. Penguin Classics, 1977.

Matthews, John. *The Grail Tradition*. Element Books, 1990.

McIntosh, Christopher. *The Rosicrucians*. The Aquarian Press, 1987.

McLuhan, T. C. *Touch The Earth*. Abacus/Sphere, 1973.

McManners, John, ed. *The Oxford History of Christianity*. Oxford University Press, 2002.

Merton, Thomas. *The Way of Chuang Tzu*. Shambhala, 2004.

Mesaros, I. *Marx's Theory of Alienation*. Merlin Press, 1970.

Miller, Alice. *Thou Shalt Not Be Aware*. New American Library, 1986.

Millar, Hamish and Paul Broadhurst. *The Sun and the Serpent*. Pendragon Press, 1990.

Mommsen, Wolfgang J. *Max Weber and German politics 1890–1920*. University of Chicago Press, 1984.

Montague, Ashley. *Growing Young*. Bergin & Garvey, 1988.

Moore, R. I. *The Formation Of A Persecuting Society*. Basil Blackwell & Co.: Oxford, 1990.

Murphy, Roland. *The Tree of Life: An Exploration of Biblical Wisdom Literature*. Wm. B. Eerdmans, 2002.

Mutwa, Vusamazulu Credo. *My People*. Blond Ltd.: London, 1969.

N.

Neihart, John G. *Black Elk Speaks*. Washington Square Press, 1959.

O.

Osman, Ahmed. *Moses: Pharaoh of Egypt*. Grafton, 1990.

Ouspensky, P. D. *A New Model of The Universe*. Alfred A. Knopf, 1934.

Ozak, Muzaffer. *Love Is The Wine: Talks Of A Sufi Master In America*. Hohm Press, 2009.

P.

Parfitt, Will. *The Living Quaballah*. Element, 1988.

Pauwels, Louis and Jacques Bergier. *The Dawn Of Magic*. Gibbs & Phillips, 1963.

Pedler, Kit. *The Quest for Gaia*. Granada, 1981.

Q.

Querido, Renee. *The Masters of Chartres*. Floris, 1987.

R.

Ravenscroft, Trevor. *The Cup of Destiny*, Weiser, 1995.

Ravenscroft Trevor and Tim Wallace-Murphy. *The Mark of The Beast*. Sphere: London, 1990.

Ravenscroft, Trevor. *The Spear of Destiny*. Weiser, 1982.

Rich, John M. *Chief Seattle's Unanswered Challenge*. Glen Adams, 1977.

Richards, Mary C. *The Crossing Point*. Wesleyan University Press, 1973.

Ricour, Paul. *The Symbolism of Evil*. Beacon Press, 1986.

Robertson, Roland. *Sociology of Religion*. Penguin, 1969.

Robinson, James M., ed. *The Nag Hammadi Library*. Brill, 1997.

Robinson, John J. *Born in Blood*. Arrow, 1993.

Roszak, Theodore. *The Making Of A Counter-Culture*. Faber & Faber, 1971.

Roszak, Theodore. *Unfinished Animal: The Aquarian Frontier and the Evolution of Consciousness*. Faber & Faber, 1976.

Roszak, Theodore. *Where The Wasteland Ends*. Doubleday, 1972.

Russell, Bertrand. *The Wisdom of the West*. Rathbone Books Ltd.: London, 1959.

S.

Serrus, Georges. *The Land of the Cathars*. Editions Loubatieres, 1990.

Shah, Idries. *The Sufis*. Jonathan Cape: London, 1969.

Shah, Idries. *The Way of The Sufi*. Penguin, 1991.

Sinclair, Andrew. *The Sword And The Grail*. Crown, 1992.

Sjoo, Monica and Barbara Mor. *The Great Cosmic Mother*. HarperOne, 1987.

Smith, Adam. *An Enquiry into The Nature and Causes of the Wealth of Nations*. University Of Chicago Press, 1977.

Snelgrove, L. E. *The Modern World Since 1870*. Longman, 1977.

Spretnak, Charlene. *Lost Goddesses of Early Greece*. Beacon Press, 1978.

Spretnak, Charlene. *The Spiritual Dimensions of Green Politics*. Bear & Co., 1986.

Steiner, Rudolf. *Goethe's World View*. Mercury Press, 1985.

Steiner, Rudolf. *Knowledge of the Higher Worlds*. Rudolf Steiner Press, 1985.

Stevens, Anthony. *Archetypes: A Natural History of the Self*. William Morrow, 1982.

Swan, James A. *The Power of Place*. Quest, 1995.

T.

Tart, Charles T., ed. *Altered States of Consciousness*. Doubleday, 1972.

Tawney, R. H. *Religion And The Rise Of Capitalism*. Pelican: London, 1940.

Teilhard de Chardin, Pierre. *L'Avenir de l'Homme*. Editions de Seuil, 1959.

Teilhard de Chardin, Pierre. *Le Milieu Divin*. Editions de Seuil, 1957.

Teilhard de Chardin, Pierre. *Human Energy*. Harcourt Brace Jovanovich, 1969.

Teilhard de Chardin, Pierre. *The Phenomenon of Man*. Collins, New York, 1959.

Toqueville, Alexis de. *Journeys to England and Ireland*. Transaction Publishers, 1987.

Turner, Frederick. *Beyond Geography: The Western Spirit Against The Wilderness*. Viking, 1980.

U.

Uhlein, Gabriel. *Meditations with Hildegard of Bingen*. Bear & Co., 1982.

Upton-Ward, J. M. *The Rule of The Templars*. Boydell Press, 1992.

W.

Wallace-Murphy, Tim. *An Illustrated Guide Book To Rosslyn Chapel*. The Friends of Rosslyn, 1993.

Wallace-Murphy, Tim, Marilyn Hopkins and Graham Simmans. *Rex Deus*. Element Books, 2000.

Wallace-Murphy, Tim and Marilyn Hopkins. *Rosslyn Guardian of the Secrets of the Holy Grail*. Element Books, 1999.

Wallace-Murphy, Tim. *The Templar Legacy and the Masonic Inheritance Within Rosslyn Chapel*. The Friends of Rosslyn, 1994.

Weber, Max. *The Protestant Ethic And The Spirit of Capitalism*. Routledge, 2001.

Wilhelm, Richard, trans. *The Secret of the Golden Flower*. Harvest, 1962.

Williams, Charles. *The Descent of the Dove*. Fontana, 1963.

Wilson, Bryan. *Magic and The Millennium*. Heinemann, 1973.

Wilson, Colin, ed. *Men of Mystery*. W. H. Allen: London, 1977.

Wilson, Colin. *The Occult*. Grafton, 1979.

Woods, Richard. *Understanding Mysticism*. Image, 1980.

ENDNOTES

1   Frank Barnaby, ed., *The Gaia Peace Atlas*, p. 13.

2   Theodore Roszak, *Where The Wasteland Ends*, pp. 131–132.

3   Joseph Campbell and Bill Moyers, *The Power of Myth*, p. 163.

4   *Where The Wasteland Ends*, p. 134.

5   Fritjof Capra, *The Turning Point*, p. 410.

6   *The Power of Myth*, p. 5.

7   Jacob Bronowski, *The Ascent of Man*, p. 45.

8   Ibid., pp. 45–48.

9   Colin Wilson, *The Occult*, p. 182. Also *The New Scientist*, no. 1772, 8 June 1991.

10 *The Occult*, pp. 78–79.

11 Julian Jaynes, *The Origin of Consciousness and the Breakdown of the Bicameral Mind*, pp. 9–10.

12 Julian Huxley's introduction to Pierre Teilhard de Chardin's *The Phenomenon of Man*.

13 Shakespeare, *King Richard the Second*, Act I.

14 Hamish Millar and Paul Broadhurst, *The Sun and the Serpent*, p. 21. Also James A. Swan, *The Power of Place*, p. 245.

15 *The Power of Place*, p. 123.

16 Robert Bauval and Adrian Gilbert, *The Orion Mystery*.

17 Charlene Spretnak, *The Spiritual Dimensions of Green Politics*, p. 32.

18 Joseph Campbell, *The Masks of God, Vol. 1: Primitive Mythology, Vol. 2: Oriental Mythology* and *Vol. 3: Occidental Mythology*.

19 Trevor Ravenscroft and Tim Wallace-Murphy, *The Mark of the Beast*, p. 44.

20 *The Ascent of Man*, pp. 76–77.

21 *The Orion Mystery*, pp. 13, 22, 24–25.

22 Ibid., pp. 22, 24, 29, 162, 196.

23 Ibid., pp. 57–58.

24 G. Masparo, *Rec. Trav.* vol. V, Fasc 1–11, p. 157.

25 I. E. S. Edwards, *The Pyramids of Egypt*, p. 177.

26 Robert Faulkner, *The Ancient Egyptian Pyramid Texts*, p. v.

27 Peter Dawkins, *Arcadia*, pp. 40–44.

28 Emile Block, *Moses*, p. 21.

29 Ahmed Osman, *Moses: Pharaoh of Egypt*.

30 *The Major Gods of Egypt*, p. 155.

31 *The Major Gods of Egypt*, p. 169ff. Also Exodus Ch. 2, vs. 11–15.

32 *Moses: Pharaoh of Egypt*, pp. 155, 215–216.

33 Sabbah Bros., *Les Secrets de L'Exode*, p. 7.

34 Exodus Ch. 14, vs. 27–28.

35 Norman Cantor, *The Sacred Chain*, p. 7.

36 Sigmund Freud, *Moses and Monotheism*.

37 Eli Barnavi, ed., *A Historical Atlas of the Jewish People*, p. 22.

38 John M. Allegro, *The Dead Sea Scrolls and the Christian Myth*, p. 65.

39 *The Sacred Chain*, p. 11.

40 2 Kings, Ch. 22, v. 8. Also 2 Chronicles Ch. 34, vs. 14–21.

41 Dan Cohn-Sherbok, *A Concise Encyclopedia of Judaism*, pp. 61–62.

42 Robin Lane Fox, *The Unauthorized Version*, p. 72.

43 *Moses and Monotheism*.

44 Karen Armstrong, *A History of God*, p. 75.

45 *The Dead Sea Scrolls and the Christian Myth*, p. 173.

46 The Wisdom of Solomon, Ch. 10, v. 17.

47 Proverbs, Ch. 9, v. 1.

48 *A History of God*, p. 82.

49 Paul Johnson, *A History of Christianity*, p. 13.

50 1 Chronicles, Ch. 3, v. 18.

51 *A Historical Atlas of the Jewish People*, p. 28.

52 The Book of Esdras.

53 Ezra, Ch. 1, vs. 2–4. Also 2 Chronicles, Ch. 36, v. 23.

54 *A Historical Atlas of the Jewish People*, p. 30.

55 Robert Feather, *The Copper Scroll Decoded*, p. 319.

56 *The Unauthorized Version*, p. 91.

57 *The Phenomenon of Man* p. 165.

58 *The Illiad*, XVII.

59 *The Mark of the Beast*, pp. 48–49.

60 Ibid.

61 *The Occult*, pp. 243–244.

62 Ibid., p. 244.

63 *The Masks of God, Vol. 3: Occidental Mythology*, pp. 255, 366.

64 *The Occult*, p. 248.

65 *Encyclopaedia of the Occult*.

66 G. S. Faber, *A Dissertation of the source of the Cabiri*, OUP 1803.

67 Strabo, *Geographica*. Ammanius Marcelinus, *Works*. Clement of Alexandria, *Stromata*.

68 *The Occult*, pp. 249–250.

69 Betrand Russel, *The Wisdom of the West*, pp. 21–26.

70 *The Occult*, p. 253.

71 *The Wisdom of the West*, p. 39.

72 Ibid., p. 66.

73 Ibid., p. 69.

74 *The Mark of the Beast*, p. 124.

75 *The Wisdom of the West*, p. 151.

76 Ibid., p. 152.

77 *The Masks of God, Vol. 3: Occidental Mythology*, pp. 264, 337.

78 Clement of Alexandria, *Stromata*.

79 E. W. MacKie, *Science and Society in Pre-Historic Britain*.

80 Peter Beresford Ellis, *The Druids*, p. 212.

81 Caesar, *Commentarii de Bello Gallico*, IV.

82 Ammianus Marcellinus, *Works*.

83 Diogenes Laertes, introduction to *Vitae*.

84 Cicero, *De Divinatione*.

85 Diodorus Siculus, *Histories*, V.

86 Pliny, *Historia Naturalis*, XIV, XX.

87 Tacitus, *Annals*, XIV. Also *Histories*, IV.

88 Pomponius Mela, *De situ orbis libri III*.

89 Lucan, *Pharsalia*, I.

90 *Commentarii de Bello Gallico*, IV.

91 Tim Wallace-Murphy and Marilyn Hopkins, *Templars in America*.

92 The New Catholic Catechism, 1990.

93 Tim Wallace-Murphy, *Custodians of Truth*.

94 Acts of the Apostles, Ch. 2, v. 6.

95 Robert Eisenmann, *James the Brother of Jesus*, p. xxvii.

96 Gospel of Matthew, Ch. 2, v. 1.

97 *The Mark of the Beast*, p. 51.

98 Gospel of Mark, Ch. 6, v. 3.

99 Gospel of Matthew, Ch. 13, v. 55.

100 Ibid., Ch. 27, v. 6.

101 *James the Brother of Jesus*, p. 936.

102 Gospel of John, Ch. 20, vs. 27–29.

103 James M. Robinson, ed., *The Nag-Hammadi Library*, p. 127.

104 Acts of the Apostles, Ch. 4, v. 36.

105 The Damascus Document, found among the Dead Sea Scrolls, translated by Eisenman and Wise in *The Dead Sea Scrolls Uncovered*.

106 Epiphanius, *Haeres*, lxxviii.

107 *The Dead Sea Scrolls Uncovered*, pp. 68–69.

108 Genesis, Ch. 9, v. 4. Also in *The Dead Sea Scrolls Uncovered*.

109 1 Corinthians, Ch. 9, vs. 1–3.

110 1 Timothy, Ch. 2, vs. 5, 7.

111 For Paul's attack on James, see Eisenman's *James the Brother of Jesus*, Ch. 16. For his relationship with the Herodian family, see *James the Brother of Jesus*, pp. 349–350, 389, 412, 441.

112 *A History of Christianity*, p. 4.

113 Pseudo-Clementine Recognitions, *Homilies*, 11.35.

114 Irenaeus, cited in Gardner's *Bloodline of the Holy Grail*, p. 154.

115 H. R. Ellis Davidson, *Gods and Myths of Northern Europe*.

116 *A History of Christianity*, pp. 46–48.

117 T. R. Glover, *The Conflict of Religions in the early Roman Empire*, Ch. 10.

118 *A History of Christianity*, pp. 50–52.

119 John McManners, ed., *The Oxford History of Christianity*, pp. 50–52.

120 *A History of Christianity*, p. 55.

121 Ibid., p. 58.

122 Hubert Jedin, ed., *The History of the Church*, vol. 1, pp. 416–417.

123 Robin Land Fox, *Pagans and Christians*, p. 655.

124 *The Oxford History of Christianity*, p. 66.

125 *Moses: Pharaoh of Egypt*.

126 *The Mark of the Beast*, p. 23.

127 Matthew Fox, *The Coming Of The Cosmic Christ*. pp. 31–32.

128 *A History of Christianity*, pp. 112–119.

129 Ibid., p. 116.

130 Ibid., p. 121.

131 Matthew Fox, *Original Blessing*, pp. 45–51.

132 Ibid., p. 47.

133 Herbert Haag, *Is Original Sin in the Scripture?*

134 Ashley Montague, *Growing Young*.

135 *Original Blessing*, pp. 48–49.

136 *Growing Young*.

137 *A History of Christianity*, pp. 116–117.

HIDDEN WISDOM

138 Ibid., p. 117.

139 Ibid., p. 116.

140 Bertrand Russel, *The Wisdom of the West.*

141 Tim Wallace-Murphy, *The Templar legacy and the Masonic Inheritance within Rosslyn Chapel.*

142 *The Wisdom of the West.*

143 Meister Eckhart.

144 *The Templar Legacy and the Masonic Inheritance within Roslyn Chapel.*

145 *A History of Christianity*, p. 130.

146 Ibid., p. 168.

147 *The Templar Legacy and the Masonic Inheritance within Roslyn Chapel.*

148 *A History of Christianity*, pp. 196–197.

149 *The Oxford History of Christianity*, p. 220.

150 *Original Blessing*, p. 75.

151 Ibid., p. 108.

152 Ibid., p. 35.

153 Ibid.

154 Ibid., p. 57.

155 Julian of Norwich, cited by Fox in *The Coming of the Cosmic Christ.*

156 Francis of Assissi, *The Canticle to the Sun.*

157 Mechthild of Magdeburg, cited by Fox in *The Coming of the Cosmic Christ.*

158 *The Occult*, p. 242.

159 Jacob Boehme, *Signatura Rerum.*

160 *The Mark of the Beast*, p. 79.

161 Ibid., p. 75.

162 Ibid., pp. 75–76.

163 *Commentarii de Bello Gallico*, IV. Also Y. Delaport, *Les Trois Notre-Dame de la Cathedral de Chartres*, p. 15.

164 Tim Wallace-Murphy and Marilyn Hopkins, *Rosslyn Guardian of the Secrets of the Holy Grail.*

165 Frederic Lionel. *Mirrors of Truth.*

166 *The Mark of the Beast*, p. 39.

167 *A History of Christianity*, p. 113.

168 Tim Wallace-Murphy and Marilyn Hopkins, *Rex Deus*, p. 138.

169 Andrew Sinclair, *The Discovery of the Grail*, p. 27.

170 See *Rex Deus* for a full exposition of this tradition.

171 *The Mark of the Beast*, p. 51.

172 For a full explanation consult Trevor Ravenscroft's masterwork, *The Cup of Destiny*.

173 *Rex Deus*, p. 140.

174 Trevor Ravenscroft, *The Spear of Destiny*, p. xv.

175 *The Nag Hammadi Library*.

176 *The Power of Myth*.

177 Discovered in the course of a conversation between the author and Sheik Reshad Field of the Mavlavi Sufi order.

178 Robert Graves in his introduction to Idries Shah's work, *The Sufis*.

179 Ibid.

180 Obedyah Maimonides, *The Treatise of the Pool*, p. ix.

181 *The Mark of the Beast*, p. 51.

182 *The Power of Myth*.

183 Simon de St. Bertin, *Gesta abbatum Sancti Bertini Sithensiu*, vol. 13, p. 649.

184 Helen Nicholson, *The Knights Templar, a New History*, pp. 23–24.

185 Ibid., p. 27.

186 Ibid., p. 29.

187 Ivo, *Epistolae* no. 245, Pl. vol., 162, cols. 251–253.

188 Michael of Albany and Walid Amine Salhab, *The Knights Templar of the Middle East*, p. 66.

189 Baigent, Leigh and Lincoln, *The Holy Blood and the Holy Grail*, p. 65.

190 Graham Hancock, *The Sign and the Seal*, pp. 95–100.

191 For a deeper analysis of the *Compagnonnage*, see Louis Charpentier's *Mysteries of Chartres Cathedral*.

192 *La Régle de St. Devoir de Dieu et de la Croisade*.

193 Fred Gettings, *The Secret Zodiac*, p. 11.

194 P. D. Ouspensky, *A New Model of the Universe*.

195 Keneth Rayner Johnson, *The Fulcannelli Phenomenon*, p. 214.

196 *The Templar legacy and the Masonic Inheritance within Rosslyn Chapel*.

197 Michel Kleber's article *Une vie pour reformer l'Eglise* in the journal *Source*.

198 Gospel of Matthew, Ch. 7, vs. 16–20.

199 Bernard Hamilton, *The Albigensian Crusade*, p. 13.

200 Arthur Guirdham, *The Great Heresy*, p. 98.

201 Ibid., p. 95.

202 Georges Serrus, *The Land of the Cathars*, p. 44.

203 *The Great Heresy*, p. 9.

204 *The Albigensian Crusade*, p. 6.

205 Ibid., p. 7.

206 David Christie-Murray, *The History of Heresy*, p. 31.

207 *The Great Heresy*, p. 18.

208 *The Albigensian Crusade*, p. 6.

209 *The Great Heresy*, p. 9.

210 *The Albigensian Crusade*, p. 4.

211 Wakefield and Evans, *Heresies of the Middle Ages*, pp. 122–124.

212 *The History of Heresy*, p. 105.

213 Yuri Stoyanov, *The Hidden Tradition in Europe*, p. 156.

214 *Heresies of the Middle Ages*, pp. 140–141.

215 *The Great Heresy*, p. 54.

216 *The Land of the Cathars*, p. 15.

217 G. K. Barnes, *The Institution of a Persecuting Society*, p. 26.

218 Michele Aue, *Cathar Country*, p. 15.

219 *The History of Heresy*, p. 108.

220 *The Great Heresy*, pp. 56–57.

221 *Cathar Country*, p. 20.

222 *The Great Heresy*, p. 63.

223 *Cathar Country*, p. 22.

224 *The Great Heresy*, p. 64.

225 *Cathar Country*, p. 26.

226 *The Land of the Cathars*, p. 27.

227 Ibid., p. 32.

228 *The Great Heresy*, pp. 78–87.

229 Ibid., p. 72.

230 *The Albigensian Crusade*, p. 27.

231 *The Great Heresy*, p. 89.

232 *The Albigensian Crusade*, p. 27.

233 The original *Codex Callestinus*, or *Liber Sanct Jacobi*, is kept in the archives of the Cathedral of Santiago de Compostella.

234 Described in detail in *Rosslyn, Guardian of the Secrets of the Holy Grail*.

235 Ibid., pp. 99–100.

236 The author heard this charge leveled against the Templars by a Catholic priest at a meeting of an historical society in Draguignan in 1993.

237 *The Templar Legacy and Masonic Inheritance within Rosslyn Chapel*.

238 *The Mark of the Beast*, pp. 52–53.

239 *Rex Deus*, p. 124.

240 *The Holy Blood and the Holy Grail*.

241 *The Mark of the Beast*, pp. 52–53.

242 *A History of Christianity*, p. 313.

243 Malcolm Barber, *The Trial of the Templars*, p. 3.

244 *The Templar Legacy and Masonic Inheritance within Rosslyn Chapel.*

245 Begg Ean, *The Cult of the Black Virgin*, p. 103.

246 *Histoire du Chef de Saint-Jean Baptiste conserve a Amiens.*

247 William Anderson, *The Rise of the Gothic.*

248 Baring and Cashford, *The Myth of the Goddess*, pp. 411–412.

249 *The Templar legacy and Masonic Inheritance within Rosslyn Chapel.*

250 Ibid.

251 *The Mark of the Beast*, p. 67.

252 John J. Robinson, *Braga in Blood.*

253 Traditional call for help from a Freemason in distress.

254 Gedricke, 18th century Masonic historian.

255 *Mirrors of Truth.*

256 Tim Wallace-Murphy, *An Illustrated Guidebook to Rosslyn Chapel.*

257 *The Templar legacy and Masonic Inheritance within Rosslyn Chapel.*

258 *Templars in America.*

259 Andrew Sinclair, *The Sword and the Grail.*

260 *An Illustrated Guidebook to Rosslyn Chapel.* Also *The Sword and the Grail.*

261 *Rosslyn Guardian of the Secrets of the Holy Grail.*

262 *An Illustrated Guidebook to Rosslyn Chapel.*

263 *The Mark of the Beast*, p. 69.

264 For information on initiatory ritual and practice, see Ravenscroft's *The Cup of Destiny.*

265 Commemorated by a superb carving in the North Portal of Chartres, the Portal of the Initiates.

266 Philip Heselton, *The Elements of Earth Mysteries*, p. 78.

267 Peter Dawkins, *Arcadia.*

268 Emile Bloch, *Moses.*

269 Elyn Aviva, *Following the Milky Way: A Pilgrimage Across Spain.*

270 Ibid.

271 Ibid.

272 Colin Wilson, *Men of Mystery.*

273 *The Mark of the Beast*, pp. 79–81.

274 *The Turning Point*, p. 38.

275 *The Ascent of Man*, p. 142.

276 Carlo Cipoloa, *The Economic History of World Population.*

277 Orton Previte, *Outlines of Medieval History*, p. 469.

278 Geoffrey Godwin, *Islamic Spain*, p. vii.

279 *The Holy Blood and the Holy Grail*, p. 109.

280 *A History of Christianity*, p. 271.

281 Ibid., pp. 281–287.

282 Ibid., p. 275.

283 Ibid., p. 272.

284 From a letter from Marx to Engels, 1854, cited by Schlomo Avineri in *The Social and Political Thought of Karl Marx*, pp. 154–155.

285 Max Weber, *The Protestant Ethic and the Spirit of Capitalism.*

286 R. H. Tawney, *Religion and the Rise of Capitalism.*

287 *The Social and Political Thought of Karl Marx*, pp. 154–155.

288 *Where the Wasteland Ends*, p. 124.

289 Francis Bacon, *Novum Organum.*

290 *Where the Wasteland Ends*, pp. 125–131.

291 Martin Luther, *Theologica Germanica*, preface.

292 *Rosslyn Guardian of the Secrets of the Holy Grail*, p. 126.

293 *Position Paper of the Native American Project of the Theology in the Americas* (Detroit II conference, July–August 1980), p. 3.

294 William Shakespeare, *Julius Caesar.*

295 *A History of Christianity*, p. 401.

296 Ibid., p. 402.

297 Ibid., p. 403.

298 *The Coming of the Cosmic Christ*, pp. 24–26.

299 *A History of Christianity*, p. 437.

300 Frederick Turner, *Beyond Geography: The Western Spirit Against the Wilderness.*

301 Chief Seattle's address to the U.S. president in 1854.

302 John G. Neihart, *Black Elk Speaks*, pp. 70–71.

303 Ibid.

304 Mutwa Credo, *My People*, p. 178.

305 Ibid.

306 *A History of Christianity*, pp. 409–412.

307 Richard Wilhelm, trans., *The Garden of the Secret Flower.*

308 Gabriel Marcel, *The Decline of Wisdom*, p. 42.

309 *The Turning Point*, pp. 330–331.

310 *A History of Christianity*, p. 413.

311 Ibid., p. 412.

312 Eric Hobbesbawm, *The Age of Capital*, pp. 49, 99, 156–159, 180.

313 Raghavan Iyer, *The Moral and Political Thought of Mahatma Gandhi*, p. 93.

314 Carolyn Marchant of Berkeley University, cited by Fritjof Capra, *The Turning Point*, p. 24.

315 Julius Bronowski, *William Blake and the Age of Revolution*, p. 7.

316 *The Economic History of World Population*.

317 Ibid.

318 Eric Hobsbawm, *The Age of Revolution*, p. 207.

319 Ibid., pp. 228–231.

320 Ibid., p. 115.

321 Ibid., p. 88.

322 Edmund Burke, *Reflections on the Revolution in France*.

323 *William Blake and the Age of Revolution*.

324 Ibid., p. 180.

325 Ibid., p. 15.

326 John Davy, *On Hope, Evolution and Change*.

327 Theodore Roszak, *Where the Wasteland Ends*, p. 329 and *Unfinished Animal*, p. 205.

328 Rudolf Steiner, *Goethe's World View*, p. 13.

329 Eric Hobsbawm, *The Age of Empire*, pp. 24–25.

330 Ibid., p. 4.

331 Christmas Humphreys cited by Colin Wilson's *Men of Mystery*.

332 Ibid.

333 Ibid.

334 Colin Wilson, *Rudolf Steiner*.

335 Ibid.

336 Kit Pedler's essay on Tesla in Colin Wilson's *Men of Mystery*.

337 Ibid.

338 *The Mark of the Beast*, p. 189.

339 *The Spear of Destiny*, p. 112.

340 *The Age of Empire*.

341 Georges Clemanceau.

342 *The Age of Empire*, p. 307.

343 Line from a poem by W. B. Yeats describing the 1916 rising.

344 *The Mark of the Beast*, p. 28.

345 L. E. Snellgrove, *The World Since 1870*, p. 126.

HIDDEN WISDOM

346 *The Age of Empire*, p. 334.

347 Ibid., pp. 333–335.

348 *The Mark of the Beast*, p. 139.

349 Robert Jungk, *Brighter than a Thousand Suns*, pp. 39–52.

350 Ibid., pp. 53ff.

351 *The Mark of the Beast*, p. 140.

352 *Brighter than a Thousand Suns*, pp. 110ff.

353 Ibid., p. 80.

354 Ibid., p. 235.

355 *The Gaia Peace Atlas*.

356 *The Phenomenon of Man*.

357 *The Occult*, p. 47.

358 *Evolution and Change*.

359 *The Mark of the Beast*, p. 83.

360 *The Spear of Destiny*, p. 262.

361 Ibid., p. 264.

362 Bernard Defgaauw, *Evolution. Theory of Teilhard de Chardin*, p. 59.

363 Julian Huxley's introduction to Teilhard de Chardin's *Phenomenon of Man*.

364 *Evolution. Theory of Teilhard de Chardin*, pp. 36–37.

365 Ibid., pp. 51–53.

366 Bernard Towers' introduction to Delfgaauw's *Evolution. Theory of Teilhard de Chardin*.

367 *Evolution. Theory of Teilhard de Chardin*, p. 43.

368 Julian Huxley's introduction to *The Phenomenon of Man*.

369 The introduction to *Where the Wasteland Ends*, pp. xxii–xxiii.

370 Pierre Teilhard de Chardin, *The Vision of the Past*, p. 217.

371 Pierre Teilhard de Chardin in 1936.

372 *The Turning Point*, p. 326.

373 Marilyn Fergusson, *The Aquarian Conspiracy*, p. 47.

374 *The Aquarian Conspiracy*.

375 *The Gaia Peace Atlas*.

376 Nichidatsu Fujii, founder of the Nipponzan Myohoji Buddhist Order, cited by Marilyn Fergusson in *The Aquarian Cosnipracy*.

377 *Original Blessing*.

378 *The Moral and Political Thought of Mahatma Gandhi*.

379 Alexis de Toqueville.

380 M. C. Richards, *The Crossing Point*.

381 *The Aquarian Conspiracy*, p. 200.

382 Ibid.

383 *The Occult*, p. 34.

384 James Lovelock, *Gaia* and *The Ages of Gaia*.

385 *The Aquarian Conspiracy*.

386 Joseph Campbell, *The Hero with a Thousand Faces*.

387 *The Mark of the Beast*, p. 188.

INDEX

A.

Abaris the Druid, 49, 60
Aborigines, Australian, 83
Abraham, 37, 75–76
Abraham, Karl, 30
Abrasax, the, 162
Abydos, Egypt, 180
Academy, the, 51–52
Afghanistan, 270
Africa, 206, 209–210, 214–215, 219
agnosticism, 182, 230, 236
Ahura Mazda, 17
Aimery, Arnold, 148
Akhenaten, Pharaoh, 20, 28–32, 89
Alchemist's Pilgrimage, 156, 171 see
    Pilgrimage of Initiation
Alchemy, 1, 26, 179, 184, 190, 200
Allegro, John, 36
Alsace, Philippe d', 119
Altimera, France, 8
Amarna, Egpyt, 31–32, 180
Amenhotep III, 30
Ammianus Marcellinus, 59
Ammonius Saccas, 243
Anatolia (Turkey), 15–17, 112
Anderson, William, 129
Andes mountains, 208
Andreae, Johann Valentin, 183, 185,
    200–201
Anglican Church, 184, 209
Anschluss, the 265
Anthroposophy, 245–246, 276, 292
Anti-Christ, The, 248–249
Anubis, 24
Apartheid, 215
Apocalypse, 303
Apollo, 59
Apostles, the, 66, 70–73, 75, 77–79, 104,
    142

Aquarian Age, 288, 304
Aquarian Conspiracy, The, 300–301
Aquinas, Thomas, 106
Arabic civilization, 105, 156–157, 160,
    190, 218
Aragon, Crown of, 137
Aramaic language, 38
archaeology, 16, 21–22, 24–25, 35–36, 45,
    57, 59, 61–62
Archimedes, 187
Ariège, France, 8
Aristides, Saint, 73
Aristotle, 299
Ark, the, 127, 132
Armageddon, 269
Armstrong, George, 210
Armstrong, Karen, 38
Ascent of Man, The, 187, 205, 292
Asclepius, 23
Ashe, David, 294
Ashen Path (also Track of Souls), 178
Assyrian civilization, 35, 57
Astarte, festival of, 94
Atbash Cipher, 160
Aten, 28–29, 31–32, 89
Athelstan, King, 170
Athens, Greece, 45, 51
Atlantic Ocean, 156, 171, 303
atom bomb, 254, 261, 264–265, 267–270
Attis, 163
Augustine, Saint, 90–93, 118, 153, 196
Austria, 252, 263, 265
Autun, France, 56
Avebury, England, 11, 15, 61
Aviva, Elyn, 182
Aztec civilization, 303

B.

Babylonian Empire, 38, 40–41, 49, 55, 161

Babylonian Exile, 31, 35–36, 41
Bacon, Francis, 198–199, 201, 223
Bactrian people, 57
Baigent, Michael, 123
Balkans, 142, 144
Baltic states, 166, 224
Balzac, Honoré de, 231
Bannockburn, Battle of, 166, 170
Banti, Cristiano, 136
Bantu people, 213
Baphomet, 160–161
baptism, 47, 141, 210
Barnabas, Saint, 72, 77
Baudrillart, Henri, 230
Beauseant, the, 162, 164
Beethoven, Ludwig van, 231
Behedet Temple, Egypt 180
Belgium, 224
Belle Époque, 252, 260
Benedict XVI, Pope, 151
Benedictine Order, 126, 155
Bentham, Jeremy, 235
Berit, the, 36
Berlin, Germany, 245, 262, 265
Bernard of Clairvaux, Saint, 124–125,
    132–133, 144–145, 158, 161
Bernardus, 110
Bertalanffy, Ludwig von, 296
Beshara School, the, 292
Bethlehem, 67
Béziers, France, 148–149
Bible (or scripture), the, 31–32, 36–41,
    70–73, 91–92, 104, 193, 200; Acts of
    the Apostles, 72, 78; Chronicles, 36;
    Deuteronomy, 36; Epistles, 77–78, 80;
    Genesis, 92; Kings, 32; Proverbs, 39;
    Song of Songs, 125 also see Gospels
Bishop, Anselm, 123
Black Madonna, 75, 160, 172
Black Virgin, the, 179, 181
Blake, William, 1, 109, 201, 222, 232–
    233, 242, 285
Blavatsky, Helena Petrovna, 238, 243–
    244, 273, 285

Bloch, Ivan, 255
Boehme, Jacob, 108–109, 232, 234
Boethius, 104
Bogomilism, 118, 143–144
Bohr, Niels, 261
Boney, Jean, 129
Book of Splendor, 118
Book of Two Ways, 178
Born, Max, 261
Botticelli, 185, 197, 200
Boyle, Robert, 185, 201
Braga, Portugal, 70
Brahmanism, 50, 60
Brazil, 205, 241
Brighton Museum, 58
Bristol, England, 213
Britain, 10, 53, 57, 62, 103, 163, 215, 219,
    225, 227–229, 235, 251, 256, 258, 265,
    268, 290 also see England
British Museum, 25
Bronowski, Jacob, 16, 187, 205, 292
Bronowski, Julius, 233
Bruce, Robert the, 166, 170
Brundtland, Gro Harlem, 296
Buddhism, 114, 216, 289, 292–293,
    299–300
Buhen, Egypt 181
Builders, Schools of, 130 see cathedrals
Bulgaria, 143
Burgundy (region), 56, 102, 176
burial practices, 8, 12–13, 15, 17, 30
Burke, Edmund, 229
Bushmen, the, 214
Byzantium (Constantinople), 144

C.

Cabaret, Castle of, 149
Caesar, Julius, 59–60, 62
Caligula, 87
Calvin, John, 196
Cambridge, England, 109, 261
Camiño de las Estrellas, 182 see Pilgrimage
    of Initiation

Camiño de Santiago, 182–183 see
   Pilgrimage of Initiation
Campbell, Joseph, 7, 17, 120, 301
Canaan, 32, 35
Cantor, Norman, 35–36
capitalism, 2, 159, 194–196, 258–260, 268
Capra, Fritjof, 187, 205, 217, 223, 282,
   285, 293
Carmel, Mount, 177
Carnac stones, 11
Carnuntum, 62
Cassiodorus, 60
castles, 140, 148–149, 170, 181; Cabaret,
   149
Castor and Pollux, 162
Castres, France, 148
Çatalhöyük, 15–17
Catharism, 97, 113, 118, 134, 139–153,
   155–156, 158, 164, 166
cathedrals, 1, 104, 114, 124–125, 127–
   128, 130–131, 155, 161–163, 172, 181,
   183; Amiens, 127, 161–162, 172, 176;
   Béziers, 148; Chartres, 100, 110–111,
   123, 127, 155, 162, 172, 175; León,
   182; Rheims, 127, 162; Orleans, 172,
   174; Santiago de Compostela, 172,
   182; Wittenberg, 191 also see Notre
   Dame
Catholic Church, 1–3, 66, 70, 75, 83,
   85–86, 88–89, 92, 95–97, 101–103,
   111, 123, 138–140, 148, 156, 160–161,
   150, 154–155, 165, 184, 188–195, 197,
   199–201, 207, 210, 227, 231, 235–236,
   277–278, 281, 299
Cave paintings, 4, 8–9, 214
Celts, 55, 57–62, 137, 140, 144
Central America, 21, 303
Cephas, 72, 77 also see Peter, Saint
chakras, 26, 61–62, 114, 172–181
Chaldeans, the, 49, 57
Chamberlain, Neville, 265
Champagne, France, 118–119, 123, 142
chariot mysticism, 163, 177
Charlemagne, 97
Charney, Geoffroy de, 159
Children of Father Soubise, 125–126

Children of Master Jacques, 125–126,
   166
Children of Solomon, 125, 127–128, 164
Chile, 205
China, 8, 14, 18, 21, 83, 217–220, 224,
   293–294
Chomsky, Noam, 295
Christmas, 67, 95
Chuma dynasty, 208
Churchill, Winston, 259
Chymical Wedding of Christian Rosenkreutz,
   183
Cicero, 60
Cintra (also Sintra), 172–173, 181
Cipolla, Carlo, 225
Cistercian Order, 104, 125, 127, 132–
   133, 145–146, 148, 161
Clairvaux, 124–125, 132–133, 145, 158,
   161
Clan Gunn, 171
Clemanceau, Georges, 255
Clement of Alexandria, 57, 113
Clement, Pope, 146
Cluny, France, 123
Codex Calixtinus, 155
College of France, 230
Columbus, Christopher, 171
Comedie Humaine, 231
Commentarii de Bello Gallico, 62
communism, 259, 266, 268, 279
Compagnonnage, the, 112, 125–128, 156,
   162
Compostela (also Santiago de
   Compostela), 69, 155, 165, 172–174,
   182
Compte, Auguste, 277
Confucianism, 216
conquistadores, 205, 208
consolamentum, 141–142 see Catharism
Constantine, Emperor, 82, 88–89
Constantinople, 144, 161
Coomaraswamy, Ananda, 7
Copernicus, Nicolaus, 187, 189
Cornwall, England, 62

cosmogenesis, 281

Craftmasons, 112, 125, 166, 170 also see *Compagnonnage*

Crazy Horse, 212

Crimean War, 240

Crotona (also Crotone), Italy, 49

Crown chakra, 173–177, 180

Crusades, the, 137–139, 144, 150–152, 157, 161, 164, 206; Albigensian, 134, 147; Cathar, 148–152, 164; First, 122–123, 129, 191

Cuba, 241

Cuéllar, Javier Pérez de, 296

Cup of Destiny, The, 119

Cybele, 50

Cyrus, King, 41–42

Czechoslovakia, 258, 264–265

D.

Da Vinci, Leonardo, 1, 185, 197, 200

Dancing Wu Li Masters, The, 293

Dark Ages, 63, 118, 178, 218

Darwin, Charles, 10

David, King, 37–38

Davidson, H. R. Ellis, 83

Dead Sea Scrolls, 2, 36, 70, 76, 78, 133

Decembrists, 231

Declaration of the Rights of Man, 228

Demeter, 48, 50

Descartes, René, 176, 188, 198–199, 223, 234–235, 241, 294

Dharma, 290

Diaspora, the, 41–42, 72, 79, 84

Dickens, Charles, 231

Didymus Judas Thomas, 70 see Gospel of Thomas

Diodorus Siculus, 60

Diogenes Laertes, 49, 60

Dionysus, 17, 48

divine, the, 17, 22, 26–27, 39, 48, 60, 65, 67, 74–75, 79–80, 85, 93, 98, 111–113, 121, 140, 151, 161, 175, 179, 188, 198, 229–230, 274–275, 281, 289–290

Djoser, King, 23, 61

Documentary hypothesis, 37

dogmatism, 68, 85, 90, 92, 96, 101–103, 105, 113, 190, 218, 276, 289

Dominican Order, 148, 150–151, 206

Domitian, Emperor, 87, 112

Donatists, 90

Donne, John, 220

Dostoyevsky, Fyodor, 231

Dresden, Germany, 266

drugs, 214, 264, 286

Druidism, 14, 23, 49, 57–63, 110, 114, 140, 144, 172–173, 175, 181–182, 303

Dudimose, Pharaoh, 30

E.

Earth goddess, 172, 202

Easter, 95, 256

Eastern Church, 92, 96, 113, 248

Ebionites, the, 76, 78–80, 84 also see Nazoreans

Eddington, Arthur, 248

Edwards, I. E. S., 25

Egeria, 17

Egypt, 17–18, 21–26, 28–31, 35–36, 41–42, 49, 55, 57, 74, 96, 106, 113, 126–127, 140, 160, 178–181; two kingdoms, 26, 28, 178–179

Egyptian Antiquities Services, 24

Egyptology, 22, 30, 178

Einstein, Albert, 263, 266, 290

Eisenman, Robert, 70, 78

El Khidir, 120, 164

Elena Petrovna Gan, 238 see H. P. Blavatsky

Elephantine, Egypt, 42, 179

Eleusis, 48

Elijah, 120, 177

Elisha, 177

Elohim, the, 37

Engels, Friedrich, 239

England, 10, 58, 62, 112, 125, 132, 162–163, 166, 170, 184–185, 201, 209, 213, 220, 224, 227, 235, 242, 245–246, 287 also see Britain

Enlightenment, the, 199, 250, 278

Ephesus, Anatolia, 112
Erasmus, 192–193, 196, 201
Eroica, The, 231
Eschenbach, Wolfram von, 119
Essenes, the, 47, 49, 60, 67, 72–73, 80, 140, 142
Etham, 33
Ethiopia, 133, 263
Eure river, 62
Eusebius, 73, 87
evolution, 6, 10, 47, 50, 87, 196, 273–274, 277–281, 285, 289, 300
Exile, the, 31, 35–41, 51, 152, 231
Exodus, the, 30–32, 35, 39, 42
Fadeef, Helena de, 243

F.

faith, 30, 48, 59, 65–66, 73, 87, 148, 150–151, 188, 192–194, 199, 293, 300
Falkland Islands, 256
Father, the, 85–86, 89, 177, 180, 193
Faulkner, Raymond, 25
Feather, Robert, 31–32
feng shui, 14
Ferguson, Marilyn, 300–301
Fermi, Enrico, 261
feudalism, 2, 97, 103, 138, 144, 197, 228–229, 259
Few, the, 9, 18, 25, 46, 239, 241
Fiedler, Leslie, 287
Filipepi, Sandro, 200
Final Solution, the, 267
Flanders, 119, 256
Florence, Italy, 189, 197
Fludd, Robert, 185, 200
Foch, Ferdinand, 259
Foster, David, 108
Fox, George, 109
France, Anatole, 241
France, 8, 53, 59, 125, 127, 132, 137, 142, 145, 147, 156, 159, 162, 166, 178, 215, 224, 227–228, 230, 235–236, 241–242, 246, 251, 258, 268, 287
Francis of Assisi, Saint, 106

Franciscan Order, 206–207
Franck, James, 261
Frankl, Victor, 295
Franklin, Benjamin, 232
Franks, the, 102
Freemasonry, 1, 27, 120, 166, 168–170, 183–185, 231, 242, 246
French Revolution, 224–231, 235, 239–241
Freud, Sigmund, 28, 30–31, 35
Fulbertus, Bishop, 110
Fulcanelli, 130–131

G.

Gabanon, Léonard, 168
Gaia, 46, 50
Gaia hypothesis, 248, 296–297
Gaia Peace Atlas, The, 5
Galatia, 57
Galician Catholics, 137, 148
Galilee, 72
Galileo, 136, 187, 198, 214
Gallipoli, 256
Gama, Vasco de, 165
Gandhi, Mohandas K., 204, 220, 290
Garbutt, Simon, 154
Gauls, the, 57, 63
Gelasius, Pope, 163
general systems theory, 296–297
genius loci, 13
Genoa, Italy, 144
genocide, 2, 66, 139, 148, 208, 211–212, 259, 263, 266
Georg-August-Universität, 262–263
George, Saint, 163–164
Germany, 53, 96, 165, 184, 191, 195, 215, 224, 242, 244–246, 251, 257, 260–269
Gestapo, 152
global warming, 296–297, 302
gnosis, 18, 22, 59, 96, 140–141, 157, 160–161, 232–233, 245, 273, 288
Gnosticism, 65–66, 74, 118, 125, 140, 143, 153, 161, 231–232, 234, 290

Goethe, Johann Wolfgang von, 1, 109,
201, 231–234, 242, 245–246, 272, 277,
294, 296
Goetheanum, the, 276
Golden Dawn, Order of the, 246
Golden Fleece, Order of the, 176
Golgotha, 79
Goshen, Land of, 29
Gospel(s), the, 67–69, 81, 84, 90, 120,
123, 137, 299; Gnostic, 70, 139;
of John, 113, 140; of Luke, 91; of
Matthew, 299; of Philip, 161; of
Thomas, 70–72, 120, 142
Göttingen, Germany, 261–263
Goya, Francisco, 231
Grail, Holy, 96, 112, 114, 117–122, 126,
134, 158, 171, 175–177, 185
Granada, Spain, 189
Graves, Robert, 16, 60, 75, 112, 120, 170
Great Slump, 260, 262
Greek civilization, 14, 23, 42, 45–55, 57,
60, 76, 83, 86–87, 96–97, 104–105,
114, 118, 126–127, 157, 160, 174, 176,
187–190, 199–200, 217, 231, 275
Green Man, the, 154, 162–163
greenhouse effect, 301–302
Greenland, 156
Gregory, Pope, 102
Gurdjieff, G. I., 286
Guzman, Dominique, 145–146
Gypsies, 143, 209, 266

H.

Hagia Sophia, Council of, 275
Hahn, Otto, 243, 262, 267
Hals, Frans, 197
Hammurabi, 17
Hancock, Graham, 124
Hanseatic League, 189
Harvey, William, 223
heaven, 13, 25–26, 43, 61, 71, 83, 107,
114, 164, 177, 180, 191, 303
Hebrew civilization, 28–29, 31–33,
38–39, 42, 57, 60 see Israelites
Hegel, G. W. F., 232, 277

Heisenberg, Werner, 262, 267
Heliopolis, Egypt, 180
Henry the Navigator, 165
heresy, 30, 32, 52, 65, 79, 85–86, 89,
91, 93, 97, 104, 106, 112, 137–138,
143–153, 159, 164, 166–167, 171, 190,
193, 200, 214
Hermes Trismegistos, 48, 174
Hermeticism, 46–49, 52, 55, 84, 117, 188,
200, 202, 234
Hermopolis, Egypt, 180
Herod, 73, 78
Hewitt, Peter, 294
Hibbert, David, 261
hierarchy, Church, 5, 66, 68, 87, 93–95,
102–106, 109–110, 124, 174, 184,
191–194, 230
Hieratic, 27
Hildegard of Bingen, 106–108, 284, 298
Hinduism, 50, 60, 216, 219, 235, 292,
299, 303
Hiroshima, Japan, 268, 285
*Historia general de las cosas de Nueva
Espana*, 207
Hitler, Adolf, 249, 262, 265, 267
Hobbes, Thomas, 223
Hobsbawm, Eric, 226, 239
Holland, 215
Holocaust, 17, 139, 209, 267, 269, 285
Holy Land, 41, 122, 124, 128–129, 133–
134, 143–144, 147, 151, 155, 157
Holy of Holies, 73
Holy Spirit, 83, 96, 98, 105, 138, 193
Homo sapiens, 297, 302
Horeb, Mount, 177
Hugh of Champagne, Count, 118–119,
123
Humphreys, Christmas, 244
Hungary, 57
hunter-gatherers, 7–8, 10, 106
Huxley, Julian, 10, 281, 295

I.

Illuminati, 170
Imago, 28

Imhotep, 23

imperialism, 89, 239, 242, 250–251, 259, 290

Inca Empire, 208

Index Librorum Prohibitorum, 98

India, 21, 57, 204, 216, 219–220, 224, 244, 290

Indissolubisten, 184

Industrial Revolution, 195, 202, 220, 223–229, 239–240, 249, 279

initiation, 1, 18, 25–28, 37, 46–49, 52, 54, 57–62, 67–68, 71, 74–75, 79–80, 96–98, 105–106, 111–114, 117–122, 124–127, 130–131, 134, 141, 156, 158, 160–161, 164, 167–169, 171–185, 188, 200–202, 214–218, 231, 235, 243, 276, 290, 302–303

Innocent II, Pope, 124

Innocent III, Pope, 147

Inquisition, the, 91, 93, 97–98, 103, 136–137, 139, 144, 146–147, 150–153, 164, 245

intelligent universe, 295

Invisible College, 183, 201

Invisibles, 184

Irenaeus, Saint, 79–80, 112

Ireland, 12, 14, 59, 62, 137, 256

Iron Curtain, 268

Ishtar, 26, 50, 163–164

Isis Unveiled, 244

Isis, 27, 48, 50, 54, 74, 160–161, 180–181

Islam, 21, 32, 74, 105, 120, 129, 157, 159, 206, 215, 219, 235–236, 299

Isle Louvier, 159

Israel, biblical, 35–36, 38, 41–42, 47, 57, 60, 74, 106, 110, 119, 127

Israelites, the, 30–33, 35–36, 41–42, 80, 122, 175, 177

Issa, 74–75

Italy, 49, 52, 57, 102, 138, 156, 189, 195, 197, 215, 224, 258, 260–263

Ivo, Saint, 123

J.

jackal god, 23–24

Jacques of Compostela, Saint, 172

Jacquin, 126

Jahweh, 37–38

Jainism, 220

James the Greater, Saint, 70

James the Just, Saint, 64, 68–80, 84, 102, 139, 156

James the Less, Saint, 69–70, 74

Janus, 162

Japan, 224, 258, 268

Jarl of Orkney, 170–171 see Sinclair

Jebusites, the, 37

Jehoiachin, King, 41

Jehovah, 17, 177, 266

Jericho, 35

Jerusalem, 36, 38, 41–42, 70–73, 78–80, 84, 102, 112, 122, 124, 126–129, 132, 139–140, 155–156, 170, 176, 304

Jesuits, the, 206, 278

Jesus (Christ), 2, 32, 53, 62, 65–80, 84–85, 89–91, 96, 98, 102, 106, 111–112, 114, 118–120, 122, 127, 132–133, 137–145, 148–149, 152–153, 156, 161, 192, 232, 280, 296, 300

Jews, 36–37, 39–42, 66, 73–76, 80, 137, 139, 209, 235, 263, 266 also see Israelites

John the Baptist, Saint, 68, 73, 80, 95, 120, 140, 143, 161

John the Divine, Saint, 69, 71–72, 112–114

Johnson, Kenneth Rayner, 130

Johnson, Paul, 40

Johnson, Samuel, 250

Joliot-Curie, Frédéric and Irène, 261

Joseph of Arimathea, 62, 119

Joses (Joseph), Saint, 68–69

Judaism, 21, 32, 38–41, 66–67, 80, 91, 94, 106, 121, 159, 177, 298

Judas, 68–70

Judea, 41, 68

Judge, W. Q., 243

Julian of Norwich, 106, 108

Jung, Carl, 233

Jupiter, 59, 83, 172, 175

Just War, 90–91, 98, 193

Justinian, Emperor, 52
Jutland, 256

K.

Kabbala, 118, 232
Kabeiri (also Cabeiri), 49, 57, 62
Kabeiros, 49, 180
Kant, Immanuel, 198
Kariba, Zimbabwe, 214
Kelvin, Lord, 294
Kennedy, John F., 185
Kerygmata Petrou, 76
Keynes, John Maynard, 260
KGB, 152
King, Jr., Martin Luther, 291
Kings College, London, 260
Klein, Felix, 261
Knight, Charles, 56
Knights Hospitaller, 147, 165–166
Knights of Alcantara, 158
Knights of Calatrava, 158
Knights of Christ, 127, 165–166
Knights of Santiago, 165
Knights Templar, 1–2, 74–75, 114, 119, 121–122, 124–128, 132–134, 143, 147, 149, 152–153, 155–159, 161–162, 165–167, 170–171, 181, 185, 246 also see Templar Order
Kolchak, Aleksandr, 258
Krishnamurti, J., 286
Kundalini, the, 173, 176

L.

La Rochelle, France, 156
Lady Guiraude, 149
Lake Balaton, Hungary, 57
Languedoc, France, 137–138, 142, 144, 146–147, 151–152
Lao Tse, 217
Laplace, Pierre-Simon, 230
Lascaux, France, 4, 8
Law of Moses, 17, 36, 38, 40, 42, 66, 73, 75, 80, 118
Law, William, 109

Le Conte del Graal, 118–119
League of Nations, 258
Leigh, Richard, 123
Lenin, Vladimir, 256–259
Leontopolis, Egypt, 42
Les Tignarii, 127
Levi, Eliphas, 160
Levites, the, 73
Lewis, C. S., 138
Liebnitz, Gottfried, 198
light (and enlightenment), 14, 74–75, 79, 111, 119, 121–122, 141, 161, 167, 176, 183, 185, 220, 230, 235, 277, 294, 303
Lionel, Frederic, 117, 169, 303
Lithuania, 165
Loire river, 62
Lombardy, Italy, 142–143, 158, 166
London, England, 29, 244, 277
Longinus, Saint, 163–164
Louis VII, King, 118
love, 45, 63, 67, 85, 89–90, 92, 98, 103, 107, 113, 129, 138, 144, 146–147, 152–153, 180, 193, 212, 275
Lovelock, James, 248, 295–296
Low Countries, the, 195, 197
Lucan (Marcus Annaeus Lucanus), 60–61
Lug's Chain, 178
Luther, Martin, 106, 186–187, 189, 191–192, 199–200, 209

M.

MacDonald, Ramsey, 185
Madonna, 75, 160–161, 172
Magi, the, 47, 49, 57, 60, 68
Magic Flute, The, 231
magic, 8–9, 14, 18, 21–22, 27, 59, 61–62, 67, 113–114, 118, 181, 188, 246, 273
Mahabharata, 299
Mahatma Letters to A.P. Sinnet, 244
Maimonides, Moses, 121
maize, 171
Majorca, Spain, 156
Manhattan Project, 266
Manichaeism, 118, 143

HIDDEN WISDOM

Marcel, Gabriel, 216

Marchant, Carolyn, 223

Marcion of Pontus, 84

Marian apparitions, 302

Mariette, Auguste, 24

Marmande, sack of, 149

Mars, 59–60, 172, 175

Martin, P. W., 286

Marx, Karl, 117, 197, 200, 239, 277, 279

Mary Magdalene, 69, 143, 161

Mary (Mother of Jesus), 68–70, 73, 90, 111, 161

Maslow, Abraham, 295

Masonry, 23, 126–128, 130–132, 162, 164, 170, 184 also see Freemasonry

Masparo, Gaston, 24–25

Matthew, Saint, 137, 299

Mauritius, Saint, 163–164

May Queen, the, 163

Mayan Long Count Calendar, 303

McLoughlin, William, 287

Mechthild of Magdeburg, 106, 108

Medici, Cosimo de', 189–190

medieval period (or Middle Ages), 1, 31, 51–52, 60, 103, 105–108, 110–111, 117–118, 125, 130–131, 137, 163–164, 167, 178, 181, 187, 189, 194–195, 197, 200, 236, 270, 292, 297–298

Mediterranean, 42, 53, 83, 156

Megara, Greece, 51

Meister Eckhart, 101, 106–107, 200, 289

Meitner, Lise, 262

Melchizedek, 37

Memphis, Egypt, 180

Mercury, 59–60, 172, 174

Merneptah, Pharaoh, 35

Mesopotamia, 18, 49, 114, 160

Messiah, the, 65–66, 71, 73, 75, 80

Mexico, 156, 207

Michael of Albany, Prince, 124

Michael, Saint, 163

Michelangelo Buonarroti, 1, 197

Micmac Indians, 171

Milan, Edict of, 81, 88, 90

Milky Way, 26, 172, 178–179, 182

militiae Christi, 123 see Templars

Minerva, 59

Minerve, France, 148

Ming dynasty, 218

missionaries, 78, 84, 103, 206, 209–210, 215

Mithras, 54, 143

Mohammed, 206

Moissac, France, 151

Molay, Jacques de, 159

Mongols, the, 218

monotheism, 28–31, 38–39, 73, 77, 89, 159, 206

Mont Saint-Michel, 155

Montdidier, Payen de, 119

Montfort, Simon de, 149

Montségur, France, 150, 152

Moon, 60, 172, 182

Moors, the, 105, 118, 165

Moriah, Mount, 76

Moses, 17, 22, 28–30, 32–33, 36–38, 42, 74–75, 118, 121

Mother Earth (also Earth Mother), 16, 45–46, 107–108, 179, 181

Moyers, Bill, 7

Mozart, Wolfgang Amadeus, 231

Mühlhiasl, 302

Muller, Herbert J., 92

Muret, Battle of, 149

Mussolini, Benito, 262

mutually assured destruction, 268–269

Mystery schools, 27, 37–38, 46–50, 54, 61–62, 74, 81, 86, 110, 121, 127, 140, 174–176, 190, 200, 276

mysticism, 13–14, 26, 37, 39, 47–50, 59–61, 98, 101, 105–110, 113–114, 118, 129–130, 156, 164, 171–172, 175–179, 182–184, 188, 199–202, 217, 228, 232–233, 237, 248, 286–288; 291–304

mythology, 6–7, 10, 17–18, 22, 26–28, 31, 36, 39, 44–48, 50, 54, 57–60, 62–63, 68, 83, 94, 113, 118, 120–121, 132–133, 150, 161–164, 169, 173–174, 178–179, 206, 243, 257, 287, 294

N.

Nag Hammadi, 71, 120, 139

Nagasaki, Japan, 254, 268

Napoleon, 228, 230–231

Nasafi, Aziz, 294

nationalism, 66, 78, 80, 163, 194, 239, 250–252, 262

Native Americans, 11, 208, 210–212

natural selection, 10

nature (environment), human relationship to, 5, 9, 38, 50, 61, 92, 96, 106–107, 111, 162, 179, 188, 196–202, 208, 211–212, 214, 220, 223–224, 234–235, 241–243, 245–247, 260, 276, 280, 282, 285, 288–290, 296–298

Nazarenes, 76, 161 also Nazoreans

Nazareth, 65, 67

Nazi Party, 209, 262–263, 266–267

Neolithic period, 9–10, 13–15, 17, 45, 60

Nernst, Walther, 264

Nero, Emperor, 87

New Testament, 25, 70, 72, 78, 84, 86, 112 also see Bible, Gospel

New York, NY, 243

Newgrange, Ireland 12, 14

Newport, Rhode Island, 171

Newton, Isaac, 185, 187–188, 198–199, 201, 222–223, 232, 234

Nicaea, Council of, 88, 113

Nicholson, Helen, 123

Nietzsche, Friedrich, 242

Nile River, 22, 26, 42, 178–179, 181

Nirvana, 114

Nobel Prize, 217, 262, 264, 301

Notre-Dame de la Dalbade, Church of, 172, 174

Notre Dame de Paris, 172, 175, 235 see cathedrals

Notre Dame Sous Terre, 175 see cathedrals, Chartres

Nova Scotia, Canada, 171

Numa Pompilius, 17, 127

numerology, 61–62, 114, 181 see seven

Nuremberg trials, 267

O.

obedience, 85, 87, 96–97, 101, 104, 157, 161, 173, 181, 236, 299

occult, the, 48–49, 130–131, 174, 177, 180, 246, 273, 276, 288

Odium theologicum, 85

Ogham script, 58

Olcott, H. S., 243

Old Testament, 25, 26, 39, 75, 84, 92 also see Bible

Olympus, gods of, 44, 46, 50, 174

Omer, Saint, 122

Onias, 42

Opium Wars, 219

Oppenheimer, Robert J., 262

oracles, 60–61, 86, 114, 172–177, 181–182, 303

Orden der Unzertrennlichen, 184

Order of St. James, 165

Origen, 87

original sin, 90–93, 193, 280

Orkney, Scotland 170–171

Orpheus, 47

Osiris, 17, 24–26

Osman, Ahmed, 29–30

Ouspensky, P. D., 130

Ovingdon trephined skull, 58

P.

Padovano, Anthony, 299

Palestine, 133–134, 220, 270

papacy, the, 51, 72, 95–97, 101–103, 117, 124, 137–140, 144–148, 152, 157–159, 165, 192, 236–237; papal infallibility, 101, 236, 280

Paraguay, 205

Parzival, 119

Patmos, Greece 112 see Revelation of St. John

patriotism, 249–252

Paul, Saint, 70–73, 75–81, 83–84, 156, 192, 220; Road to Damascus, 78; the Scoffer, 76; Spouter of Lies, 66, 76; Wicked Priest, 76

Pax Romana, 63

HIDDEN WISDOM

Payens, Hugues de, 132
Pedler, Kit, 247
Pentecost, 72–73
Perceval, 118
Peregrino a Santiago, 182
Persia, 17, 41–42, 47, 53–55, 57, 68, 80, 113, 118, 175
perspectivism, 296
Peter, Saint, 71–72, 79, 112, 147, 156
Pharisees, the, 67
Philae, Egypt, 179, 181
Philip of Spain, King, 207
Phoenicians, the, 62, 112
Pibram, Karl, 293
Pictet, M., 62
pilgrimages, 13, 124, 128, 133–134, 151, 155–157
Pilgrimage of Initiation, 156, 164, 171, 171–183
Pillar of Cloud, the, 39
Pioneer of Allahabad, *The*, 244
Planck, Max, 261
Plato, 14, 51–52
Pliny the Elder, 60
Poland, 242, 258
Polanyi, Michael, 295
Polynesia, 17
Pomponius Mela, 60
Portugal, 165–166, 181, 206, 215
Posidonius, 49, 60
prayer, 26, 28, 38, 125, 155, 278
prehistoric humans, 5–9, 18, 25
Priestley, Joseph, 232
priests, 18, 23–24, 31–32, 36–37, 40, 60, 67, 73, 94, 132, 145, 176, 194
Prigogine, Ilya, 217, 301
Princip, Gavrilo, 252
Priscillian, 146
prophecy, 24, 37, 39, 57, 60, 67, 69, 79, 83, 92, 94, 105, 110, 113, 120, 146, 248, 255, 260, 299, 302–303
Protestant work ethic, 196, 213
Protestantism, 192–193, 198, 201, 209–210, 227, 235–236, 242

Pseudo-Clementine Recognitions, 78
psychedelic drugs, 286
psychic phenomena, 243–244
Pure Ones, 143 see Cathars
Puritans, the, 210
Pushkin, Alexander, 231
Pyramid Texts, 23–26, 178
pyramids, 22–24, Cheops, 285; Djoser, 23–24, 61; Giza, 15; Unas, 24
Pythagoras, 49–52, 55, 60, 143

Q.
Quakerism, 109, 227
quantum physics, 267, 293–294

R.
Raine, Kathleen, 7
Ramtha's School of Enlightenment, 292
Rashi (Rabbi Shlomo Yitzhaki), 31
Ratzinger, Joseph Alois, 150
Ravenscroft, Trevor, 119, 172, 263, 267
Reconquista, the, 189
Red Army, 256–257, 259
Red Sea, 33, 39
Reformation, the, 152–153, 183, 188, 190, 192, 194–197, 199, 260
Reich, Third, 263, 265
relativity, 285
Rembrandt, 197
Renaissance, the, 1–2, 84, 138, 144, 153, 166, 176, 185, 188–190, 197–199, 207, 217, 223, 275, 292
Revelation of St. John, 112–114, 161, 232, 248
revelation, 37, 39, 63, 92–93, 104, 142, 198, 232, 281, 289
Rhineland, the, 195
Richard of Poitou, 123
Robinson, John J., 166
Rocamadour, France, 155
Roman Empire, 13, 17, 21, 38, 42, 53–55, 59–63, 67, 76, 78, 80, 86, 88–90, 95, 101–102, 114, 127, 132, 181, 190, 207, 218

Roosevelt, Franklin Delano, 266

Rosenkreuz, Christian, 200

Rosicrucian Manifestos, 201

Rosicrucianism, 1, 166, 169, 183–184, 200

Rosslyn Chapel, Scotland, 153, 163–165, 167, 170–174, 177

Rostock, Germany, 245

Roszak, Theodore, 1, 7, 233, 282

Royal Arch degree, 184

Royal Homoeopathic Hospital, 277

Royal Navy, 229

Royal Society of London, 201

Rule of St. Devoir de Dieu et de la Croissade, 127

Rumi, Jalaluddin, 129

Ruskin, John, 250

Russell, Bertrand, 95

Russia, 164, 209, 224, 229, 243, 256–259, 262, 266, 268

Russian Revolution, 257–259

Rutherford, Ernest, 261, 264

S.

Sabbah, Messod and Roger, 32

Sadducees, the, 67

Sahagún, Bernardino de, 207

Saint James of the Sword, Order of, 165

Samaria, 36, 112

Samaritans, the, 42

San Marco, Florence, 189

San Sebastian de Garabandal, Spain, 302

Santiago de Compostela, Spain, 69, 155, 165, 173, 182

Saqqara, Egypt, 23–24

Saracens, the, 157

Sargon, 28

Sargon II, 35

Sarsen stones, 61

Saturn, 60, 172, 177

Scandinavia, 229

Schaubach, F., 236

Schonfield, Hugh, 160

Schubert, Franz, 231

science and scientific revolution, 1, 6–7, 22–23, 27–28, 36, 46, 49–52, 57, 105, 167, 187–188, 190, 192, 197–202, 213–220, 223, 226, 231–234, 237–239, 241–249, 261–266, 268–270, 273–281, 286, 290, 293–297, 300–304

Scotland, 49, 129, 132, 153, 162–163, 166–167, 170–172, 178, 292

Secret Doctrine, The, 244

Sefer ha-Zohar, 118

Sellars, Jane, 178

Senzar, 27

seven, degrees of initiation, 110–111, 119–121, 172–183, Raven, 121, 173; Peacock, 121, 174; Knight, 121, 174; Swan, 121, 175; Pelican, 121, 175; Eagle, 121, 175; Crown, 121, 173–176, symbolism, 23, 26, 39, 61–62, 114

Shah, Idries, 112, 160

Shakespeare, William, 1, 13, 205

shamanism, 8–9, 18, 25, 36, 60, 106, 188

Shamash, 17

Shavu'ot, 72

Shell Pilgrimage, 156 see Pilgrimage of Initiation

Sheshbazzar, 41

Sieyes, Abbé, 228

Signatura Rerum, 108–109

Silbury Hill, England, 61

silver, 32, 69, 178

Sinai, Mount, 17, 29

Sinclair family (originally St. Clair), 153, 167, 170–171, 176–177, 184

Sinclair, Henry, 171 also Henry St. Clair

Sinclair, William, 163, 167, 170, 176–177 also William St. Clair

Sinnet, A. P., 244

slavery, 32, 93, 103–104, 146, 205–213, 241

Smith, Adam, 226

Snail Men, the, 178

socialism, 251–252, 256, 258–259, 266, 301

Socrates, 51, 97

Sol Invictus, 54, 82, 88

Solomon, King, 36, 39, 112, 124–128, 132, 164

Solovyov, Vladimir, 248, 255, 296

Sommerfeld, Arnold, 261

Son(s) of God, 26–30, 68–69, 75–76, 140, 163–164, 193 see Jesus

sons of the widow, 27, 169, 180

Sophia, 138, 160–161

soul, the, 23, 59, 91, 111, 140–142, 150, 174–178, 191, 205, 275, 282, 290

South Africa, 213

Spain, 53, 105, 118, 121, 137, 146, 156, 165–166, 172, 182–183, 189, 208, 210, 215, 263

Spear of Destiny, The, 267

Spretnak, Charlene, 16

St. Petersburg, Russia, 255

Stalin, Joseph, 259, 262–263

Stein, Walter Johannes, 267

Steiner, Rudolf, 200, 245, 274–281, 285, 287, 294, 296

Steppes, the, 16, 218

Stieler, Joseph Karl, 272

Stonehenge, England, 11, 14–15

Strachan, Gordon, 129

Stromata, the, 57

Succoth (Sukkot), 33

Sufism, 112, 120–121, 129, 164, 170

Sumerian civilization, 21, 26

Sun, the, 17, 60, 89, 172, 175, 177, 187, 214

Sung dynasty, 218

Swedenborg, Emanuel, 109, 232, 285

Switzerland, 257

Szilárd, Leó, 262, 266

technological progress, 5, 17, 23, 124, 158, 218, 223–224, 239, 247–249, 264, 288, 294, 297

Teilhard de Chardin, Pierre, 10, 45, 248, 273–274, 278–279, 281–282, 295–296

Teller, Edward, 262, 266

Templar Order, 1, 114, 116, 121–125, 128–131, 133, 143, 153, 155–166, 170–172, 174, 195, 200 also see Knights Templar

Temple Mount, 124, 129, 132

Temple of God, 26, 179

Temple of Solomon, 37–38, 41–42, 66, 73, 80, 84, 112, 122, 124, 126–128, 132, 170, 176

Temple Scroll, 133

Templi Omnium Hominum Pacis Abbas, 160

Ten Commandments, 36 also see Law of Moses

Tertullian, 85

Tesla, Nikola, 246–248

Teutonic Knights, 158, 1661166

Thebes, Egypt, 49, 179–180

theology, 54, 66, 70, 80–81, 83, 90–92, 190–193, 198, 205, 241, 280, 290 also see Bible, Gospel(s), Old and New Testament

Theosophical Society, 238, 243–246, 292

Therapeutae, the, 49, 140, 142

Third Force, 201

third wave, 282

Thoreau, Henry David, 301

Thoth, 48

Thuthmose, 29

Tiahuanaco dynasty, 208

Tibet, 242

Titus, Emperor, 132

Toffler, Alvin, 282

Toledo, Spain, 189

Tolstoy, Leo, 250

Toulouse, France, 142, 145, 172, 174

Transcendentalists, the, 285

Trinity, 29, 89

Trotsky, Leon, 259

Troyes, Chrétien de, 118

T.

Tacitus, 60

Talmud, the, 40, 298

Tammuz, 26, 163–164

Tao of Physics, The, 293

Taoism, 216–217, 219

tarot, the, 185, 190

Tawney, Richard Henry, 197

Troyes, Council of, 125
Tunisia, 263
Turkey, 229 see Anatolia
turning point, 41, 187, 205, 223, 282, 285, 302
Tuscany, Italy, 142, 153
Tutankhamun, Pharaoh, 22, 27, 30
Tutu, Desmond, 289

U.

uncertainty principle, 267
United States, 131, 184–185, 196, 209–210, 213, 224–225, 236, 258, 265–268, 287
universe, concept of, 108–109, 187–188, 199, 201, 214, 217, 227, 237, 241, 247–249, 274, 281, 295
Upuaut (or Wepwawet), 24
utilitarian philosophy, 240

V.

Venice, Italy, 144, 156, 197
Venus, 60, 172, 174
Verdi, Giuseppe, 231
Verges, Raoul, 125
Versailles, Treaty of, 257
Vesalius, Andreas, 187
Vienna, Austria, 29, 231
Vikings, the, 103
Virginii Pariturae, 62, 111

W.

Waddington, C. H., 295
Wagner, Wilhelm Richard, 231
Wallace, Alfred Russel, 10
Walpole, Robert, 185
Warmund of Picquigny, 122
Watkins, Alfred, 14
Wealth of Nations, The, 226
Weber, Max, 196–197
Weimar, Germany, 232, 245, 275
Westford, Massachusetts, 171
White Russian Army, 258–259
Wilberforce, William, 235

Wiesel, Elie, 92
Wilhelm, Richard, 216
William of Tudela, 149
William of Tyre, 122–123
Wilson, Colin, 9, 46, 49, 108, 244, 273, 294
wine, ritual use, 47–48, 59, 75, 84
wisdom goddesses, 27, 39, 138, 160–161
women, status of, 8, 62, 90, 138, 142, 223, 239
Word of God, 35, 65, 225
Wordsworth, William, 233–234
World War, First, 240, 245, 255, 257–260
World War, Second, 209, 264, 268–269
worship, 26, 38, 42, 42, 45, 49–50, 54, 59, 62–63, 73, 84, 86, 89, 111, 131, 138, 141, 160, 172, 181, 183, 198
Wouivre, 61, 173

X.

X-rays, 247

Y.

Yeats, William Butler, 1, 256
Yeb, Egypt, 42 see Elephantine

Z.

Zadok the Priest, 37, 119
Zebedee, 69–70
Zeitler, Andreas, 302
Zep Tepi, 25
Zerubbabel, 41
Zeus, 46, 83
zodiac, 60
Zoroastrianism, 17, 47, 80, 143, 299
Zukav, Gary, 293
Zumárraga, Juan de, 207

HIDDEN WISDOM